HISTORICISM

Paul Hamilton

LONDON AND NEW YORK

First published 1996
by Routledge
11 New Fetter Lane, London EC4P 4EE

Simultaneously published in the USA and Canada
by Routledge
29 West 35th Street, New York, NY 10001

© 1996 Paul Hamilton

Typeset in Adobe Garamond and Scala Sans
by Keystroke, Jacaranda Lodge, Wolverhampton

Printed and bound in Great Britain by
Clays Ltd, St. Ives PLC

British Library Cataloguing in Publication Data
A catalogue record for this book is available from the British Library

Library of Congress Cataloging in Publication Data
A catalogue record for this book has been requested

ISBN 0–415–13311–4 (hbk)
ISBN 0–415–11051–3 (pbk)

CONTENTS

SERIES EDITOR'S PREFACE

The New Critical Idiom is a series of introductory books which seeks to extend the lexicon of literary terms, in order to address the radical changes which have taken place in the study of literature during the last decades of the twentieth century. The aim is to provide clear, well-illustrated accounts of the full range of terminology currently in use, and to evolve histories of its changing usage.

The current state of the discipline of literary studies is one in which there is considerable debate concerning basic questions of terminology. This involves, among other things, the boundaries which distinguish the literary from the non-literary; the position of literature within the larger sphere of culture; the relationship between literatures of different cultures; and questions concerning the relation of literary to other cultural forms within the context of interdisciplinary studies.

It is clear that the field of literary criticism and theory is a dynamic and heterogenous one. The present need is for individual volumes on terms which combine clarity of exposition with an adventurousness of perspective and a breadth of application. Each volume will contain as part of its apparatus some indication of the direction in which the definition of particular terms is likely to move, as well as expanding the disciplinary boundaries within which some of these terms have been traditionally contained. This will involve some re-situation of terms within the larger field of cultural representation, and will introduce examples from the area of film and the modern media in addition to examples from a variety of literary texts.

ACKNOWLEDGEMENTS

Historicism is an enormous subject; I have tried to use the most readily available translations and selections of the different languages and literatures in which I have been obliged to travel. Part of chapter 5 reworks bits of an article published in *English* (Autumn 1993). Almost all the research was done in the British Library, a neglected institution, wonderfully staffed.

I am grateful to John Drakakis for suggesting that I write this book and for his constructive criticism and support. The book derives much of its energy from the stimulus of working in the University of Southampton's English Department, and I owe especial intellectual debts of one kind or another to Tony Crowley, Ken Hirschkop and Jonathan Sawday. My thanks to Peter Ucko, then Dean of Arts, who manufactured a vital term's study-leave *ex nihilo*, and worried me with his prehistoric thoughts. Elsewhere, Richard Bourke shared ideas and was encouraging at an early stage. My thanks to Michael Bird for help with the typescript.

But I wrote it for Reeta and Daniel, who were in on the action throughout.

INTRODUCTION

The protagonists of progress in historical understanding are always isolated individuals who are led by such historical convulsions as wars and revolutions to put new questions. Thucydides was induced to undertake his history because he regarded the Peloponnesian War as the greatest war of all times. Augustine wrote his *City of God* under the impact of Alaric's conquest of Rome. Machiavelli's political and historical writings are his reaction to the French expeditions into Italy. The revolution of 1789 and the Napoleonic wars provoked Hegel's Philosophy of History. Upon the defeat of 1871 followed Taine's revision of French history, upon the establishment of the Hohenzollern empire, Nietzsche's 'unseasonable' essay on the 'Advantages and Disadvantages of History for Life' – a precursor of the modern discussions of 'historism'. The end of the first World War was responsible for the resonance Spengler's *Decline of the West* found in Germany. Deeper in intent and saturated with the entire yield of German philosophy, theology, and history was Ernst Troeltsch's unfinished work, *Der Historismus und seine Probleme* [Historicism and its Discontents].

(Curtius 1979: 3–4)

What is historicism? Historicism (or 'historism' in this translation of Curtius' *Historismus*) is a critical movement insisting on the prime importance of historical context to the interpretation of texts of all kinds. It has enjoyed a long tradition of influence upon many disciplines of thought, recently experiencing a lively renewal in contemporary literary criticism. The most prominent late 20th-century critical fashions, poststructuralism and postmodernism, have ended up being understood through the images of history they imply. Yet this historical turn rejoins a well-worn tradition of historicism. At present, historicism is tempted to present itself as 'new', the latest way forward for literary theory. That alone might be a good reason for a book on it. In addition, though, to briefing students on the current state of the critical art, a book on historicism should identify an underlying pattern of historical explanation recurring at different times in different forms.

While human beings have generally tried to understand themselves historically, they have not always done so as historicists. Historicism emerges in reaction to the practice of deducing from first principles truths about how people are obliged to organize themselves socially and politically. The natural laws governing human behaviour at all times are formulated, and cultures evaluated by the degree to which they approximate to this ideal pattern. Historicists oppose this tradition, which, primarily associated with the Enlightenment, stretches, in different versions, from the 17th-century natural-law theorists to the sophistications of Kant and Hegel. They argue instead that human nature is too various for such legislation to be universally applicable. They therefore have to evolve a model for apprehending social and cultural diversity different from the scientific, law-governed paradigm of the Enlightenment. Romantic aesthetics, that sense of a human richness unmeasured by scientific calculation and best equated with a natural grandeur similarly exceeding computation, immediately offers itself for this purpose. In Ernst Troeltsch's summary, Romanticism was 'ultimately a metaphysic in which individuality, plurality and pantheism are combined' (Troeltsch 1934: 211). From Schleiermacher to Gadamer, though, the hermeneutic tradition has struggled to recast this aesthetic heritage in order to show that history, properly understood, demonstrates that we can have a kind of knowledge complementing the natural sciences, and that all experience not falling under scientific jurisdiction need not be consigned to a non-cognitive aesthetic which lays no claim to being true.

Simply put, such anti-Enlightenment historicism develops a characteristically double focus. Firstly, it is concerned to situate any statement – philosophical, historical, aesthetic or whatever – in its historical context. Secondly, it typically doubles back on itself to explore the extent to which any historical enterprise inevitably reflects the interests and bias of the period in which it was written. On the one hand, therefore, historicism is suspicious of the stories the past tells about itself; on the other hand, it is equally suspicious of its own partisanship. It offers up both its past and its present for ideological scrutiny.

We can call the first focus of historicism hermeneutical. The past is to be understood on the model of interpreting a text; and texts, literary or otherwise, only have meaning within an economy of other texts, which both limits their possibilities and facilitates the distinctiveness of their utterances. A poetic statement, for example, amounts to one thing in Plato's philosophy, but it might possess an altogether different status in Renaissance, Enlightenment, Romantic or postmodern treatises. In each case, its value is relative to that accorded to adjacent discourses of science, politics, history and so on.

Hermeneutics was originally the science of interpreting Scripture. Secular hermeneutics retains the idea of relating the individual work to a larger purpose into whose pattern it meaningfully fits. Understood hermeneutically, a text's meaning is limited by the value accorded its discourse within the culture of its first audience. Nevertheless, between that past reception and our present attempts to understand it, the text will in all likelihood have generated many more interpretations. The historicist usually claims to be more aware of the conventions governing the first set of expectations than the original readers, for whom they may well have been internalized, unconscious assumptions, and for whom reading the text consisted in straightforward exegesis. Historicists also claim to have gained more knowledge of the text's meaning because of their acquaintance with the new meanings it had for subsequent historical periods.

As soon as the critical heritage of a text becomes an issue in its interpretation, my second question of relativism comes into focus. Is hermeneutics a circular process? Do critical interpreters always find what they want to find? Or, are historicists, by contrast, so effectively aware of this problem that they can break out of the hermeneutical circle? Can they distinguish between the meaning a piece of writing had for its first audience and a *real* meaning, unclouded by that original audience's or any subsequent period's ideology? A notion of ideology – here a society's unconscious tailoring of criteria of objectivity to fit its own interests – comes into play, because historicists, especially nowadays, frequently define themselves as critics who refuse to take the past on its own terms, regarding the economy with which it regulated the possible meanings of different genres as *the* ideological constraint to be broken. We shall see that the deregulation of original economies of meaning which historicists claim to achieve characterizes the transition from modernity to postmodernity. Modernity's typical insistence on the 'new' is overridden by postmodernity's refusal to accept the fixed sense of the past against which modernity asserted its novelty.

Modernity itself is defined by the idea that we can break from the past by claiming to be the measure of all things and not vice versa, and that this subjectivity is not an embarrassment for science but the grounds of its possibility – an attitude shared by otherwise opposed modes of thinking from the Renaissance onwards. The critique of modernity is an historicizing one, which exposes the ideological content of the logic of a subjectivity that supposedly transcends local interests. To the extent, therefore, that they criticize modernity, Marx, Nietzsche and Freud write as historicist critics of the traditions by which we make sense of the past. Their postmodern successors, Foucault, Derrida and Lacan, pursue especially the reflexive implications of this scepticism. They distrust not only tradition but also any interpretation which does not acknowledge that its history of the past is relativised by being also a history of the present. The way around this problem, though, cannot be to provide yet another interpretation of the bias of their own interpretations. Postmodernists have to find alternative expressions explaining how they can 'think differently' from both their past and their present.

While this book is a survey of historicism and a short history of some of its main effects in the history of critical thought, it also argues towards certain conclusions. One of these is that postcolonial and feminist writings most effectively provide the alternative expression sought by postmodernism. So-called 'new historicism' tends helpfully to isolate the problems from which those critical efforts take off, and, when it goes further, itself mutates into one or the other. The philosophical ingenuity and range of commentary arising from their rewriting of history has not been fully appreciated; nor is the degree to which their idiom is shared and links widely differing critics to the postmodern moment. Another conclusion is that, while we seem able to examine critically the idea of progress, we still cannot do without some idea of redemption. Its theological overtones, no doubt embarrassing to critical theorists, belong to a language they are obliged to use. So this book follows Theodor Adorno, Walter Benjamin and, to some extent, Jurgen Habermas, but also, by implication and more controversially, a host of others starting from Schleiermacher, in thinking that to strive for a just estimation of or undistorted communication with the past is simultaneously to believe that the present can be significantly altered for the better. The result might not be progress, with all the questionable assumptions of continuity that entails, but it would make a difference.

1

HISTORY AND HISTORICISM

THE POETICS OF HISTORY

From ancient times, philosophers have been eager to separate history from fiction. Like many others, this disciplinary boundary proved fragile from the start. Despite having expelled poets from his ideal republic, Plato was still constrained to use myth in his descriptions of the ultimate truths of philosophy. In books 7 and 10 of Plato's philosophical dialogue, *The Republic*, his master, Socrates, enlightens his listeners by having them picture two imaginary scenarios for philosophical purposes. The myth of the cave invents a viewpoint from which we can survey the processes of knowledge which normally circumscribe us; the myth of Er imagines a comparable escape from the boundaries of mortality in order to explain the progress of the soul. In both cases, the contradictory recourse to art of a philosopher who has just condemned art as intellectually and morally disreputable implicates history in fiction. Plato's justification of myth here is that it tells a true story in the only terms available. His myths aspire to be history, but in the absence of facts they must resort to fictions. We can only understand them, though, if we read them as supporting his philosophy with imagined histories.

In his *Poetics*, Aristotle had difficulty in seeing why this serious philosophical purpose could not straightforwardly be attributed to art. Why was history required to accredit the philosophical use of fiction to explain the nature of knowledge and mortality? For Aristotle, history was distinguished from poetry not by greater seriousness of purpose but by the different balance of probability and possibility proper to each discourse. Thus, while Oedipus thinks it impossible that he could have killed his father and married his mother, the narrative power of Sophocles' play *Oedipus Tyrranus* shows how each step he took to avoid this outcome made it more probable. History, on the other hand, is full of examples of victory snatched from the jaws of defeat, or vice versa, in total defiance of what we expect to happen, of all probability. In fact, poetry was more philosophical than history because of its greater freedom to represent the complete understanding desired by philosophy. In poetry, probability was all; history, on the other hand, had to attend much more to what was possible. Provided a fiction was coherent, provided it contained a beginning, middle and end and reached a cathartic conclusion, it served its purpose: one that modelled the philosophical end of apprehending events in their entirety, with nothing necessary to their elucidation left out. History must resign itself to what could have taken place, however improbable this might be, and however its improbability might threaten the coherence of history's relation of events, leaving readers frustrated rather than cathartically purged of their desires for explanation.

History, then, appears to be as vulnerable to criticism as poetry is safe from it. This is an unusual way of looking at Aristotle's *Poetics*; usually the standards of coherence he imposes on fiction are viewed as restrictive and parochial, canons to be broken by creative writers down the centuries. It is worth stressing the comparable dilemma in which the *Poetics* leaves history. If the historian tells a coherent tale, one that has point and purpose, its probability may undermine its possibility and leave the author justified as a philosopher and discredited as an historian – probability, we recall, being the sign that poetry's is a philosophical imagination. If, instead, the history in question records a host of improbabilities, however possible, faithfulness to what happened or could have happened will produce a discourse without point and purpose, philosophically negligible, random in its accuracy and literal in its confusion. Faced with this choice, it is fair to say, most historians reach a compromise. 'It is sometimes fiction. It is sometimes theory', wrote Macaulay of his craft in 1828 (Stern 1970: 72). They find their own ways of making the possible and the probable interact, balancing truth to the facts against the need for those facts to make sense. Equally, though, writers of fiction have often had to confront the resistance of the individual fact to ordinary explanation. They have taken it as their task to devise a context for understanding or even just tolerating the exception to probability, the event which cannot be regularized. Some things, one might say, have to be remembered because they cannot be imagined. It may take as great a creative effort to step outside our criteria of probability as it did to reanimate them from within. Art and history inflect each other in commemoration and elegy, hypothesis and vision, record and story. Memory – Mnemosyne – was, after all, the mother of the Muses, and the leading muse, Clio, presided over history.

When we look back to the ancient historians, we find just this tangle of common concerns rather than Aristotle's clear demarcation of purposes. In a famous aside in *De Legibus*, Cicero tries to stick to the Aristotelian agenda, but he is obliged to concede that in practice distinctions become blurred: 'different principles are to be followed in history and poetry . . . for in history the standard by which everything is judged is the truth, while in poetry it is generally the pleasure one gives; however, in the works of Herodotus, the father of History, and in those of Theopompus, one finds innumerable fabulous tales' (I.5). In his classic review of Herodotus' reputation, 'The Place of Herodotus in the History of Historiography', Arnaldo Momigliano shows that Herodotus' standing as the inaugurator of ancient history persists alongside the assumption that he did not tell the truth. Momigliano is rightly fascinated by the fact that Herodotus' alleged unreliability clearly counts against him, yet does not diminish his importance to his detractors. Partly this results from Herodotus' historical situation: commentators have noted that he was as much the son of the fabulists, Homer and Hesiod, as the father of subsequent historians (Vandiver 1991: 239). Looking forward, we find that his immediate successor, Thucydides, though not attacking Herodotus by name, was eager to distinguish his own style of history writing from that of previous poets and chroniclers. Thucydides successfully 'imposed the idea that contemporary political history was the only serious history' because there was supposedly no room in it for the art of fable, myth and unproven anecdote associated with Herodotus (Momigliano 1966: 131).

But it is only by contrast with Herodotus that Thucydides' history can appear as strict documentary. His own magisterial statement of principles at the start of his account of the Peloponnesian War fatally allows that 'it has been difficult to record with strict accuracy the words actually spoken'. As a result, 'the speeches are given in the language in which, as it seemed to me, the several speakers would express, on the subjects under consideration, the sentiments most befitting the occasion' (Thucydides 1972: 47–8). In the absence of possible documentation, then, Thucydides relies on probability, on his own sense of what sounds inevitable and fitting. Again, history no longer looks opposed to fiction, but within history we encounter different genres of writing, in which it is appropriate to tell different kinds of story. Or we could say that different kinds of historical evidence need to have different kinds of construction put upon them. Herodotus writes not about contemporary political history, but about the past, and about different cultures, Lydian, Scythian, Egyptian. His evidence is oral, anecdotal, antiquarian. While Thucydides' success in setting a pattern for future historians meant that few had a good word to say for Herodotus, the distinctive legitimacy or propriety of Herodotus' kind of history to the sort of evidence available – Thucydides' own criterion – remained undeniable, and so his lasting reputation was assured.

Momigliano notes that, subsequent to Herodotus, when Western archivists recorded the wonders of the New World, classical scholars were quick to point out that Herodotus and not Thucydides was now the useful historical precedent. Momigliano believes too that historical writing since the 18th century has become, more and more, a discourse within which you can find that mixture of geography, ethnography, mythography, sociology and any other human science originally conflated in Herodotus and condemned by his critics as the mixing of poetry and history (137, 141, 220). Eventually Herodotus arrives on the agenda of American 'new historicism' when a study of him appears in a series under the aegis of the journal, *Representations*, by François Hartog, who concludes that a 'return' to Herodotus is possible because of 'a shift . . . in the historical field' especially signalled by 'recent inquiries into the imaginary representations of various societies' (Hartog 1988: 378).

This coincidence raises the question of how to historicize the historians Herodotus and Thucydides. We see our reflections in the historical mirror by which they make us more aware of our own preoccupations, methods and practice. But their power to make modern historians conscious of their own preoccupations, methods and practice may, in turn, inspire these historians to still more productive meditations on Herodotus and Thucydides. Hartog notes that Herodotus wrote his more documentary histories of the Persian Wars, closest to what was to become Thucydides' model, later than his more ethnographic work, and probably during his stay in Athens. History, then, becomes the discipline into which Herodotus matures, 'one which – naturally – could ripen only in Athens' (312). His pre-Athenian writings were therefore retrospectively constructed as mythologies and fables; they were in this way distinguished from the greater seriousness which belonged ideologically to an Athenian history representing its cultural supremacy past and present. Sophisticated scholarship of Classical historiography is now attentive to the ways in which historical meaning can change with the reception of its audience; how, for example, 'the language in which Greece once celebrated itself can come into its own to celebrate Rome' (Fox 1993: 47).

One can easily point to passages in the *Histories* which support the view of Herodotus as an Athenian ideologue: 'Thus Athens went from strength to strength, and proved, if proof were needed, how noble a thing freedom is' (Herodotus 1972: 369). Here is that mixture of civic optimism and chauvinism recognizable in the funeral speech Thucydides gives to Pericles in his history and which is taken up, ironically, by the Chorus in Sophocles' *Oedipus Tyrannus*. The conclusion to be drawn by someone writing up the Greek campaign against Persia is straightforward: 'one is surely right in saying that Greece was saved by Athens . . . It was the Athenians who – after God – drove back the Persian king' (487). While there are qualifications and caveats built into Herodotus' account of Athenian glory, many more appear in his tentative records of other cultures. When he has lived in the environment in question he happily turns his experience against home prejudices:

> The Greeks have many stories with no basis of fact. One of the silliest is the story of how Heracles came to Egypt and was taken away by the Egyptians to be sacrificed to Zeus, with all due pomp and the sacrificial wreath upon his head; and how he quietly submitted until the moment came for the beginning of the actual ceremony at the altar, when he exerted his strength and killed them all. For me at least such a tale is proof enough that the Greeks knew nothing whatever about Egyptian character and

custom. The Egyptians are forbidden by their religion even to kill animals for sacrifice, except sheep and bulls and bull-calves as have passed the test for 'cleanness' – and geese: is it likely, then, that they would sacrifice human beings?

(Herodotus 1972: 148–9)

Famous and fabulous stories of Indian ants bigger than foxes, or snakes that fly, either characterize his ethnography – his interest is as much in the Persian character of the anecdotes – or, in the case of the snakes, are checked against the bones themselves, viewed by Herodotus and graphically described for our supposedly wiser interpretations. By way of contrast, we could argue that Thucydides in his history was repeating the sin he deplored, a self-destructive introspection in Greek culture typified by the internecine quarrel between Athens and Sparta after their combination to forge an emancipating Greek identity in the war against Persia. The historiographical corrective here would have been the interest in other cultures, devoid of imperialist design, found in Herodotus' histories, and the significance of his writing of a history of the Persian wars while the unity it epitomized collapsed all around him.

Both historicizings of Herodotus situate him ideologically, the first making him a tool of Athenian propaganda, the second placing him in opposition. It is perhaps not possible for both interpretations to be true, but what has been historically transmitted to us is the probability of both. In this endless shuttle, though, questions of probability return us to the present and the task of deciphering the rationale for choosing one interpretation over another. Hartog, consistent with his new historicist setting, has a Foucauldian suspicion that all writing, in one way or another, ends up conniving at the political power that permits it. Yet, as Momigliano has demonstrated, it is then necessary to explain the consequent misreading of Herodotus' writing as possessing, above all, a liberating alternative to the sad tales of contemporary political history.

THE NATURE OF HISTORICAL EXPLANATION

What is it to offer an historical explanation of an event or action? History and aesthetics do seem to have this vital fact in common, that they are concerned with events which are particular and individual rather than instances of the application of a scientific law. The Battle of Waterloo is not a member of the class of Battles of Waterloo about which we might then generalize. We may certainly learn from such an event and utilize this knowledge in our interpretations of other battles or analogous events. But this knowledge could not be formulated, in the way that knowledge derived from the scientific observation of phenomena might hope to be, in terms of causes and effects and the laws deducible from them. As Schopenhauer stated, a science of history would 'be a science of individual things, which implies a contradiction' (Schopenhauer 1958: 440). Causal explanation characteristically allows us to predict when such events will occur again, and obviously this is not the case with historical events. Part of the meaning of a thing's being historical is that it has happened once and for all. Santayana's warning that those who do not remember the past are condemned to repeat it only makes sense in tandem with the realization that history may repeat itself symbolically but not literally, and it is the duty of the alert interpreter of events to realize when such figurative coincidences occur. No more could we learn from Bernini's statue of *David* or Manet's *Déjeuner sur l'herbe* how to repeat their achievement or predict the time and circumstances under which they might occur again. Bernini's sculpture owes something essential to Michelangelo's *David* as does Manet's painting to the *Fête champêtre* once attributed to Giorgione but now thought to be by Titian; but to say in either case that one caused the other seems as wide of the mark as to expect a modern reworking of their achievement to be comparably transparent. Artworks and historical events, like our reworkings of them, are inseparable from their moment.

Let us look more closely at 'the Battle of Waterloo', or rather at one novelist's attempt to show the difficulties in taking that close look. In Stendhal's novel *The Charterhouse of Parma* (1839), the hero, Fabrice, attaches himself, disguised as a hussar, to a series of leading figures on the battlefield who, instead of illustrating the battle's course in their purposeful galloping about and supposedly decisive actions, lead him into total confusion.

> The sun was already very low, and it was on the point of setting when the escort, coming out of a sunken road, mounted a little slope three or four foot high to enter a ploughed field. Fabrice heard a curious little sound quite close to him. He turned his head; four men had fallen off their horses; the general himself had been thrown off his horse, but he was getting up again, covered in blood. Fabrice looked at the hussars who had been flung to the ground. Three of them were making convulsive movements, the fourth cried: 'Pull me out from underneath!' The serjeant and two or three men had dismounted to assist the general, who, leaning upon his aide-de-camp, was attempting to walk a few steps. He was trying to get away from his horse, which lay on its back on the ground, struggling and lashing out furiously with its hooves.
>
> The serjeant came up to Fabrice. At that moment our hero heard someone behind him say quite close to his ear: 'This is the only one that can still gallop.' He felt himself seized by the feet: they were taken out of the stirrups at the same time as someone gripped his body under the arms. He was lifted over his horse's tail, and then let slip to the ground where he landed in a sitting position.
>
> The aide-de-camp took Fabrice's horse by the bridle; the general, with the help of the serjeant, mounted and rode off at a gallop; he was quickly followed by the six survivors of the escort. Fabrice got to his feet in a furious rage and began to run after them shouting '*Ladri! Ladri!*' (Thieves! Thieves!). It was

rather comical to be running after thieves in the middle of a
battlefield.

(Stendhal 1958: 63)

The passage is packed with inconsequential detail. It speaks for
itself by telling us nothing. The reader of this and the rest of
Stendhal's description of a decisive historical moment has, like
Fabrice, to hang on to individual concerns and make sense of
things privately in the absence of any alternative point of view.
And, yes, Fabrice ends up a comical figure, grotesquely out of
place in a vast tragic arena, proclaiming his own small loss, his
own 'curious little sound'. Stendhal's technique suggests with
equal force that to try to place an intelligible grand historical
construction on this mess would be just as comical. Either way, as
the follower of the comic tale of Fabrice or of the tragic history
of Waterloo, the reader is unseated, and also ends up in the mud,
on his or her rear. The event of Waterloo is written as a confusion
of genres. Whichever interpretative vehicle we mount, it is liable to
be commandeered by the narrative and dispatched in another
direction. Tolstoy, who saw active service in the Crimea, claimed
to have learned all he knew about war from Stendhal's description
of Waterloo (Berlin 1992: 48).

Nevertheless, we do try to explain historical events and to
interpret works of art consistently. What can be the content of
these explanations and interpretations if not scientific? Thinkers
as different as Condorcet and Croce, the late Enlightenment
philosophe and the 20th-century follower of Vico and Hegel, have
claimed that there is a 'science' of history. For Condorcet, the
scientific analogy was unproblematic:

If man can, with almost complete assurance, predict phenomena when he knows their laws, and if, even when he does not, he
can still, with great expectation of success, forecast the future
on the basis of his experience of the past, why, then, should it
be regarded as a fantastic undertaking to sketch, with some

pretence to truth, the future destiny of man on the basis of his history?

(Condorcet 1955: 173)

Cause is, undeniably, a word which frequently crops up in history books. The same aura of elucidation hangs over the word 'influence' in books of art history and literary criticism. But here the idea of cause may well have the function ascribed to it by Michael Oakeshott when he writes that in historical discourse it is 'no more than an expression of the concern of an historical enquiry to seek significant relationships between historical events' (Oakeshott 1983: 88). In his vigorous attack on the belief that we can predict the course of human history, Karl Popper insists on the uniqueness of its events and the absence of the antecedents required for scientific generalization: 'the most careful examination of one developing caterpillar will not help us to predict its transformation into a butterfly' (Popper 1986: 109). Popper's famous polemic against historicism, *The Poverty of Historicism*, is therefore not directed against historicism as defined here, and which Popper Englishes as 'historism' (17). By historicism, Popper means a philosophy which, like Condorcet's, claims to predict the course of human history on the basis of past behaviour. If we accept his refutation of this unwarranted extension of scientific generalization, then we are left with the question of which interpretative categories we can use without raising false expectations of historical and aesthetic understanding.

Oakeshott describes the writing of history as a restorative act in which we discover from fragmentary survivals 'what may be inferred from them about a past which has not survived' (52). This act of salvage looks much more like learning a language or reconstructing a cultural context than conducting an experiment under laboratory conditions. The latter practice prescribes and limits our speculations; the former grants us entry into a linguistic or cultural medium in which we can find our own standpoint. This freedom, though, produces uncertainty: familiarity with a language increases our awareness of the multiple idioms and meanings of which it is capable. We can produce an entirely probable gloss on an historical event or a convincing interpretation of a literary text, but, in the face of equally probable competitors, we are still tempted to reach for an external scientific proof that ours is the only possible one. We might claim that the agent or author intended our meaning, but this fact would only verify our reading if we could add convincingly that such a motive *caused* things to turn out as we have understood them. As philosophers such as Donald Davidson and, here, Carl Hempel argue, 'the presentation of an action as being appropriate to the given situation, as making sense, cannot, for purely logical reasons, serve to explain why in fact the action was taken' (White 1978: 105). But although the artefacts of culture and history have been produced once and for all, their interpretations have not. There is no reason why our understanding should be foreclosed in this way. The particularity of historical event and artwork fixes them in time yet opens them up to a mode of explanation which changes over time. The events subsumed under scientific laws are not one-offs; they can recur, and their recurrence can be predicted – that is what is meant by their conformity to law.

But the scientific law, to remain valid, cannot change. By contrast, historicism shows, fundamentally, as in the case of Herodotus just looked at, that the historical character of interpretation allows us as critics continually to refocus a present that is always changing, always sliding out of focus again. We should therefore expect the process of understanding the past to be as unending as is the future.

We can conclude from this necessary but difficult summary of some of the main principles of historical explanation that history and aesthetics have cleared the way for a kind of understanding of their subjects different from scientific understanding. The Augustan historian, Dionysius of Halicarnassus, is especially remembered for his aphorism that 'history is philosophy teaching by examples'. This aptly fits our discussion if we regard each example as irreplaceable, and teaching by examples as an alternative to abstracting from them the general principles to which philosophical explanation aspires on other occasions. Instead, we must infer from each example an explanatory context, and through this act of restoration or archaeology resurrect the medium in which the example makes sense. At the same time, this effort is bound to reflect back to us a sharper picture than perhaps we hitherto possessed of our own typical assumptions and methods. Setting the historical example in context is like learning the language in which it speaks, but the greater our proficiency in that language the more conscious we become of the variety of senses in which our example's speech may be taken. Our interpretative decisions, therefore, will be based on a judgement between different possibilities of the time; and the history of interpretations shows such adjudications to be abundantly and primarily expressive of their own periods of utterance. Historicism is the name given to this apparent relativizing of the past by getting to know the different interpretations to which it is open and deciding between them on grounds expressing our own contemporary preoccupations. Fears then grow that this amounts to uncontrolled relativism on the part of the historian or critic. All one can say so far in mitigation is that changeability in our view of the past is a condition of getting our present into proper perspective. A fixed view of one would entail a contradictory curtailing of our alertness to the formative historical processes still at work in the other.

This book, though, is devoted to examining a theoretical resource for contemporary criticism. It examines the contribution of historicism to our current critical idiom. Pursuit of the logic of historical explanation suggests that understanding the past is much more like the literary/critical activity of interpreting a text than that of discovering a new object of science. But within this linguistic competence, crucial issues of judgement and questions of justice have to be resolved. Which past meanings should we choose out of a number for which our historical research has identified the rules or grammar? Are Herodotus' writings limited by a hegemonic Athenian view of the world or are they critical of that view? The art of interpretation here is that of hermeneutics, and this methodological crux explains why a substantial section of this book has to be devoted to the hermeneutic tradition and *its* constitutionally self-critical history. As E.H. Carr saw, history is neither 'a hard core of facts' surrounded by a 'pulp of disreputable interpretation' nor 'a hard core of interpretation surrounded by a pulp of disreputable facts' but a dialectic between the two (Carr 1986: 4,18). Hermeneutics, we shall see, is the traditional means of negotiating this historicist dialectic. But now let us take a preliminary look at historicism in more detail.

HISTORICISM AND HISTORIOGRAPHY

So far, we have been suggesting, the emphasis on truly individual examples which distinguishes aesthetics and history leads to an art of interpretation different from scientific generalizations. This hermeneutic appears vulnerable to accusations of relativism. On my description, the critic appears obliged always to read past works on their own terms without ever formulating a general theory of their why and wherefore. Relativism, though, always works in relation to something fixed; but the logic of historicism is to imply, as we saw, that the point from which the critic speaks is as unsettled by historicism as the object he or she interprets. This is not to say that interpretative theory can on this basis happily contradict itself. Some stability and degree of internal generalization must be established by our interpretations; for to speak the contextual, cultural language which makes sense of the example from the past is still to possess on its terms a general competence – to be capable, as the ethnologist Clifford Geertz phrases it, 'of continuing to yield defensible interpretations as new social phenomena swim into view' (Geertz 1993: 26–7). It is just that the shelf-life of such competence is limited at both ends, by the epoch in which the language is spoken and by the present one whose interested judgements decide between different senses within that language.

Two main points emerge as a consequence of this for our understanding of historicism. The first is that historicists and historicisms can be differentiated by how they measure and define these crucial epochs. They may do so in broad, intermittently illustrated cultural outline, as does the 'archaeology' of Michel Foucault which, in turn, develops the equally bold but less specific 'genealogies' of Nietzsche. Both these thinkers can be seen to be reacting to the over-systematic historicism, as they thought, of a Hegelian tradition. Or, historicism may work more informally, producing, like Jan Kott, a Shakespeare who is 'our contemporary', a 'poststructuralist Joyce', or, historicizing the other way round, revive a neo-Platonic (Northrop Frye, Harold Bloom), Aristotelian (the Chicago School), Kantian (New Critics) or, indeed, Marxist criticism. In these cases it is usually left to others to explain, sometimes polemically, the informal coincidence of past and present which the critic has effected.

This leads to the second point, growing out of this informality, which is that if to understand the historical example is to establish the language in which it takes on significance, then criticism may come increasingly to be a question of style. Issues such as how persuasively we write in that language, how good our vocabulary is, how expressive our periods, become paramount. Our convincing *use* of the interpretative language is what matters, compelling the reader's agreement through rhetorical skill. Even after we as readers have ceased to be convinced, looking back at dated historical interpretations, what we notice are the master-tropes employed, the strategies for persuading us that evidence is being used in the proper sense, the mechanics of articulation. The justification of an interpretation is lodged in its expression. Explanation and historiography, history and its writing, appear to have become the same thing.

This conflation is characteristic of recent, usually poststructuralist writings about history and criticism. In texts ranging from Derrida's *Spurs – Nietzsche's Styles* (1979) to Hayden White's *Metahistory* (1973) we find contemporary theorists redescribing the content or depth of reference of a piece of writing as an effect of the play of rhetorical figures across its surface. In his more popular condensation of his main thesis, White asserts that 'the rhetoric of the historical work is ... the principal source of its *appeal* to those of its readers who accept it as a "realistic" or "objective" account of "what really happened" in the past' (White 1973: 3). The criterion of valid history here becomes the subject-matter of literary criticism: what is possible is a function of what is probable. White notes that, for example, in the 19th century a conspicuously narrative style in history, the undisguised attempt to tell stories about the past, purported greater objectivity than a display of formal analysis (8–9). Historians were thought to murder when they dissected, perhaps in their wish to attack a tradition or to vindicate a new methodology with radical political implications. In England, this conservative suspicion, passed on from Burke and Wordsworth, was very influential. Nowadays, we would probably see things the other way round and believe an engaging story more likely to have been told for ulterior motives than a dry-as-dust analysis. If White is right, though, his scholarship works at the level of style, giving us lessons in how to read history books without introducing us to new facts from outside which they may have omitted. When Peter Gay published *Style in History* in 1974, a year after White's *Metahistory*, he was keen to assert against Carr that history privileges a core of facts over their interpretations (Gay 1974: 197–8). But the facts to which his stylistic rendering of interpretation leads back turn out to be facts about the historian's present. His description of what the historian is about is more in keeping with the historicist dialectic we have been outlining:

Gibbon's way of pairing phrases, Ranke's resort to dramatic techniques, Macaulay's reiteration of antitheses, Burckhardt's informal diction, taken by themselves, as single instances, mean what they say on the page. They describe a battle, analyze a political artifice, chronicle a painter's career. But once characteristic and habitual – that is, recognizable elements in the historian's mode of expression, of his style – they become signposts to larger, deeper matters. Partly idiosyncratic and partly conventional, partly selected and partly imposed by unconscious, professional, or political pressures, the devices of literary style are equally instructive, not always for the conclusive answers they supply but for the fertile questions they raise about the historian's central intentions and overriding interpretations, the state of his art, the essential beliefs of his culture – and, perhaps, about his insights into his subject.

(Gay 1974: 7–8)

Interpretation, then, is not necessarily a usurper of facts, and its medium – style – may be our surest means of access to some of them.

One of Gay's main examples of an historian whose style releases facts, Jakob Burckhardt, set himself the task of writing about individuality – not just as a characteristic of people but as a feature of political states. Burckhardt's history of *The Civilization of the Renaissance in Italy* famously opens with a chapter on 'The State as a Work of Art'. The particularity of his subject-matter, in other words, closes the gap between history and aesthetics, and he makes it his aim to have his readers understand cultural history as they would appreciate art. Burckhardt thus abandons the authority of generalization for a truth to the unique particularity of this kind of artistic statesmanship. He has to deal with princes, such as Lodovico Sforza of Milan, patron of Leonardo, who 'claimed relationship with all who, like himself, stood on their personal merits – with scholars, poets, artists, and musicians' (Burckhardt 1945: 27).

The result is a vast collection of stories, anecdotes and pictures which build up a portrait of an emerging modernity without ever venturing a theoretical explanation. Of course others drew general conclusions from his work. Carr refers to 'the familiar account in *The Civilization of the Renaissance* [of] the cult of the individual', relating it to analogous movements in capitalism and religion which do claim universal explanatory force (Carr 1986: 27). David Norbrook criticizes American new historicist writing on the Renaissance for its unconscious replication of Burckhardt's aesthetic selectivity in contrast to Sismondi's earlier republican history of the Italian states (Norbrook 1989: 95–7). Gay has him anticipating those later writings of Freud (and Freud, in turn, was one of Gay's preoccupations as an historian) which 'saw destruction at [civilization's] very heart' (Gray 1974: 182). But the historiographical paradigm set by Burckhardt's fascination for individuality tells its own historicist tale.

In Burckhardt's history philosophy teaches by examples whose aesthetic individuality resists generalization. Yet this scrupulous historical care for the integrity of the individual falls into revealing contradiction. This is not just the paradox Gay picks out, when he shows Burckhardt giving his individuals enough rope to hang themselves. The tale which particularly catches Gay's attention looks more like one expressing the frustrations of Burckhardt's own commemorative art.

> The citizens of a certain town (Siena seems to be meant) had once an officer in their service who had freed them from foreign oppression; daily they took counsel how to recompense him, and concluded that no reward in their power was great enough, not even if they made him lord of the city. At last one of them rose and said, 'Let us kill him and then worship him as our patron saint.' And so they did, following the example set by the Roman Senate with Romulus.
>
> (Gay 1974: 13–14).

Burckhardt here provides a parable of his individuals' tendency to implode under historical scrutiny – in the freedom, that is, from being made to serve as examples of anything other than themselves. He wants to honour the achievement of Renaissance individuals, but his attempt to make them the patron saints of humanism canonizes the period's 'unbridled egotism' and 'vicious tendency' as much as it does its 'healthier culture' (Burckhardt 1945: 2). At one point he praises Aeneas Sylvius' (Pope Pius II) delight in nature as being 'genuine modern enjoyment, not a reflection of antiquity' (183). In his own case, this is like being able to look affectionately on a character like Lodovico Sforza 'as a kind of natural product [who] almost disarms our moral judgement' (26). He approves Piero Valeriano's praise of the mendicant friar Fra Urbano Valeriano as 'a type of the happy scholar', because he had 'ceased to feel the compulsion under which he lived' (166–7). But this acceptance of nature, this willing of the inevitable explains nothing directly. Burckhardt asks us to believe that his examples will yield the human essence of developing modernity, a heritage undeniably ours, unsullied by didacticism. As Gay points out, however, in later years Burckhardt lamented his own work's failure to inculcate methodological practices so as to obtain a recognizable following: 'I will never found a school' (Gay 1974: 182). Almost alone of Burckhardt's commentators, E.A. Gombrich argued, despite Burckhardt's own protestations to the contrary, for the existence of a persistently Hegelian cast to his thought from his student days, a 'preconceived idea which could have attracted disciples' (Gombrich 1969: 14–25). One might then, with Hugh Trevor-Roper, see Burckhardt's methodological reticence as his commendable 'refusal to fall in with any fashionable school of thought' (Burckhardt 1959: 17). Gay, though, convincingly documents Burckhardt's genuinely expressed regret, but, like Trevor-Roper, still takes his inimitable individualism as his 'most solid claim to immortality'. Croce writes of his failure 'to develop and systematize' his historical reflections, left 'scattered and discontinuous' as a result, with a consequent embarrassment for the student of historiography wishing to 'place' Burckhardt's work (Croce 1941: 104). The Renaissance, in other words, emerges as brilliantly represented because Burckhardt has forgone the visible role of elucidator.

But Burckhardt does seem to be re-experiencing his present in the style of his historiographical dilemma; and we might expect as much when the subject of his history, Renaissance individualism, is presented as the source of his understanding of modernity. The outmoded political loyalties of his aristocratic liberalism ruled him out of party affiliations or else left him, belatedly, to cultivate like-mindedness through his lectures; but he similarly distanced himself from the intellectual centre of his profession, preferring seclusion in Basel to the Berlin professorship formerly occupied by his great teacher, Ranke. His *Renaissance* continued his habit of grasping a present in which worth excluded itself from political representation or favour because to write the truth about the present, as of the Renaissance, demanded a detachment supremely confident of its subject's aesthetic expressiveness, leading by example in contempt of anything more collective or programmatic.

To Burckhardt's mind, the Renaissance city-state identified its aesthetic form with its political content. He could, therefore, write its history as answerable style, as fluency in his topic's political poetry, a tactic which we shall see, in chapter 5, was developed by postmodern stylistics. Yet on all sides his work uncovers indirectly his specific view of that time and his own. Examples like Burckhardt reveal how historiography – the way history is written and the literary criticism this invites – contributes to an historicist dialectic. Are we to infer, then, that no stylistic extravagance on the part of the historian is counter-productive? As Stephen Bann argues in *The Clothing of Clio* (the style of history's muse) we must beware of thinking of the historian as a taxidermist. The stuffed animal of the past may appear, incontrovertibly, to be the thing itself; but such history's lack of a living relationship with our present is more of a disadvantage than the new shape, altered to fit modern needs and prejudices, in which it can continue to live with us. At some stage, though, the alteration may no longer be recognizable; it may cease to tell the historical tale of the difference between past and present which made it necessary. No longer recognizable *as* an alteration, it will become like Popper's singular insect, only this time a butterfly of which no amount of observation will lead us to deduce the antecedent caterpillar. Roland Barthes, for example, celebrates the writings of the 19th-century French historian Michelet, with the claim that Michelet's characteristic 'theme' or 'myth' in fact 'resists history' (Barthes 1987: 201–2). Michelet, thinks Barthes, inherits various models of historical explanation – 'History-as-Plant (Herder), and History-as-Spiral (Vico)' (30) – but rejects them in favour of a pattern of equivalences. These 'equalities', as Barthes calls them, constitute the grid of themes with which Michelet replaces received modes of understanding.

> History does not advance by cause but by equalities. From the peasant Jacques to Jeanne d'Arc, the successional is not of causal but of equational order. Jeanne is not the result of a certain number of anecdotal data. She is essentially a relay of identities . . . all are weak, all are Christ, all are the People.
>
> (Barthes 1987: 36)

Michelet's metaphorical equivalences, here, are not eccentric but thoroughly concentric, describing Michelet's self-defining choice of a coherent world-view which his reader has to understand *in toto*. 'The three ages of coffee are those of modern thought', he startlingly announces at one point; and indeed they are, he brilliantly persuades us, if we make his mythic choices. But Barthes' Michelet seems to possess myths without any sense that they are mythologizing something else. Everything is metaphorically equivalent, hence Barthes' sense that although history might inflect Michelet's present in many ways, 'it could not change his myths' (201–2). It was not the object of them in any way; they did not interpret it.

At this point, though, we might want to say that such an inter-pretation of Michelet best describes a stage in Barthes' own career. We catch him in the mid-1950s, suspended between the ruling Sartrean existentialist phenomenology and the Saussurean semi-otics in which he was about to create the brilliant initiatives for which he would be remembered. He is still drawn towards Sartre's analysis of the mythic constitution of the self, the mixture of authenticity and betrayal uncovered in Sartre's sequence of studies of Baudelaire, Flaubert, Genet and others. Also, the metaphorical equivalences this tradition uses to thematize individuals are begin-ning to look like the menus of Barthes' general semiotics of culture. In either case – Michelet's or Barthes' – historical difference, and the dialectic between past and present we have seen it make possible, disappears. A synchronic tropology of the present – a treatise on figures of speech – displaces a diachronic map of the past. The writer no longer describes how meaning changes across time, diachronically, but the idiosyncratic choices with which he struc-tures his own experience at any one time, synchronically. In Barthes' *Michelet*, the aptness with which we grasp Michelet's or Barthes' present concerns progressively sidelines their ostensible interest in writing about the past.

Can we therefore assume that when the content of history and its writing or stylistics become the same thing we may gain a vivid rendering of the writer's present, but we necessarily lose a more revealing articulation of past and present through mutual dialogue? In my reading of Barthes' *Michelet*, the past which is discussed – represented by 'Michelet' – becomes an increasingly obvious substitute for a nearer past not discussed – post-war French intel-lectual life. But if the choice of metaphor for the present is to be informative, that bit of the past thus used to stand for the present must have its own significance, a significance added to by the fact that it can be made equivalent to the present in this way. Historicism is hard to eliminate from any interpretative inquiry. Even in historical stylistics, historical difference creeps in as the distinction between tenor and vehicle, or a word's meaning and the new use to which it is put. And the historicist dialectic is refigured here as the interaction by which the new use sheds more light on the old use that makes it possible. My account of Barthes' *Michelet* implies that however contemporary or synchronic may be writers' ambitions, their self-understanding will be worked out diachronically. There are no laws against using one period of the past as a metaphor with which to understand another; and the substitution will change our view of both. But we can no longer postpone a fuller history of the historicism relied on here.

2

THE RISE OF HISTORICISM

ENLIGHTENMENT BY NATURAL LAW

'The Rise of Historicism' virtually translates the title of Friedrich Meinecke's great book on the subject, *Die Entstehung des Historismus*, a tome situating itself at the end of a tradition which, in reaction to the Enlightenment, had progressively relativized all historical truth, making it a function of the particular culture or group to which it belonged. Its essence, according to Meinecke, was 'the substitution of a process of individualizing observation for a generalizing view of human forces in history' (Meinecke 1972: lv). Meinecke conceded that the desire to find law and typicality in the past will never go away and will always have to be accommodated by the historian. He also acknowledged that the rise of historicism had caused harm, but held 'that it has the power to heal the wounds it has caused by the relativising of all values' (lvi). How had this come about?

The story Meinecke tells is of a growing resistance in Europe to the strongly influential idea that human beings observe laws of their own nature that are everywhere invariable and constant.

History, like any other form of thinking about humankind, should therefore take its bearings from this foundation, whose rationality had been proclaimed with a new confidence from Descartes onwards. In its social and political applications, essential, male humanity was given definitive form by 17th-century political theorists such as Hobbes, Pufendorf, Grotius and Selden. By observing human beings in general, therefore, a view abstracted from the peculiarities and differences they displayed within existing institutions, these thinkers deduced the character of a society fit to cater for their basic needs and wants and so most likely to prove viable and to last. Equally, according to this method, in observing different societies we can expect to detect the efforts by which their citizens endeavour to keep the laws governing their communities in line with natural law. Ideally there would be no difference. Natural law is not a rule justifying a state of nature prior to political organization; it embodies the rationality by which we contract out of that dangerous and fraught condition into the benefits of society. Only if natural law is universal in its rational appeal can we be sure that it will bind all our fellow citizens in so far as they are reasonable and prudent.

For the 18th-century historians succeeding to this tradition, the possibility of a universal history loomed large. All human societies were perceived as being ruled by the same rationality whereby they had formed themselves to escape the perils of the lawless state of nature. The choice, as represented by Samuel Pufendorf in *On the Duty of Man and Citizen According to Natural Law* (1673), which reveals the aims and logic of any society, is straightforward. 'There [in the state of nature] is the reign of the passions, there is war, fear, poverty, nastiness, solitude, barbarity, ignorance, savagery; here is the reign of reason, here there is peace, security, wealth, splendour, society, taste, knowledge, benevolence' (Pufendorf 1991: 118). Everywhere these evils and these goods are the same for all people. Pufendorf is recognizably writing just after the Thirty Years War and in support of the Peace of Westphalia, a settlement keen to identify common interests rather than religious differences as essentially defining human features. When Voltaire writes an essay on universal history, the immense variety of nations covered is meant simply to reflect the order in which civilization chronologically progressed. He begins with China because he wants 'to consider [the globe] in the same order as it seems to have been civilized' (Voltaire 1759: 4,10). Of course he was well aware that this could embarrass the *amour propre* of his European audience, and he delighted in attacking their pride by beginning with 'a people who had a connected history in a language already fixed, before we knew how to write' (10). But the nature he studied, its vices and its virtues, remained the same, irrespective of temporal, geographical or cultural difference.

Inheritors of the natural law tradition may disagree as to how human nature is furthered by society. Hobbes, like Pufendorf, believed that we move from a natural state of war into one of artificial pacification; Montesquieu argued that it is only in society when men 'lose their feeling of weakness' that 'the state of war begins' (Montesquieu 1989: 7). Montesquieu's interest in cultural difference, like Voltaire's, aims to tell truths about his own society. Like parts of Voltaire's *History of Candide* (1759), Dr Johnson's *History of Rasselas* (1759) and Diderot's *Les bijoux indiscrets* (1748), Montesquieu's *Persian Letters* (1721), a supposed exchange of letters between Persian visitors to France and their homeland, defamiliarizes his society by constructing its Orientalized mirror-image. In 'Some Reflections on the Persian Letters' of 1754, Montesquieu ascribed their 'whole effect . . . to the perpetual contrast between the reality of things and the odd, naive or strange way in which they were perceived' (Montesquieu 1973: 284). The freshly presented reality stayed the same, in Persia as in France. As C.J. Betts aptly points out in the introduction to his translation, even the book's most exotic fantasies of Oriental sexual licence and pleasure are evidently 'the perfection of 18th-century social and sexual pleasures' (22). Montesquieu is fascinated by the differences in the particular cases 'to which human reason is applied' through the rule of law. Laws differ but their rationale remains the same. Montesquieu's famous experiment of microscopically watching taste-buds expose themselves as a tongue unfroze led to his conclusion that people in cold countries enjoyed less vivid sensations. 'A Muscovite has to be flayed before he feels anything' (Montesquieu 1989: 233). Laws and penalties could therefore be expected, reasonably, to alter in conformity to climatic difference, but the constant here is of course 'reason'. And the shapes reason takes keep the histories of other times and places germane to interpretations of the present. Otherwise, they would merit Descartes' criticism of those immethodical and fabulous histories contributing nothing to enlightenment: 'when one is too curious about things which were practised centuries ago one is usually very ignorant about those which are practised in our own time' (Descartes 1967: I, 84). On the conservative rather than liberal side of 18th-century thought, Dr Johnson's poem, *The Vanity of Human Wishes*, published ten years before *Rasselas* and *Candide*, takes its survey like Voltaire 'from China to Peru' but reposes on the 'just observation of general nature' for which Johnson praised Shakespeare. An earlier English Augustan, Alexander Pope, begins his *Essay on Man* (1733) by exhorting his friend Lord Bolingbroke to 'Expatiate free o'er all this scene of Man;/ A mighty maze! but not without a plan'. Bolingbroke did just that in his *Letters on the Study and Use of History* (1752), admired and defended by Voltaire, where the plan emerging from the study of history is again Montesquieu's spirit of the laws, here described as the reduction of 'all the abstract speculations of ethics, and all the general rules of human policy, to their first principles' (Bolingbroke 1791: 93).

Despite such unanimity of conservative and progressive thinkers, English Augustans and French philosophers, their interest in the particular examples they subsume under first principles appears to exceed the use to which they are put. Montesquieu's sense of the ridiculous – the mark so he claims, of sociability – leads to a delight in paradox as expressive of this social tone as the general reasonableness which otherwise predominates (333). He becomes if not a raconteur, then an anecdotalist. Both his and Voltaire's studies of history and culture evince what Meinecke calls 'an avid hunger for facts and a tendency to collect enormous masses of material' (93). Where Meinecke saw pragmatism, a willingness to use empiricism instead of rationalism if that would have the desired rhetorical effect, the major critic of the Enlightenment, J.G. Herder, saw only confusion. Montesquieu's *The Spirit of the Laws* was 'a Gothic edifice in the philosophical taste of the century . . . a frenzy of all times, nations and languages like the Tower of Babel' (Herder 1969: 217). This, as Herder put it in his sarcastically entitled *Yet Another Philosophy of History for the Enlightenment of Mankind: A Further Contribution to the Many Contributions of the Century* (1774), was the result of modern historians 'modelling all centuries after the pattern of their time' (185). Historical facts remained obstinately expressive of more than the general principles to which Enlightenment history reduced them. More charitably, we might say that Montesquieu is a classic liberal and appreciates above all the difference between tolerating social practices other than his own and approving of them. But for Herder, the scope of Montesquieu's toleration makes a nonsense of his explanatory principles; Montesquieu's understanding of the variegated nature of different societies leaves his unifying principle, the spirit of their laws, looking hopelessly abstract. Accordingly, the historian's facts accumulate in proportion as his sense of their connection refines itself out of existence. Herder thinks the logical conclusion here is the intellectual perversity he attributes to the *Encyclopédie*, the massive collaborative work of the *philosophes*: 'what the art of printing is to the sciences, the *Encyclopédie* is to the art of printing: the highest peak of perfection and durability' (211). As the principle of historical organization fades, so the facts it adduces but cannot process correspondingly multiply. Good news for printers.

CRITIQUES OF ENLIGHTENMENT – VICO AND HERDER

Before Herder, however, an obscure Neapolitan philosopher had evolved a new science which could accommodate historical variety without loss of principle. In his *New Science*, first published in 1725, Giambattista Vico argued that the error of 'the three princes' of the doctrine of natural law, Grotius, Selden and Pufendorf, had been to begin 'in the middle; that is, with the latest times of the civilized nations' (Vico 1970: 394). The kind of understanding Vico proposed was, in the word of his translators, 'ontogenetic', or one which grasps its object in its development through time. In this development, a nation, society or normal object of historical study follows a pattern or 'course', as Vico calls it, analogous to that of the individual human life – childhood, maturity, decline and dissolution. To view historical explanation in this way is to anticipate much with which this book deals later on. Vico interprets the cultural self-understanding with which the historian has to cope as divisible into three principal stages – the first peopled by Gods, the next by giants or heroes, and only the last by people themselves. To begin with the final demythologized view of the world is to neglect its explanatory origins and so to fail to understand it. And here lies 'the master key' of Vico's science: the discovery of the mythological or *poetic* sources of civilization. Historical chronicles often begin too late 'because with our civilized natures we [moderns] cannot at all imagine and understand only by great toil the poetic nature of these first men' (399). But only by this exercise in poetic interpretation can we comprehend from what modern society has evolved, and only in grasping this development can we begin to understand the society it produced. Furthermore, Vico believed that the 'course' run by ancient civilizations such as those of Greece and Rome was recapitulated in a 'recourse' played out by modern nations. History is cyclical in the sense that individuals constitutionally rework an inherited pattern of evolution on their own terms. Our lives are repetitions of the same self at different stages of its development.

The expressiveness of historical fact, therefore, which was incidental to Enlightenment history, is fundamental to Vico. And as the individuality of different histories comes to the fore, so the arts of literary interpretation grow in importance for the historian. Vico anticipates two cardinal aspects of hermeneutics: its affinity, given the first of Vico's stages, with 'divination . . . meaning the science of the language of the gods' (379); and its characteristic distinctiveness from sciences of natural objects we have neither made nor experienced as having the connectedness of different parts of our life. Vico, to use his own terminology, gives us in advance the heroic, mythological sources of major ideas of Schleiermacher and Dilthey, studied in chapter 3 – Schleiermacher's theory of hermeneutic divination and Dilthey's separation of science (*Naturwissenschaft*) from the human or cultural sciences (*Geisteswissenschaften*).

Historicism, then, takes its rise from the convergence of literary interpretation and historical explanation demanded by the particular modes of expression of different nations at different times. Vico seeks to establish the 'natural law' of the nations, certainly, but this universalist ambition is dissipated by his computation of the different stages of cultural development as different levels of literary interpretation. In Isaiah Berlin's summary, Vico evolves 'a way of conceiving the process of social change and growth by correlating it with, indeed, viewing it as conveyed by, the parallel change or development of the symbolism by which men seek to express it' (Berlin 1976: xix). Primarily this requires a projection back into the past in order to reconstruct the past on its own terms. To do this is not to feign a sentimental forgetfulness of modernity, but to credit past symbolic practices with meanings which, translated, would have significance now. Berlin describes the remorseless grind of the demythologizing by which Vico takes the past seriously. 'He is the father of economic interpretation of ancient legends . . . No myth is safe from Vico's zeal: every legend is grist for his socio-economic mill' (54). This Vico is like a latter-day cultural materialist, preserving the value of myth by showing that it can be translated into an historical commentary on material conditions still governing life today. Thus the myths of Poseidon, the story of Zeus in the shape of a bull abducting Europa by swimming off with her on his back, the legend of the Minotaur, all describe fears of piracy or trade wars. Continuity with present canons of significance is thus preserved, but we should be aware that Vichian interpretation does not, as the term 'demythologizing' usually implies, devalue past mythic expression. Vico often insists that when the mythic animation of the world is taken figuratively, the result is not necessarily enlightenment. Ignorance of the past can be screened by a modern rhetorical sophistication which the good historical interpreter should see through.

> For when we wish to give utterance to our understanding of spiritual things, we must seek aid from our imagination to explain them, and, like painters, form human images of them. But these theological poets, unable to make use of the understanding, did the opposite and more sublime thing: they attributed senses and passions . . . to bodies, and to bodies as vast as sky, sea, and earth. Later, as these vast imaginations shrank and the power of abstraction grew, the personifications were reduced to diminutive signs. Metonymy drew a cloak of learning over the prevailing ignorance of these origins of human institutions.
>
> (Vico 1970: 402)

By contrast, a romantic like Blake tells us in *The Marriage of Heaven and Hell* not to forget 'that all deities reside in the human breast' (153). For Blake, the cardinal sin is to forget that all our categories of authority and reality are metaphors, human constructions, poetic figures answering to the imagination in each one of us. For this forgetfulness to be possible, though, he seems to have to postulate an original rhetorical awareness which Vico would have thought anachronistic. Vico encourages a further effort of imaginative sympathy with the past to try to understand how ancient peoples could take their myths literally, as the proper description of the truth. Only by doing this can we preserve the historical difference which demythologizing would otherwise erase. We will look at this dialectic in more detail when considering the hermeneutic tradition's attempt to break with its own Romantic origins.

There is, in Vico, a respect accorded to the historical specifics of cultural expression which goes well beyond the Enlightenment's liberal tolerance of national diversity. When Pufendorf writes a chapter 'On Interpretation' and considers particular exceptions to the rule of law, he refers them to equity. 'For equity is the correction of what is deficient in the law because of its universality' (Pufendorf 1991: 110). Equity, however, is still law; it effects in Pufendorf's argument a startling reversal whereby the unfairly universal application of laws is suddenly revealed not to be universal enough, fallibly human rather than unarguably natural. The surest sign that we should have recourse to equity is 'if it is apparent that natural law would be violated if one followed closely the letter of human law' (111). Vico's poetics, as we have seen, contrastingly assert that we have not understood the claims of particular exceptions to our notions of what is everywhere the case unless we can imaginatively reconstruct the historical situation in which it would be possible for the exception to be literally true. In Herder, this sympathetic effort becomes the means to a 'higher criticism'. For the purpose of understanding 'the Hebrew scriptures', he urges the reader to 'be a shepherd with shepherds, a peasant in the midst of an agricultural people, an oriental among the primitive dwellers of the East' (Berlin 1976: 186). The philosophical point to be taken here helps specify Herder's historicism in two ways. First it highlights his linguistic determinism, his belief that it is in the use of language that we become human. As Charles Taylor points out, Herder thinks that this definitive use of language is displayed not simply in designating things but in communication. It is because we understand each other that we know to what the words we use refer and not vice versa (Taylor 1991). The humanity revealed in language, therefore, is a cultural manifestation bound to conventions of time and place, pastoral and Oriental in the case of the 'Hebrew scriptures'. And this diverse, cultural determination of what is human is the second main aspect of Herder's historicism.

In his *Politics* Aristotle defined man as a political animal because he believed that it is in political association that the purpose of human nature is achieved (Aristotle 1988: 1252b–1253b). This view could be cited by Enlightenment theorists to support their idea that human nature is elucidated by the reasons why men (and it is always men – the feminist project of writing a history of women's systematic exclusion from such representative activities will be examined in chapter 5) contract into society. Or else it could be used by anti-Enlightenment historicists, like Herder, to assert that we become human in as many ways as there are languages, cultures and societies. 'Nature', Herder tells us, 'exhausted all the varieties of human form on Earth, that she might find for each in its time and place an enjoyment, to amuse mortals through life' (Herder 1968: 78). The task remains, though, of saying what those different manifestations have in common without reducing their individuality to that bland conformity which Vico's imaginative reconstructions and Herder's sympathetic projections were meant to disprove. Like Vico, Herder models cultural variety on the stages of an individual life – childhood, maturity, age – each understood proportionately to the overall narrative.

> The youth is not happier than the innocent, contented child; nor is the peaceful old man unhappier than the energetic man in his prime . . . And yet the striving never ceases. No one lives in his own period only; he builds on what has gone before and lays foundation for what comes after.
>
> (Herder 1968: 188)

Again anticipating the hermeneuticists of the 20th century, Herder holds that our historical knowledge must be internal to its object in the way that self-knowledge is. The stories we tell to make our own experiences look coherent provide models for history. To illustrate further why this insight does not produce a uniformly applicable science we can enlist for Herder an unlikely ally in another critic of the Enlightenment, Jonathan Swift.

Now Swift would have had little time for Herder's championing of cultural diversity; but he would have agreed with the classical dimensions of the individual discovered elsewhere by Herder's comparative historical studies. In Book 3 of *Gulliver's Travels* (1726), Gulliver encounters the Struldbruggs, people who never die but age endlessly. Their life is one of perpetual decay and progressive deprivation. The eventual ghastliness of their existence – 'Sans teeth, sans eyes, sans taste, sans every thing' – seems worse than death. But when Gulliver heard of their immortality, he waxed lyrical, before meeting any Struldbruggs, on the good he could have achieved, had he been born one. Swift's satire on Gulliver's gullibility shows indirectly the extent to which we are obliged to understand our world in human proportions. Conceive human life as free of the requirement that it be embodied in historical individuals, and it loses all meaning. The Struldbrggs, we can say, have outlived themselves. But also – and here he is even closer to Herder – Swift argues that the most important knowledge cannot be learned theoretically at a remove from historical experience. Gulliver initially fancies himself one of a community of Struldbruggs who would have:

> the Pleasure of seeing the various Revolutions of States and Empires; the changes in the lower and upper World; antient Cities in Ruins, and obscure Villages become the Seats of Kings. Famous Rivers lessening into shallow Brooks; the Ocean leaving one Coast dry, and overwhelming another: the Discovery of many Countries yet unknown. Barbarity overrunning the politest

Nations, and the most barbarous becoming civilized. I should then see the discovery of the *Longitude*, the *perpetual Motion*, the *universal Medicine*, and many other great Inventions brought to the utmost Perfection.

(Swift 1959: 210)

But the wider this historical panorama becomes, the more it loses authority and returns us to the nonsense of its supposed author, the Struldbrugg. The gestures towards universality and perfection towards the end of the passage are comically unconvincing because the prior inventory of events intended to support the optimistic conclusion observes no principle of connection, no more than does the unstructured, purposeless tedium of a Struldbrugg's superfluous experience. For Herder, too, human progress is not a science but an 'endeavour', a growth always appropriate to the character or age of the individual (Herder 1968: 187). It is measured by the human perception of 'what has gone before' and 'what comes after', and so will exhibit variations according to cultural circumstance analogous to differences in personal biography.

Concluding his study of the rise of historicism, Meinecke wrote that it 'enabled the process of individualization to become aware of itself by teaching men how to understand all history as the development of something individual, though always conditioned by typical successions of events and regularities' (Meinecke 1972: 492). Historicism, therefore, could be seen by him as healing the wounds its relativism had caused through an assuaging humanism: it humanized our notions of historical continuity. History for Vico and Herder had to be understood as something we are actively implicated in, like purposeful living, not external to, like the phenomena rationalized by scientific investigation. Its 'succession of events and regularities' were thus more like those of an individual's experience than happenings instantiating law-like regularities. The primacy accorded to their expressiveness denotes the convergence in historicism of historical, cultural and poetic interpretation.

KANT AND HEGEL – TOWARDS HERMENEUTICS

It would be misleading, however, to tell a story in which Enlightenment was gradually superseded by historicism. The Enlightenment in Western Europe was highly complex and many-faceted. It could be characterized by the scepticism of Pierre Bayle's *Historical and Critical Dictionary* (1697–1706) and David Hume's *Treatise on Human Nature* as aptly as by the rationalistic confidence of the Cartesian tradition. The very abbreviated accounts given here of some main features fit the image of it invoked by the self-defining attack on it by an emergent historicism. The Enlightenment proceeded to grow still more sophisticated, assimilating its basis in natural law theory to juridical and historical aspects of philosophical logic. When we try to understand what Kant and Hegel had to say about historical interpretation, we are dealing with thinkers who believed that the Enlightenment ideal of universal truth was attainable, but not immediately – as a practical idea of reason for Kant and a truth grasped in its historical production for Hegel.

In his *Idea for a Universal History with a Cosmopolitan Purpose* Kant proposes the writing of a history which will not be an empirical record of facts but the interpretation of world events as conforming to certain rational ends. He concedes that the idealism of his project might turn it into a novel rather than history (Kant 1970: 52). But this fictional latitude must be set against Kant's belief that the history of a people only begins when they produce annals for an enlightened readership, 'an educated public'. He had no time for the relativism of a Herodotus or a Herder. Like Hume, he believed that authentic history began with Thucydides. Two years after publishing his *Idea* he reviewed Herder's *Reflections on the Philosophy of the History of Mankind* with notorious severity, and was bound to do so given this fundamental premise that a people only become historically articulate when their annals observe standards so abstract and universal that they can be shared by all. That, Herder would have thought, is the problem.

Nevertheless, Kant's cosmopolitanism is not as dismissive of cultural and historical individuality as it at first appears. He does think that scientific laws of cause and effect apply to human history to the extent that it is a history of desire, will, passion – everything he takes to be different from the exercise of reason. But the history of the latter is the history of a different kind of thing and so escapes causal explanation. Nevertheless Kant holds that nature orientates all these disparate causes and effects, making up the history of unreason, towards a single end. Only on this assumption can we explain how nature can hang together as a coherent whole and science be systematic. In the case of mankind, nature's unifying purpose is to develop our distinctive rationality. Such an achievement exceeds the scope of any single individual, and so nature in this purposive, teleological aspect describes a striving for enlightenment characterizing the human species from generation to generation. Historical interpretation, then, detects this progressive fulfilment of rationality which connects the present with the past.

Moreover, Kant holds that such progress, philosophically understood, shows his two kinds of history, causal and purposive, joining together. Like cultures which have not yet entered the rational world of Kant's 'educated public', the non-rational urges which make us, like animals, susceptible to scientific explanation produce discord and antagonism of a kind which encourages our contrastingly authentic rational nature to sort things out. Adapting Rousseau's ideas on the state of nature and the social contract, Kant maintains that the strife of animal existence is not the natural law theorists' barren and perilous state; nor is it a Rousseauistic utopia. But it is the ideal existence for developing our innate rational capacity to establish a civil society which can administer justice universally (45).

Also, just as the species rather than the lone individual is the vehicle of nature's purpose, so society is needed to align individuals' naturally competitive desires with their natural vocation for rational improvement. Kant's elucidatory paradox here is that, in society, a person's natural unsociability – all the selfish desires incompatible with other people's satisfactions – works to the advantage of society. For the greater the competitiveness fostered by the state of nature, the more ingenious will be the social solution which has to be evolved, and, correspondingly, the greater the advance in intellect. Like Montesquieu, Kant does not think that strife ends in society, but that it is resolved by a rational self-discipline which will, by definition, intellectually animate and persuade the other members of a human community. Culture and art, argues Kant, 'are fruits of [man's] unsociability' (46). They testify to how the social order enlists our common animal drives in the service of the distinctively rational fulfilment nature intends for us. The two meanings of nature, understood causally and purposively, now work in tandem. Sounding more like Herder, Kant can claim the highest purpose of nature to be 'the development of all natural capacities' (45).

This same contested diversity carries on to the larger stage of relations between societies. Their natural competitiveness must be harmonized within a commonwealth once more rationalizing this natural unsociability for the furtherance of human progress. Even wars, Kant tells us, are nature's way of realigning states in patterns more productive of its purpose for us. Faced with so unworried a sublimation as this of the messy events described, say, in the earlier extract from Stendhal (see pp. 15–16), we may feel queasy. Our credulity is similarly tried when Kant casts us as one of the citizens he imagines winking at the selfish motives of the ingeniously just law-giver. How can he live on two planes at once, as nature's servant and as a selfish nature? But Kant's accommodation of these two aspects of human nature, one moral and the other pathological, show him, like Vico and Herder, contributing to the next move in historicism, that of hermeneutics. He has formulated the grounds of a science complementing the natural sciences, a distinction leading to one that is potentially definitive for hermeneutics – that between the natural and the cultural sciences. He does so not in a mythological fashion, like Vico, but in such a way as to make precise some of the problems belonging to this distinction over which hermeneutics would subsequently labour.

Two in particular stand out. The first is that Kant is unable to picture the goal of nature. His conception of human fulfilment is purely formal, descriptive of a logical possibility not a real existence. What would the entirely moral society, the kingdom of ends, look like? As Kant's guiding idea for human development, it regulates, but never constitutes, social behaviour. Law-givers, however moral, will still possess the mixed nature described in Kant's *Idea*. We, at least, will never know if they are prompted by desires belonging to their animal natures or by universal moral reason, for nature has geared the unsociability of the first to promote the latter. In Kant's famous phrase (46), we are composed of warped wood or crooked timber (*aus so krummen Holze*). But doesn't this return us to Herder's cultural determinism? Humanity, it now appears, only emerges in particular cases, in specific, historical examples of the compromise between its animal and rational natures – crooked timber – not in a timeless, rational essence.

The second difficulty follows from the first and suggests an answer. Culture and art are still not the proper objects of Kant's new discipline. Their expressiveness is symptomatic of the larger groupings – species and society – in which progress takes place. Acceptance of law, rather than the continuous effort to produce civilization, is paramount. Kant wrote his *Idea* in 1784. By 1790 he had published his *Critique of Judgement* in which the faculty investigated, judgement, subsumes both teleological and aesthetic judgement – both, that is, the logic of historical explanation and the logic of critical appreciation.

History and culture now display equally nature's purpose for us, showing that we are right to assume nature's cooperation in making possible our distinctively rational activities. Kant never quite explains how reason evolves out of nature; that transformation remains as much an 'idea' as the translation of competitiveness in the state of nature into social and then cosmopolitan finesse in his *Idea*. We will have to look at this crux and his successors' solutions in the coming discussion of hermeneutics. For the moment, though, we should note the convergence of historical and critical methods. According to *Idea*, we are only interested in the past by the evidence of a rationality distinctively human and alive now in the moral law we prescribe ourselves. To be famous, in other words, be virtuous! In the *Critique of Judgement*, however, history and aesthetics are valued for their common expression of nature's connivance at our fulfilment. This fulfilment is certainly a rational vocation too narrowly defined for Herder; but it is one whose expressivity calls for a philosophical appreciation distinct from that of the natural sciences, a historical poetics. Such a poetics of history binds together the rift between reason and nature which Herder never acknowledged and begins to address the problem unresolved by Herder's intuitive appeals to the coherence of biography – how to define as an intellectual discipline this alternative to the natural sciences.

Kant's attempt to describe the continuity of human history enlists the help of aesthetics. In aesthetic appreciation we judge of the fitness of nature to those purposes defining our rational vocation. We make sense of history by detecting these progressive accommodations of reason by nature, and their differences, across time. Herder's intuitive appeal to autobiography – the stories we tell to explain how we are what we are – is replaced by a more rigorous demarcation of different intellectual disciplines. Aesthetic experience, as described by Kant, then fills out the formal logic of his universal historiography with particular sensuous content. Culture and art now contribute to our understanding of nature's cooperation in our rational progress. As a corollary to this, though, we might expect Kant to insist upon the historicity of art and culture, or the tailoring of our critical appreciation of them to the stage they evoke in nature's purpose for us. That he does not do so shows his understandable unwillingness to fall back into a relativism akin to Herder's. But here lies a still deeper problem.

Why should we grasp nature's plan for our rational fulfilment in the same way at different times in our history? Why shouldn't progress have the effect of so transforming our understanding of the world that it is changed utterly for us? The expression of human aspiration in one age can seem barbaric, misguided or just completely *different* in another. Vico's cyclical answer is to rely on a vestigial natural law guaranteeing that the 'courses' he is charting will have their modern 'recourses', and to use his ability to detect these repetitions as evidence for the regularity of the underlying 'natural law of the nations'. Kant avoids this circle; our poetic understanding of history is of a different order from that detecting scientific regularities. But for him to say that we can still appreciate the expressiveness of different cultures aesthetically does not help if he wants aesthetics to support, not to be the exception to, history's continuous disclosure of enlightenment. In other words, Kant assumes that progress and historical continuity are the same thing. He allows, as we have seen, for a fair degree of conflict and rivalry in the material out of which progress emerges, but not for contradictions embodying real discontinuities.

It is in contrast to this uniformity that Hegel's *Phenomenology of Spirit* (1807) accounts for knowledge as the progressive self-recognition of 'mind'. The mind which rationalizes nature in the course of scientific improvement comes to see in nature only its own self-image reflected back to it. Nature is now intelligible, but at the cost of its own distinctive otherness. Dissatisfied with this contradictory outcome, the mind then strives for a fuller rendering of nature's otherness which will, in turn, be defeated by its own success. Philosophy, consequently, becomes a history of these contradictory encounters, a dynamic chronicle revised at each stage by the transformation of what it is about. The history of the mind's constructions of reality is, then, as much a history of discontinuity – since both terms, mind and nature, repeatedly change their meanings – as it is one of continuity. Eventually we reach an absolute identity of mind and nature beyond which progress is impossible, but whose meaning can still only be experienced by going through the whole journey of its production again, each stage of which will now be seen definitively in context. The trouble, though, is that this context looks much more like Hegel's *Phenomenology* than the real world, and its discontinuities and contradictions appear the kind acceptable within a single narrative. As a colonizing model of knowledge, too, Hegel's phenomenology, as we shall see in chapter 5, will inspire postcolonial and feminist theory to imagine still more radical dissociations within history. In the meantime, though, we can usefully set off the literary unity of its philosophy against the contents of literary history.

In 1917, T.S. Eliot tried a more accessible Hegelian formulation on the readers of *The Athenaeum* when he asserted that:

> what happens when a work of art is created is something that happens simultaneously to all the works of art which preceded it. The existing monuments form an ideal order among themselves, which is modified by the introduction of the new (the really new) work of art among them. The existing order is complete before the new work arrives; for order to persist after the supervention of novelty, the *whole* existing order must be, if ever so slightly, altered.

> (Eliot 1932: 15)

For Eliot, poet and critic are lodged within this process. Here, literary creation and critical understanding model the flexibility needed to overcome Kant's rigidity. The contradiction between new literature and received canons of critical understanding harms neither, but sharpens the sense of the difference between past and present, refining the historical understanding of both.

We can take Eliot's view here a bit further. The fact that a literary work is not necessarily damaged by contradiction suggests one of the changes required of a Kantian understanding of history.

We need a theory to explain how historical expressiveness is created anew out of contradiction. Symbols may fail history by sublimating its struggles, or history may betray art by enrolling it as propaganda. Each time this happens, though, we don't, somewhat ridiculously, repudiate history or banish the artist. Instead we end up understanding history in more depth, glimpsing further resources of expression beyond the reach of a particular or current concept of art.

A novel in contradiction with itself is not like a failed mathematical theorem or an incoherent scientific hypothesis. It pushes its critics into formulating new standards by which they can make sense of its undoubtedly continuing expressiveness. The effect of Hegelian phenomenology on critics like Eliot is to allow them to argue for a new notion of tradition. Tradition should be a necessary part of making sense of the present. But it would not help for it to be a rigid, fixed structure; it should house what Eliot called 'the present moment of the past' (22). This mobility of understanding, though, in which an Enlightenment universal modifies to accommodate individual differences, was only a stage in Hegel's philosophy. And Eliot writes in apparent ignorance of the details of Hegel's philosophy of history and its hermeneutical development. In his *Lectures on the Philosophy of World History* (1822), Hegel distinguishes three different kinds of historical writing – original history, reflective history and philosophical history. 'Immersed in the spirit of the events he describes', the writer of original history 'does not rise above it to reflect upon it' (Hegel 1975: 13). The reflective historian, by contrast, tries to seize on 'the past as a whole', looking for what 'is as valid and present now as it was in the past and ever will be' (16, 19). This pragmatic approach, chronicling different kinds of criticism, leads to the 'higher criticism' of which Hegel now disapproves, although it is perhaps closest to his phenomenological method. The conclusion of Hegelian phenomenology, though, in which, as already described, all its stages are finally seen aright, squares with Hegel's third and favoured kind of history, philosophical history. This ultimate rationalization is 'the spirit which is eternally present to itself and for which there is no past' (24).

In this final Hegelian scenario, the expressive energies we have seen constantly historicizing our understanding of the past and the present, modifying the tradition binding them together, are superseded. That absolute perspective from which everything is at last seen in its right place is more adequately described, in Hegel's view, by philosophy than art, criticism or even religion, the end-point of Eliot's thought as he too moved towards a more static historical certainty. Nothing which might happen in the future should now alter our estimation of the past. History in that sense has come to an end. Again this sounds like Hegel substituting his own writings and their conclusions for real history. But as Raymond Plant summarizes it, Hegel's 'notion of the end of history is not primarily a chronological one. It is rather a logical one concerning the institutional patterns required for the completion or realization of certain concepts – freedom and reason in particular' (Plant 1983: 239). Hegel's absolute resting-place recreates an Enlightenment universal at a higher level; or so it seemed to the emergent hermeneutic tradition, which pictured all transactions of human understanding as historical negotiations between present and past, not their cessation. To this tradition we now turn.

3

THE HERMENEUTIC TRADITION

INTRODUCTION

Hermeneutics is the science of interpretation. It stresses the individuality of each human expression and, against scientific generalizations, claims that we choose between the several meanings any utterance might have in the light of the special circumstances under which it is made. In this way we resolve grammatical ambiguities, appreciating, for example, that commands in one situation are not intended to hold good in another. 'Children must be accompanied at all times' is usually posted in a location fortunately qualifying an otherwise eternal prescription. Hermeneutics solves cultural puzzles, so that Dr Johnson's apparently witless act of standing in the pouring rain becomes intelligible as a deed of penance. Its use in historical explanation is thus a logical consequence of this orientation towards discerning the unique circumstances of the individual example.

Historically, this tactic was most in demand for the interpretation of religious texts. By definition, religious inspiration is unprecedented: the deity is not bound by the laws of this world. However, the unavoidable constriction of divine purpose to human expression in order to become comprehensible allows for endless interpretation, as these original constraints change with the times. In the Christian tradition, criteria of relevance have been continually and controversially updated from the Church fathers to the German 'higher criticism' of George Eliot's mentor, D.F. Strauss, and Feuerbach, to Don Cupit and the last Bishop of Durham – acceptance of their revisions depending upon the needs of the interpretative community to whom they spoke. Hermeneutics, though, also survived 19th-century secularization to become a general theory of understanding. Its Greek etymology also points behind Christianity to Aristotle's *Peri hermeneias* (On Interpretation), already philosophical, not theological, in its application. But a god still lurks linguistically in the background. Hermes was the divine messenger of the Greek pantheon. Confusingly, this great communicator was also thoroughly untrustworthy, the god too of 'thieves, pickpockets, and all dishonest persons'. Yet, as Lemprière's *Classical Dictionary* also recalls, statues of Hermes sometimes 'represent him as without arms, because, according to some, the power of speech can prevail over everything, even without the assistance of arms' (Lemprière 1984: 373–4).

Hermeneutics, therefore, leaves us an ambivalent legacy. Its secularization of a religious model seems to align it with demythologizing modernity. Yet its power radically to reinterpret in the light of historical circumstance is still best caught in the figure of an antinomian god who connects hermeneutical respect for particular utterance with a significance potentially at odds with everything else. Furthermore, this supernatural patron of hermeneutics is sometimes only recognizable in the character of trickery and deceit in which he frequently appears. Mischievous, obstreperous rebellion against current norms of interpretation problematizes the tradition and continuity often thought to be hermeneutics' exclusive inheritance from religious thinking. Hermeneutics, that is to say, can perversely require us to reinterpret the very notions of tradition and continuity on which it is based. This divisiveness, we shall see, is a recurrent feature of historicism in its hermeneutical confrontations from the Reformation to modernity, and then postmodernity.

If hermeneutics has an early modern beginning or renewal, then most historians of hermeneutics would agree with Gerald Bruns in pointing to Luther's insistence on the self-sufficiency of scripture in contrast to the traditional authority of the Church which was reaffirmed at the Council of Trent (Bruns 1992: 146–7). Luther's slogan, *scriptura sola*, was intended to assert the plain sense of holy writ undeniably brought home to its readers in a collusive religious experience. The sense is understood through an effective spiritual change, a modification of being; and this existential dimension allows Luther to anticipate the much later philosophical hermeneutics based on Heidegger's ontology. But, above all, this personal hermeneutic of Luther was stabilized by scriptural prescription. The true interpretation of scripture and genuine religious experience authenticated each other in the reading process. To latter-day observers, though, this circular guarantee did not appear to have worked. Private judgement had increasingly found itself at odds with institutional norms. As Stanley Rosen puts it, 'divine commands', hermeneutically discerned, 'either found or dissolve communities': the political dimension opened up by interpretation is as likely to produce conflict as it is to cement solidarity (Rosen 1987: 88). A major tradition in social theory from Max Weber to Ernst Gellner concedes the connection between the disenchantment or demystification of ecclesiastical authority, the rise of democratic hermeneutics, and the advent of nationalism. In Gellner's summary:

> Equal access to a scripturalist God paved the way to equal access to high culture . . . society can and does worship its own

culture directly and not, as Durkheim taught, through the opaque medium of religion. The transition from one kind of high culture to the other is visible outwardly as the coming of nationalism.

(Gellner 1983: 142)

But this grounding of nationalism, with its characteristic territorial disputes, in hermeneutic liberty had been interpreted by Spinoza.

In his *Theologico-Political Treatise*, published in 1670, Spinoza lamented that 'religion is thought to consist, not so much in respecting the writings of the holy Ghost, as in defending human commentaries, so that religion is no longer identified with charity, but with spreading discord' (Spinoza 1951: 98–9). Rejected by his own Jewish community, Spinoza reaffirmed the Protestant belief of the Dutch society in which he lived that religious authority was founded on the meanings of its sacred texts and not derived from external sources, whether supernatural, natural or institutional. He sharply distinguished between interpreting the words of scripture by 'twisting about and reversing or completely changing the literal sense', his charge against Maimonides, and his own historicism (117). While he advocated understanding the Bible 'in the light of history', with respect to 'the occasion, the time, the age' of the composition of each of its books, he believed that in so doing the reader worked analogously to the scientist investigating what was common to all natural phenomena. Yet his emancipatory emphasis on reading both scripture and nature by 'the natural light of reason' defined itself in opposition to Rabbinical and Papal authority. Furthermore, despite his apparent pluralism – 'every dominion should retain its original form' – Spinoza was historically obliged to write a partisan *Treatise* in favour of states tolerant of liberty of opinion, such as his own United States of the Netherlands (244, 264). Spinoza's scientific analogy fails, and his hermeneutics remain incomplete, because the historical particularity or cultural relativity he attributes to religious utterance finally overrides its cosmopolitan pretensions.

England, intermittently at war with Holland during Spinoza's lifetime, exhibited still more starkly the tension between the universal enlightened ambitions of hermeneutics and the local rivalries it immediately provoked. The establishment of a reformed English Church on roughly Lutheran principles had not ensured the convergence of the religious experience of different individuals within a common culture. In 18th-century England, the dissenting, Puritan tradition, blamed for the Civil Wars and continuing social strife, seemed proof that hermeneutics was politically divisive. English Protestant culture had tried to reproduce reformed versions of Catholic discipline. Donne and Milton tempered individual religious enthusiasm with a Protestant form of spiritual exercise. Poets like Marvell and Dryden tried to redefine the public sphere in line with a constitutionalism which all citizens must sensibly share and critically sustain. The attack on any radical hermeneutics producing schism and sectarianism was continued by their Augustan successors who, like Swift, ironically rubbished an unspoken but in fact inalienable consensus of interpretation, or, like Fielding in *Tom Jones*, figured this broad understanding as the composition of the nation state. By the time that Burke wrote his *Reflections on the Revolution in France*, the redemptive experience characteristic of Luther's reader of scripture had been reconsecrated, this time as one of political participation apparently just as religious, and anterior to Enlightenment once more. A 'noble equality . . . through all the gradations of social life' has now, Burke deplored, 'to be dissolved by this new conquering empire of light and reason' (Burke 1987: 67).

So hermeneutic practice has its own history, and specific versions of this history. It achieves its first classic theoretical formulation in the work of a thinker sometimes called the founder of Protestant theology, Friedrich Schleiermacher.

SCHLEIERMACHER – THE GRAMMAR AND DIVINATION OF HISTORY

The two approaches

Schleiermacher argued fundamentally that hermeneutics had a particular and a general dimension. Sometimes both these aspects appear contained within his theory of language, which explains how the particular word, in order to have meaning, must inhere within a grammatical system. Language is a fluid, growing medium, whose correct usage can never be completely known or prescribed. The art of understanding, the hermeneutic art, lies in distinguishing occasions when it is right to let grammar prescribe from those when grammar should give way to the genuine innovation which 'individualizes the language anew' (Schleiermacher 1977: 49). At other times, Schleiermacher takes hermeneutic sensitivity to particular historical circumstances to license a psychological or empathetic understanding of an author's words – a process of divination which may complement but need not depend on grammar for the meaning at which it arrives.

Accordingly, Schleiermacher's hermeneutics has given rise to two main lines of interpretation, which privilege either his grammatical or his divinatory emphasis. Wilhelm Dilthey is taken to have approved and advocated the primacy of psychology, and, more recently, modern hermeneutics has followed H.G. Gadamer in criticizing this psychological Schleiermacher and encouraging scholarship to salvage his linguistic hermeneutics. The inner experience of the author is a special object for hermeneutics if one takes the view, in line with the Kantian philosophical tradition being developed by Schleiermacher's contemporaries, that our experience is never exhausted by the scientific descriptions adequate to the external world. Hermeneutic sensitivity to expressions too individual for general classification aligns hermeneutics with aesthetics, and interpretation with recreation. Were the psychological method to take over entirely, 'there would', thinks

Schleiermacher, 'be no need for hermeneutics, but only for art criticism' (48). In fact, we shall see that Dilthey joined Schleiermacher's two versions together, making it a criterion for identifying the language proper to hermeneutic exegesis that it be expressive of subjectivity. This solution has considerable problems of its own, but Dilthey's difficulties come from responding to an ambivalence in Schleiermacher's original position. If Schleiermacher is unable to stick to his linguistic version, his hermeneutics become nothing more than a general theory of understanding. We encounter the same problems in understanding a foreign language, or in interpreting the words of another author, or in deciphering a record from the remote past, as we do in understanding our own language. Once we are fluent in the different linguistic conventions, we face the usual contextual problems of judging when non-standard usage is mistaken and when it legitimately adds to the language, distinguishing solecism from neologism. The cultural determinism of Herder, for example, gives way to a kind of universal grammar. The psychological approach, on the other hand, has the merit of trying to do something not achieved in ordinary communication and description. Hermeneutics has a special task again if it takes as its object an inner life complementary to its outward expression. It also now has the problem of explaining how we can have access to someone's thoughts in a medium other than our common usage. The 'questionableness' of this alternative is the starting-point for Gadamer's critique. The linguistic Schleiermacher – the Schleiermacher, that is, of grammatical hermeneutics to the exclusion of divinatory hermeneutics – anticipates Saussure and Gadamer's own deployment of the linguistic turn Heidegger gave to hermeneutics, but more of that later. The psychological Schleiermacher is best understood with reference to his Romanticism and his Christianity.

For to grasp 'the thinking that underlies a given statement', and so a psychological experience which is not fully described in that statement, is, for Schleiermacher an act of divination.

Schleiermacher's use of 'divinatory' has definite theological resonances. In his original German he writes of *die divinatorische Methode* and *die Divination*, Latin coinages whose theological echo is not present in the more common *Ahnung* (Schleiermacher 1959: 109). The 'divinatory' supplement to our understanding of someone's words restores us to the familiar idiom of the spirit rising above the letter. With a religious – in Schleiermacher's case, Lutheran – model in mind it is easier to see how Schleiermacher might have envisaged our having thoughts which were cramped rather than facilitated by their expression. The religious context also explains how Schleiermacher could have thought of the past as hermeneutically decipherable in terms other than those in which it was actually recorded. Walter Benjamin was to rework a comparably religious 'concept of history'. From a position of religious faith or ideological scepticism, one knows that the past could always have been different. To divine God's purpose in history can be equivalent to voicing history's distortion, through human waywardness or variety, of that original purpose – our authentic purpose. The religious background of divination makes sense of the notion of a revealed but inhibited or imperfectly expressed purpose which might be conceivable in the case of *any* author. And sidelined in this quest to recover a full meaning is, precisely, history, which now appears to impose circumstantial constraints on full expression rather than to seek to tell the whole truth. But before dismissing this out of hand as a superstitious break from history, we should again note its symmetry with militant critiques of the ideology of history, such as Benjamin's, which although thoroughly political in form still seem to require the leaven of a religious perspective.

The 'higher critics' who followed Schleiermacher rebuked him for stopping short of a full historicizing of the Gospels. 'He only goes half way; he doesn't pronounce the final words', complained D.F. Strauss, whose own work, *The Life of Jesus*, inaugurated a quest for the historical Jesus extending through Albert Schweizer to works like Geza Vermes' *Jesus the Jew* (Harris 1973: 34–5). It quickly inspired Feuerbach's reduction of religion to anthropology – 'in God man has only his own activity as an object' – not intended by Strauss but fuel for Marx's critique of that supposedly natural state of human oppression which our supernatural vocation had excused. Strauss, though, does not appreciate that the 'final word' might not be to abandon theology for the historical Jesus, but to acknowledge that in confronting the relativity of historical constructions, and so describing an alternative to history, the theological idiom might once more apply. Strauss almost seems to concede as much in *The Life of Jesus* when, supposedly disagreeing with Schleiermacher, he insists that Christianity possesses only a psychological reality, but one whose radically different thinking still needs to be described by the religious category of the miraculous: 'if Schleiermacher claims a miracle for the origination of his real Christ, we have an equal right to claim one for the origination of the ideal of Christ in the human soul' (Strauss 1898: 772).

The comparative study of religion expanded strikingly in Schleiermacher's day, but he definitely associates the 'comparative method' with the grammatical sphere of hermeneutics, and the 'divinatory' with the New Testament exegesis central to his role as a Protestant pastor and theologian. Those who object that they cannot share Schleiermacher's doctrinal convictions, and that they *have* to share them in order to give content to his psychological hermeneutic, need not forfeit the *function* which the religion can play hermeneutically, as the example of Benjamin shows. But the 'cultured despisers' of religion, as Schleiermacher would call them, are usually and conversely content to collapse hermeneutics into the general theory of understanding against which the psychological, divinatory method, with its intuitions of particular deviations from the general rule, stood out. They can argue, as we will find Gadamer doing, that the conversations we can have with the past are sufficient corrective, if our hermeneutic arts are skilled enough, of our ideological preconceptions. Hermeneutic understanding of the past both indicates the tradition which makes such understanding possible and questions exactly those canons it uses through the adjustments and improvements inevitably arising from their particular applications. A mutually enlightening conversation rather than an interrogation, Gadamer would claim, is the best description for how we engage philosophically with our past. But Schleiermacher in psychological, divinatory mode, he would say, wants the past explained with reference to a principle different from the general rule by which we must anyway understand it. His linguistic opponents thus define the divinatory method out of existence.

Dialectics

A collected edition of Schleiermacher's hermeneutics has now been compiled from his many handwritten manuscripts of aphorisms, lecture notes and drafts. Its effect is to show the degree to which Schleiermacher was a dialectical thinker. His natural habit of mind is to hold two opposed positions at the same time in tension. Their differences remain unresolved, but their dependence on each other for a self-defining opposition is clarified. This is primarily the case with Schleiermacher's central opposition of grammatical and divinatory hermeneutical principles, as we shall now see in more detail. On a more general view, though, his entire hermeneutical project is dialectical in purpose. Schleiermacher is quite unequivocal in his desire for a general hermeneutics. The tradition he has inherited is too specialized; no progress can be made in hermeneutics, especially as it applies to scripture, unless the discipline can be shown to have overall philosophical coherence. For Schleiermacher, the main implication of believing this is that the central religious texts of his culture should be understood just like any other texts. Knowledge of their sacred quality can only be a consequence of having understood them. 'The customary belief', writes Schleiermacher, 'that the Holy Spirit is not to be subjected to the rules of interpretation is simply erroneous' (1977: 67). Schleiermacher squarely faces the apparently secular conclusion that 'every element' in Christian scripture 'must be treated as purely human' (106). There is nothing special, it seems, in scriptural susceptibility to interpretative procedures which Schleiermacher thinks apply equally to 'newspaper advertisements' (181). Any written text or conversation is equally fair game.

On the other hand, consistent with my conclusion above, Schleiermacher does also appear, dialectically, to restore some specificity to the religious texts he initially levels with all others. To treat the possibilities of writing in full, he has, to some extent, to return to the uniqueness, for him, of the Gospels as models of communication. On the way to that conclusion, the process of understanding has in any case been used to sanction a grasp of individuality bypassing general rules and approximating to artistic recreation. Nevertheless, especially in his early writings on hermeneutics, grammatical interpretation predominates. Schleiermacher can sound so unilateral on the importance of understanding language that little room is left for the complementary psychology we know he might claim to divine behind its conventional uses.

'Language is the only presupposition in hermeneutics', asserts one of Schleiermacher's early aphorisms; 'there is no thought without words', he declared to the Prussian Academy of Sciences in 1829 (50, 193). He separates the 'internal speaking' of thought from the 'shared language' it might come to modify, but there is no suggestion that thought can become accessible other than through the play of particular utterance and general *langue* (98–9). Indeed, in one passage, scientific renewal is described as taking place through linguistic growth, at one with 'the rejuvenated and living terminology created by this renewal' (73). Science and its paradigms are demonstrably as interconnected for Schleiermacher in explaining scientific revolutions as they are for our own philosophers of science working in the shadow of Thomas Kuhn. But a more consistent anticipation lies in his willingness to see textuality everywhere. This correlates with his persistent expansion of hermeneutics into a general principle of understanding. Dilthey will try to remedy the vagueness of Schleiermacher's expanded concept of language here, redefining as symbolic the subject-matter of the human sciences he thinks Schleiermacher's hermeneutic ambitions imply. Schleiermacher's grammatical hermeneutics, however, sounds quite undifferentiated when we hear that 'the vocabulary and the history of an author's age together form a whole from which his writings must be understood as a part' (113). Later in this same 'compendium' of 1819, in case we thought Schleiermacher was distinguishing 'vocabulary' and 'history', he emphasizes that 'the era in which an author lives . . . is a finished text' (118). Why, then, bother separating out psychological from grammatical interpretation, if whenever we go behind an author's work to intuit his personal motivations we only encounter more text, more of the same 'linguistic sphere' (118)?

Schleiermacher's most famous hermeneutical dictum – that we should understand an author better than he understood himself – trades on the idea of an all-embracing grammatical interpretation (112). As a reader, an author is potentially as good as the rest of us; authors have no hermeneutical advantages in the interpretation of their own texts. Psychological insight seems simply to intensify our linguistic understanding of the expressive resources available to an author at a particular moment. If this were true, were grammatical interpretation entirely to prevail, then, Schleiermacher concedes, 'a speaker is regarded entirely as an organ of language' (85), a view familiar to us from poststructuralism. Elsewhere, though, he is quite insistent that to understand an author is not equivalent to understanding another genre of writing. Schleiermacher clearly does not favour an exclusively linguistic interpretation, however close he may approach it on occasion. He remains a dialectician, as indeed one would expect of someone whose major philosophical work is entitled *Dialektik*. Gadamer stresses that the complementary impulse of psychological empathy in Schleiermacher's hermeneutics describes a process which may *issue* in the common language we all use to describe our world, but which, Schleiermacher's psychology implies, exists *prior* to that. Psychological hermeneutics recreates the thinking through which individuals come to understand the words they use; it must therefore do so aesthetically, invoking an attitude to words we might have prior to being able to use them grammatically. To avoid collapsing into grammatical interpretation, it must divine authorial orientation towards language in a different way – as expressive of motivation, as compositional, as style. For Gadamer, the trouble is that Schleiermacher's psychological hermeneutic can then be ubiquitous. We can find it in every act of understanding, complementing the comparative study of another person's or age's linguistic conventions. Whenever we do not understand something, we find ourselves in the same situation as children learning a language; and prior to knowledge of the rules, we have recourse to a 'divinatory boldness' (194) which creatively latches on to clues to the unknown grammatical conventions. One of Schleiermacher's aphorisms claims that 'Every child comes to understand the meanings of words only through hermeneutics' (52). When he genders divination it is as 'the feminine strength in knowing people'. The childlike and feminine character of hermeneutics both implies dependence on a dominant and masculine order of understanding and attests an irreplaceable aesthetic individuality.

Expressiveness and truth in history

Highlighted here is the general problem of the status of hermeneutics as conceived by Schleiermacher. It isn't scientific in the sense of being progressive. It does not advance on the views of the authors it understands better than themselves. Their writings just become clearer and more expressive of those views; the views themselves are not subjected to critique. Yet if Schleiermacher's elucidations are not just to be those of a philologist, then perhaps the expressive element emphasized by psychological interpretation must prevail. The interpretation of writings in their past context is either like learning a foreign language or like understanding that language as the expressive speech of historical characters. The two processes are dialectically related, and facilitate each other, but neither defines a particular subject-matter for history, distinct from though related to philology and aesthetics. That was the task Dilthey set himself – a critique of historical reason.

To follow through Gadamer's objection to Schleiermacher in this way helps us understand Dilthey's project and eventually Gadamer's, but perhaps skimps on Schleiermacher's own inventiveness. In particular, two aspects of Schleiermacher's hermeneutics need further consideration: the place it gives to aesthetics and the full extent of Schleiermacher's dialectical twisting and turning. The fact that Schleiermacher's psychological, divinatory method is based on aesthetics places him not only as a Romantic but also in a line of thought which these days is no longer dismissed out of hand. Philosophers of science are much more interested than they were in the role of metaphor in scientific investigation, especially, as my mention of Kuhn telegraphed, at those moments of scientific 'renewal' mentioned by Schleiermacher. Also, the dialectic of Schleiermacher's position means that aesthetic understanding is only vindicated as such if it results in grammatical understanding. This is obvious in the case of the child; but the adult thinker who believes something 'comes between the internal speaking and its communication' can only convince us this is so through contributing to our common language a new usage which will in turn have its grammatical rule. Equally, we could not say that we had historically understood his or her achievement could we not point to the individuality and originality involved, a divination which will dialectically return us to indicating the resulting grammatical increase: 'Often nothing at all may be concluded from new invented words' (63). A divinatory interpretation which remains uncorroborated by grammatical rules leans towards the fanatical. Schleiermacher here follows Kant in distinguishing the genius through his or her ability to experience aesthetically something which the rest of us subsequently rationalize. Nevertheless, the subjective creativity of the language-user retains its own individuality in Schleiermacher's divination. Grammatical interpretation never fully accounts for that personal inflection: 'a statement that is grammatically insignificant is not necessarily psychologically insignificant' (103). The justification of the new thought, as it were, is still kept independent of our intuition of the creativity involved in its composition. In historicist terms, we might say that we are constantly measuring the possibilities of the situation against the resources of the individuals, and, as Schleiermacher would of course add, vice versa.

Finally, we should remember Schleiermacher's dialectical turn back from a general theory of understanding to the specific problem of New Testament hermeneutics. Properly understood, this too may temper Gadamer's objections. Gadamer worries that Schleiermacher implicitly substitutes a philological project for an Enlightenment one, detaching questions of language's expressiveness from questions of its truth. His hermeneutics tries to hang on to Enlightenment philosophical credentials, but the simultaneous abandonment of critique, or the idea that advancing on someone's knowledge is measured by closer approximation to the truth, is philosophically impoverishing. The pure expressiveness which can be valued instead results in a kind of nonsense. Gadamer imagines what it would be like for Schleiermacher's hermeneutics to achieve its purpose. Were we to understand the New Testament writers completely, the meaning we could hand on through hermeneutical reconstruction would be like a galvanized corpse, connected to us only by its semblance of life (Gadamer 1989: 167). Its Rip Van Winkle aliveness would be so strange and anachronistic that it might as well be dead. We are back with the model of historian as taxidermist. Schleiermacher, that is, takes account of the special situation of the original New Testament readers and writers of the Gospels, but only in order hermeneutically to stage their discourse in the most expressive way. The truth or lack of it in what is said becomes irrelevant; our ability to understand becomes paramount. Thus, in Gadamer's words, we are 'able to grasp every text as an expression of life and ignore the truth of what was said' (197). Otherwise, though, divinatory interpretation would collapse into grammatical interpretation, as we noted above.

Gadamer is not denying that the truth is expressive in Schleiermacher's sense. He is rather questioning the adequacy of Schleiermacher's definition of expressiveness. If the question of truth is not relevant to the definition of expressiveness, is the latter's definition not too limited or artificial? To say that some-thing was true for an earlier author or writer, is to specify its expressiveness for them in relation to its expressiveness for us, which Gadamer thinks we have to do and which Schleiermacher's idea of complete understanding of the past bypasses. But how can we say we completely understand the past without caring if what was then thought was true or not – or, we could add, moral or immoral, politically desirable or undesirable, and a whole list of anachronistic criteria? Somehow the divination of our shared 'uniqueness' as individuals is meant to overcome an endless list of historical differences.

The quick answer is that Schleiermacher did think that the Gospels recorded truth. He does participate in the liberation from dogma that hermeneutics appeared to offer, but he dialectically shapes his philological/aesthetic exegeses of the Gospels to a dog-matic point of view. Concessions to the human nature of the transmitters of the good news must eventually be set aside by the truth of what they say. The change of tense in a crucial passage, from past to the present Gadamer desires, then takes place: 'For if dependence on Christ was of no significance for one's personal character and for the shortcomings of one's upbringing, then Christ himself is of no significance' (139). In this case, the nonsense of a restoration of the past to life through grammatical and sympathetic recreation must have rung in Schleiermacher's ears with all the authority of the Christian tenet of the Resurrection and its perpetually present meaning.

This is, of course, a particular case, the example of religion; and Schleiermacher's hermeneutics was meant to supply a general theory. Nevertheless, as I suggested before, embedded in his religious idiom may still lie a general hermeneutical function. In the history of hermeneutics, religious dogma appears as the claim limiting interpretative freedom. However, if, as Gadamer holds, Schleiermacher's hermeneutics does not follow an Enlightenment pattern but 'transforms its nature' from critique into something else altogether, then dogmatic contradiction of what is the case can take on a slightly different function. Here it represents the authenticity which may lie behind all ideological constructions of the past. This authenticity may be inaccessible to us, so hide-bound are we by prejudice and circumstance, but it remains an idea which cannot be gainsaid. Schleiermacher is well aware that those who try to read history against the grain risk finding secret meanings everywhere, a fanciful cabbalistic alternative to a tradition of shared meanings (108). His belief in the arbitrariness of history is highly abstract. Gadamer's quotation of one of Schleiermacher's diary entries, also quoted by Dilthey in his *Life of Schleiermacher*, is meant to show the enormous task which lay ahead of Dilthey if he was to explain how Romantic hermeneutics could become the human sciences. 'True historical significance rises above history. Phenomena exist, like miracles, only to direct our attention towards the Spirit that playfully generates them' (197). But the religious idiom remains the most uncompromising challenge to the continuity of historical tradition on which understanding is meanwhile obliged to rely.

DILTHEY'S CRITIQUE OF HISTORICAL REASON

Dilthey's Romantic heritage

Wilhelm Dilthey thought he lived in an age which demonstrated the 'dominance of science over life'. In a late lecture reviewing the current state of culture and philosophy, he pointed out their inefficacy and emptiness, and claimed these deficiencies were not unconnected with the unprecedented scientific progress enjoyed by Western civilization since the 17th century (Dilthey 1976: 111). Science crucially neglected a large area of human experience – typically represented in poetry and fiction – which it was palpably unable to regulate. Such was the dominance of a scientific world-view, however, that the aesthetic exceptions to its rationalizations appeared void of content. The cumulative effect of scientific advance had been to leave free and unmanageable an activity of 'spirit' which sadly had been reduced to nothing more than a grim reflection of this unrestricted anarchy. Art, Dilthey implied, had come to represent the ultimate failure of science to order our lives in their entirety; art had ceased to represent something positive on its own account. Despite the variations on a 'philosophy of life' which Dilthey detected in Schopenhauer, Wagner, Nietzsche, Tolstoy, Ruskin and Maeterlinck, their immediate, usually literary grasp of what science could not as yet explain inevitably took on the subjective character of irrationality in which they were dismissed by the prevailing, scientific world-view.

It wasn't always like this. Dilthey began his mature studies with work on Schleiermacher resulting in a massive but incomplete biography. There he stressed that Schleiermacher saw religion less in dogmatic terms and more as 'the free activity of the individual' (37). The biography of Schleiermacher rings with praise of the great age of metaphysics from Kant to Hegel, celebrating the intimate connection of that philosophy with the literary culture of Goethe, Schiller, Hölderlin and others. Basic to the Kantian origin of this collaboration was the idea that aesthetic experience complements scientific knowledge and makes up the whole of our grasp of life. In his essay 'The Development of Hermeneutics', Dilthey draws on his early work on Schleiermacher, and agrees with his precursor that the 'final goal of the hermeneutic procedure is to understand the author better than he understands himself'. He explicitly links this aim, though, with the Romantic development of Kant's idea that we can apprehend ourselves not just as objects of science but aesthetically and historically. Kant's critique of pure reason prescribes the logical conditions which must obtain for scientific consciousness – knowledge – to be possible. His critique of judgement, on the other hand, shows that our experience is more than can be described by the rules of cognition. For a fully philosophical picture of human life we must consider ourselves under a purposive aspect of which science is not conscious. Dilthey, then, figures Schleiermacher as already proposing a remedy for the cultural malaise of Dilthey's own age. Schleiermacher's hermeneutic ambition is to find a language for this free creativity, in which human beings escape from the causal determinism rationalizing scientific procedure to gain a sense of their own intrinsic vocation. The philosophical emphasis on spontaneity is seen as developing Kant's views on aesthetics and history which Dilthey understood as primarily showing the mysterious connection between nature and mind. He fondly quoted Schiller on Goethe in this regard: 'by, as it were, imitating Nature's creation you try to penetrate its hidden technique. A great and truly heroic idea' (57). The great artist mirrors a greater artist, nature, grasping how the world must have connived at our fulfilling experience of it through time. Again, this intuition of a scheme in which science plays a part is necessarily of something more than can lie within the compass of scientific understanding; and in the Kantian tradition access to this excess is gained by historicizing science and regarding it aesthetically, in its cultural rather than truth-telling capacity. As defined by Dilthey, post-Kantian philosophy from Schelling to Hegel set itself the task of making explicit what was implicit in Kant's thought by 'reach[ing] behind what is given in consciousness to the creative capacity which, while working harmoniously and unconscious of itself, produces the whole form of the world in us' (256). Or, as Wilhelm von Humboldt phrased it in 'The Task of the Historian':

> in order to understand each other [we] must have, in another sense, already understood one another. In the case of history, the preliminary basis of comprehension is very clear, for everything which is effective in world history is also active within man himself.
>
> (Mueller-Vollmer 1985: 112)

Science unconsciously assumes what Romanticism intuits through the aesthetic and historical understanding it especially valorizes.

Dilthey describes Schleiermacher's famous formula of the 'final goal' of hermeneutics – to understand authors better than they understood themselves – as 'a statement which is the necessary conclusion of the doctrine of unconscious creation' (Dilthey 1976: 259–60). To understand an author with true hermeneutic success, then, is to understand him or her in a manner which adds to the author's scientific effectiveness another explanatory context. This context will necessarily seem to have to do with unconscious creation, because it historicizes what the author knows, learning from it something in addition to the truth he or she tells. And this contextualization is something the author could not have said, something he or she lacked the historical distance from themselves to see.

But wouldn't this productive context still have been available to the original author in his or her own aesthetic experience? In Schleiermacher's theory, that could well be true: hermeneutics in its subjective, divinatory aspect emphasizes those formative experiences authors may have of themselves as freely creative natures but which they do not necessarily express. Dilthey's view, though, is that this added dimension is specifically historical, not just aesthetic. It depends, therefore, on an art of historical under-standing which does not reduce to science but which has scientific advantages over the original authors, suggesting the need to recog-nize another *kind* of science. Authorial perspectives are perhaps limited by comparison with the overview that is possible for the historical researcher, and of course historical self-consciousness might have been far from the writers' intentions. The historical turn in Dilthey's thought transforms a Romantic aesthetic with which he felt great sympathy into a philosophy of history grounded on a new science. If he were to succeed, he would oppose to the impoverishing scientific hegemony of his age, and its artistic mirror images, a more rounded world-view in which a new histori-cal discipline complemented traditional science within an enlarged philosophy of life.

To summarize, Dilthey's reworking of the earlier metaphysical tradition – 'Can we imagine a more magnificent conception of the universal system' (67) – in which Schleiermacher participated tries to improve on post-Kantian exploration of the space cleared beyond scientific jurisdiction by Kant's *Critique of Judgement*. The literary example retains, for Dilthey, its Kantian function of giving aesthetic expression to a wider area of social and cultural behaviour than can be known scientifically. But it was in history that he found room to consider how expressions and symbols of *all* kinds might have developed out of an original creativity. In history, too, he found the assumption that their incidence and succession might be explained, and that the logic of this explanation might ground another kind of science altogether – the cultural or human sciences (*Geisteswissenschaften*). He stands, therefore, at the point of dissemination of a poetic model of intrinsic human action, inherited from the Romantics, into other modes of study – sociological, cultural and political. He propels the specialized hermeneutics of law, religion and philology, which Schleiermacher had begun to generalize, into the service of a revitalized humanities fit to compete with science. And he does so by following the turn of Romantics like Schiller, Wilhelm von Humboldt, the brothers Schlegel and, of course, Schleiermacher from the study of 'poetic production to the understanding of the historical world' (257). He is central to our study, therefore, to the extent that he demonstrates the evolution of major questions about the nature of history and historicism out of the concerns of literary theory and interpretation.

Dilthey's new science

Let us look at how this happened in more detail. Dilthey's ambition of writing a critique of historical reason at first appears thoroughly Kantian. His drafts set up categories for understanding history that appear analogous to Kant's categories of scientific cognition. Like Kant, he seems to envisage human beings as belonging to two worlds, the phenomenal world of science and the noumenal world of freedom. The phenomenal world is rationalized by natural science, which explains natural events happening outside us by reference to law and concept. The world to be understood by Dilthey's historical reason will be grasped from the inside by the sympathetic relocation or transposition of ourselves into the lives of others. The symbols and expressions we inherit in the shape of historical records are already in the form by which we understand ourselves. The best symbol for how we sense that our personality coheres is not a theorem but a story, not a science but an aesthetic receptiveness to the relations between the parts and the whole of our life: 'a poem expresses that meaning by a free creation of meaningful connections. The event depicted in the poem becomes a symbol of life' (241).

But we have seen how Dilthey also wishes to resist the Kantian heritage and the Romantic development of it. He opposes the Kantian separation of ourselves as objects of science from our inner autobiographies. Kant had originally intended his third critique of judgement to join together the two realms of necessity and freedom through reflective judgements on their compatibility. Dilthey sees the original division as symptomatic of the obso- lescence of Kant's conceptual framework and, consequently, of Kant's ingenious resolution of its problematic divisions. He puts his position straightforwardly in a late paper on 'The Nature of Philosophy'. Kantian metaphysics is impossible because it sets up mutually exclusive views of the world while claiming for itself an inclusive point of view, a non-existent unity. Although we do live simultaneously in the different realms of cause, value and purpose, they defy unitary explanation. Our different activities express aspects of a world for which metaphysics mistakenly tries to find an essence. What, then, is there left for philosophy to do? Kant correctly diagnosed the misleading 'bias' in philosophy: its history shows a constant tendency to explain one aspect of the world in terms of the others – value in terms of cause and effect, cause and effect as divine purposiveness, and so on. But if there is no over-arching understanding of these categories, if they are not grounded in some common essence, then philosophy's totalizing metaphysical ambition is actually bound to reveal bias to one side or another in this way (123).

Dilthey believed that what philosophy *can* do is learn from precisely this dilemma. It can reflect on the historical relativity of those occasions on which philosophers have tried to persuade us that their partial world-views are views of the whole of life. 'So, of the immense labour of the metaphysical spirit', concludes Dilthey, 'only the historical consciousness remains' (123). But how does the exposure of the relativity of any philosophical world-view amount to more than the arid reflection of philosophy on its own one- sidedness? How does it constitute the initiative Dilthey desires for philosophy and not just record the oscillation of philosophy between different world-views, dogmatic and critical, which Romantics like Schelling thought characteristic of philosophy anyway?

The answer is that 'the historical consciousness' which Dilthey wants philosophy to become is one which can relate past instances of 'philosophy' to a much wider context. Philosophy, historically understood, grows out of and then theorizes unphilosophical cultural practices. These 'systems of culture', as Dilthey calls them, cover a broad band of religious, legal, political, social and aesthetic institutions. They are further specified at the time by the kind of philosophical explanations to which they give rise. The knowledge of life they exemplify prior to philosophical rationalization is practical but unmethodical. Yet Dilthey's point has been, as we have seen, that such philosophy is partial and abstract in its analyses. What is needed is a new kind of understanding, which will found the art of interpreting culture on its own terms and not just as the generator of a certain kind of subsequent philosophical gloss.

On the one hand, therefore, Dilthey's revamped 'Understanding' aims to comprehend philosophy through the history of its relations to the wider 'life' of its age. He writes that 'from the essential nature of a philosophical world-view is derived its relationship to the systems of culture' (124). On the other hand, he proposes a new kind of human sciences with which to treat cultural life in its wholeness, and not merely from the philosophical angle it naturally gives rise to. This involves the appreciation of cultural expressiveness in a manner traditionally more associated with aesthetics than systematic philosophy. Seeing how the parts of a culture might group themselves to form a whole is less like an act of scientific conceptualization and more like alternative models for the connectedness of life – autobiography, story, poetry. Dilthey argues that we typically understand ourselves in relation to our past. In detecting the values, meanings and purposive patterns which connect our past to our present, we make of our lives intelligible events rather than miscellaneous examples of the laws of science. And this, Dilthey thinks, is true of how we understand all history: 'The reflection of a person about himself remains the standard and basis for understanding history' (218).

This all sounds highly subjective, though. Isn't an individual at liberty to devise all kinds of idiosyncratic versions of self-understanding? Dilthey applies the idealist guarantee of self-knowledge to autobiography: 'the person who understands' the life related 'is the same as the one who created it' (215). It is hard to see how this creativity can be contained; misreading of the past can appear as more autobiographically relevant creativity. But Dilthey has a further, more convincing check on subjectivity which is, in effect, to make it intersubjective. The understanding of past events certainly betokens for Dilthey as much as for Schleiermacher a sort of empathy by which we 'transpose' ourselves into a past not our own so as to 're-live it' (258). But while this empathetic understanding clearly remains outside science, it is more knowing than the original, unconscious creativity of the life thus re-lived. This is because transposition is made possible by the interpretation of publicly available signs and symbols; it is 'dependent on permanently fixed expressions being available so that understanding can always return to them' (228). Dilthey does not believe in the possibility of untranslatable private languages. We understand ourselves in the same language in which we understand others, the two activities existing in constant 'interaction'. Furthermore, Dilthey believes that the forms of understanding common to individuals 'have objectified themselves in the world of the senses'. The realm of this 'objective mind' extends far and wide, embracing the most highly individual and the most communal of expressions:

> it extends from the style of life and the forms of social intercourse to the system of purposes which society has created for itself and to custom, law, state, religion, art, science and philosophy. For even the work of genius represents ideas, feelings and ideals commonly held in an age and environment.
>
> (Dilthey 1976: 221)

In this way, Dilthey tries to remove the tension between the two poles of Schleiermacher's hermeneutics – subjectivity and grammar. For he argues, in effect, that we can only identify the cultural language in which we understand a person or the past by recreating in ourselves its expression of subjectivity. There is a problematic hermeneutic circle here to which we will return. In the meantime, we should note that when Dilthey claimed that people's reflections on themselves modelled the proper understanding of history, he must have meant more than to draw a contrast with scientific investigation. Self-understanding makes use of the communal forms of objective mind already in the public sphere, automatically locating autobiography in its historical context.

Self-understanding models historical understanding for Dilthey because it is a part of which the latter is the whole. In Dilthey's thought, the hermeneutic circle, and what he describes as its aporia, occurs here. We only understand individuals from the cultural context they use to define themselves, yet this 'objective mind' is nothing other than the historical uses to which it is put by individuals. Both kinds of understanding depend on the interpretation of their common expressions. Dilthey is so keen to stress the public rather than the private character of this material that he eventually defines hermeneutics as the 'methodology of the understanding of recorded expressions' (261). The hermeneutic circle, however aporetic, allows Dilthey his own historical ambition of connecting that aesthetic sense of our natural selves, untrammelled by scientific concepts and valorized by his Romantic heritage, with an historical programme for the human sciences.

> What is usually separated into physical and mental is vitally linked in mankind. For we, ourselves, are part of nature and nature is active in our obscure and unconscious instincts; states of mind are constantly expressed in gestures, facial changes and words and have an objective existence in institutions, states, churches, and seats of learning; these provide the contexts of history.
>
> (Dilthey 1976: 170)

Despite the criticisms we can make of Dilthey, this represents a formidably single-minded reorientation of a notoriously complicated intellectual tradition. Romantic philosophy tends to be at its most suggestive when it is at its most esoteric, dealing with an unconscious natural productivity which philosophy cannot conceptualize, an experience it therefore isolates through its inability to define it. Dilthey argues that the way forward for philosophy is to understand itself historically, much in the way that we understand our past selves. This appears to invite immersion once more in processes of unconscious creativity, but Dilthey's adherence to Schleiermacher's hermeneutic dictum leads him to make empathetic, non-scientific understanding dependent on public expression and written record. The art of interpreting the historical context of philosophy leads to another sort of philosophy altogether, an hermeneutical one, in which philosophy traditionally understood is only one part of the whole cultural system which Dilthey's human sciences strive to comprehend.

Back to Romanticism

If literary understanding is the primary skill in interpreting records of the past whose value is expressive rather than scientific, then, in Dilthey's scheme of things, literary theory ought to be given central philosophical importance. Dilthey frequently seems to be searching for, as he puts it, 'a theory which transforms the history of poetry into historical scholarship' (231). At times Dilthey surely anticipates later theories of the textuality of history. Gadamer, setting up his own hermeneutical premises in the Introduction to *Truth and Method* (1960), claims that Dilthey 'was seduced' by starting with the historical school of 19th-century historians like Droysen and Ranke 'into reading history as a book' (Gadamer 1960: 241, xxxv). It is true that Dilthey emphasizes the deciphering of the past as a corrective to the subjective tendencies of a tradition of empathetic recreation of the past stemming from Herder. Still, empathy remains the source of coherent literary interpretation. Poem, narrative and story, Dilthey keeps telling us, are better models than science for self-understanding; but which poetic or fictional genres it is important for autobiographical writing to use is not self-evident. That depends on another decision as to the concept of a person they are meant to make coherent. Which aspects of a person, one suddenly finds oneself asking, would be the ones with which a person like Dilthey would empathize?

Dilthey does not historicize this concept, which he then extrapolates to the interpretation of history in general. He enumerates a series of types of world-view found in history. His own priorities in judging their expressiveness must always return him to the unexamined base of his own German, Protestant, bourgeois culture. There are various escapes from this relativist dilemma plotted in Dilthey's philosophy, but none is entirely satisfactory. As noted earlier, behind Dilthey's project of a critique of historical reason lie categories of general validity analogous to those of its Kantian precursor. When the Kantian precedent is most pressing, Dilthey writes as if the common cultural forms shaping our contemporary individuality, whose expressiveness guides our empathetic reading of the past, already release for us the transhistorical categories of historical reason. But the abstraction of these categories, such as meaning, value, purpose and development, from the actual *process* of interpretation goes against Dilthey's examples, which are empirical and interpretative (Dilthey 1976: 231,195). Historical reason is, after all, the same as historical consciousness for Dilthey, an awareness which 'takes us behind the tendency of metaphysicians to form a uniform, universally valid system' (145). Nevertheless he does repeatedly try to elucidate 'the connection between life and metaphysics', although the nearer his discussion comes to one, the fainter his delineation of the other. History, we find, teaches us that 'to enter life which is the centre of these [metaphysical] systems . . . [is] to be conscious of their continuity (in which typical attitudes persist) however we may delimit and classify them' (146). 'Typical attitudes' are a frail bridge on which to build the historical 'continuity' which makes interpretation possible.

Gadamer suggests that the more important emphasis in Dilthey is on historical consciousness as 'the intensified possession of itself', and so 'a mode of self-knowledge' (Gadamer 1989: 235). This again emphasizes an idealist strain in Dilthey's thought. When, as Dilthey proposes, philosophy reflects upon its own history, it produces 'the theory of theories' (Dilthey 1976: 125). Here Dilthey hopes his project will expand the traditional role of philosophy to include the human sciences, but does real expansion take place? For Dilthey, just as the individual has always already risen above his particularity in 'forms of expression that . . . are all forms of the objective mind', so the human sciences 'endeavour to rise methodologically above the subjective fortuitousness of their own standpoint in history through the tradition available to them' (236). But this only works because the human sciences call the shots in defining what is to count as 'tradition'. We are back in the relativist position whereby we can learn about ourselves 'through history', but only through a history rendered expressive in Dilthey's present-day terms, those made available by his grand instauration of the human sciences. In a revealing moment, Dilthey concedes the size of the historical task required to overcome this historicism.

> Only when we have grasped all the forms of human life, from primitive peoples to the present day, does it become possible to see the generally valid in the relative, a firm future in the past, greater esteem for the individual through historical conscious-ness and so recognize reality as the yardstick for progress into the future.
>
> (Dilthey 1976: 121)

It is not altogether apparent that such a philosophical generalization will ever be practicable. We may note, in passing, the Kantian plot whereby nature's cosmopolitan purpose is somehow written down in a single tome, in front of us, to read. However, to propose to write such a book, rather than to think of it only as a regulative ideal, is a Hegelian rather than Kantian endeavour. Dilthey, like Marx, understood himself to be reversing the Hegelian project by showing not how history might be rationalized but how reason might be historicized (193). Despite his revisionary ambitions, statements like the last quotation show that, having substituted the life studied by the human sciences for Hegelian reason, he attributes to it a comparable rationality. Much of Dilthey's most interesting work remained in uncollected form after his death in 1911. Evidently the critique of historical reason did remain a regulative ideal. The other Romantic assumption which may have kept Dilthey going is that of nature unconsciously producing the minds which then try to know themselves in it. Hence, throughout history, a 'common human nature' is 'vitally related to reality which is always and everywhere the same; life always shows the same sides' (140).

This vitalism is the focus of Jurgen Habermas's criticism of Dilthey. For without a philosophy of life, Dilthey's idealism looks even more pronounced. He cannot distinguish between history which is understood and that which is not, that which remains recalcitrant, brute fact. For the past to be transparent to Dilthey's human sciences, he has to violate its often typical unconsciousness of itself. The categories with which we divide the past into historical periods, for example, are almost always retrospective. Which Renaissance dramatist or Romantic poet ever knew he or she was one in anything like the detail of our literary histories? The hermeneutic critic after Schleiermacher knows their context better than they did themselves. But Dilthey also believed that to be history, the past has to be expressive. Otherwise it won't simply go unnoticed, but it won't be composed of that stuff, 'objective mind', of which history is made. Dilthey can only record history he can interpret. Lacking the open-endedness of Schleiermacher's divinations, he appears to reduce history to his own ideas of it. To avoid such idealist conclusions, Dilthey must assume that when he transposes himself into the past and re-lives it, he is participating in 'the one omnipresent stream of life', as Habermas puts it (Habermas 1978: 182–3). Also, as Gadamer points out, he has to presuppose Romantically that this shared life is intentional, it 'interprets itself . . . [it] has a hermeneutical structure' (Gadamer 1989: 225–6, 236). Together with Schelling, Dilthey believed that the life shared with the past is the same life because it has the potential to become expressive in ways of which we are now conscious. But again this appears simply to assert that, in respect of life, past and present are simultaneous, and the historical difference between them is once more explained away.

In conclusion, we have seen how Dilthey's Romanticism initially inspired his intervention in the philosophy of his times. His 'human sciences' were established to redeploy the 'power of this great conception', as he called Schelling's philosophy, and so to counter the scientific hegemony of Dilthey's day (Dilthey 1976: 42). Yet this same Romanticism, with its 'magnificent world view', unconsciously naturalized Dilthey's understanding of human expressiveness, excluding ideological worries from his theory. Its current cultural forms, which provided him with his standards of interpretation, expressed a straightforwardly 'objective mind' consecrated by vitalism. Life, perennially the same productivity, might have been more or less expressive, but not otherwise significantly different. It therefore educated us in the skills required for an empathetic reading of a self-identical past.

GADAMER AND THE EVENT OF MEANING

Gadamer's past

For Gadamer, the deficiencies in the historical sciences bequeathed by Dilthey are best explained historically. The Enlightenment attack on prejudice submitted past cultural inheritance to a withering rationalist critique. Everything that could be doubted was dismissed as the product of superstition or authoritarianism. This scepticism had to be tailored, certainly, to suit certain vested interests of the day, religious and political, too powerful to ignore. But the impulse of Enlightenment was always either to justify rationally traditions handed on from the past, or to discount them as prejudices. Gadamer's key point, though, is that the Romantic reaction to the Enlightenment produced not an alternative to it but a 'rejection' of it (Gadamer 1989: 293). Enlightenment was perpetuated by its Romantic opponents in another form.

At first, the Romantic reaction appeared straightforwardly irrational. The content of the past was worth restoring for its expressive interest, irrespective of whether or not it made sense scientifically. Thinking of German Romanticism, Gadamer enumerates various aspects of this 'revival of the past' – increased interest in forms of national and racial expression, folk literature of all kinds, the study of languages for their implicit 'world views', comparative religious and cultural research – true to European Romanticism in general (275). These movements first of all continue to think in terms of an opposition of scientific and historical interests; but they eventually so valorize the latter in contrast to the Enlightenment as to construct Enlightenment as the new prejudice and history as its philosophical scourge.

While Gadamer believes that Romantic restorations of the past are often admirable, he finds their intuitive revivals of, say, medievalism, too uncritically beholden to Romanticism's artistic and poetic ends. The polemical exhumation of the past is anachronistically put to work in a contemporary quarrel. The Romantics are untroubled by historical difference, because it is just in the empathetic recall of a distant time or exotic culture that they hope to demonstrate the imaginative faculties downgraded by Enlightenment reason. Subsequent to Romanticism there arises in Germany a genuinely historical school of research, in Gadamer's opinion, inspired by the Romantic effort of recall, but intent on founding it on historical knowledge. This had been Dilthey's starting-point, but it, too, turns out to be another 'refraction' of Romanticism.

The trouble is that the new historical school goes along with the Romantic broadening of historical interest to such an extent that, in practice, it simply magnifies the Enlightenment attack on prejudice. Now, though, prejudice and tradition are the names used to describe anything which inhibits us in our research into the past. To the dogmas of political and religious establishments, historicism now adds those of science. Science becomes as historically expressive of a particular age and society as any other methodology. Like them, it is absorbed into an all-embracing historicism, and made to reflect upon itself and the local time and circumstances of its production. Gadamer insists that this replicates rather than replaces the Enlightenment ideal. Overall, the same attack on tradition and prejudice continues, only now the methodological net has widened to include its own scientific basis. Science must not dismiss as anachronistic historical attempts to understand the orders of meaning and significance which ruled in the past by describing them as nonsensical. But, equally, historicism must show a reciprocal philosophical generosity and not discount the claims of science as themselves historical prejudices. Historicism must, in other words, avoid repeating the mistake of an unreconstructed scientism; it must not join in that self-defeating project, as Gadamer sees it, an 'overcoming of all prejudices, this global demand of the Enlightenment' (276). Gadamer holds that the historicizing of science simultaneously amounts to the rendering scientific of historicism. In this episode of intellectual history, these two categories have not been able to exclude each other, try as they might. Hermeneutics is, then, Gadamer's description of the task of untangling this dilemma: hermeneutics must be able to explain how our understanding of the world is not confined to science, but it must do so without taking up an epistemological stance opposite to but still dependent on the image of scientific success.

Gadamer takes Dilthey's attempt to free hermeneutics from scientific hegemony one step further. Like Dilthey, he sees the need to liberate historical and cultural understanding from polemically professing to be a mirror-image of scientific rationality. But, with the benefit of hindsight, he can circumvent the difficulties of Romantic alternatives. Gadamer begins to try to avoid the inherited opposition of Enlightenment and Romanticism by reconsidering the categories of prejudice and authority, which both science and historicism are united in attacking. His rehabilitation of both categories under the name of 'tradition' is part of an attempt to direct the hermeneutical tradition away from the prioritizing of expressiveness in historical explanation and towards a methodology that delivers truth. *Truth and Method* is Gadamer's title for the *magnum opus* in which he aims to demonstrate that a hermeneutical method distinct from science does just that.

Gadamer believes that the proper answer to the question of how tradition reveals the truth to us will disclose an act of understanding distinct from scientific method; that act of understanding by which, as we have seen Humboldt put it, we 'must have, in another sense, already understood one another' (Mueller-Vollmer, 112). The hegemony of science, he argues, still dictates the hermeneutical reaction of Schleiermacher and even Dilthey's attempt to found the *Geisteswissenschaften*, those moral, human and cultural studies supposedly distinct from science. Gadamer sees himself as working very much within the 'tradition' of Romantic hermeneutics and the later 'historical school' rationalized by Dilthey, but from a radically different philosophical starting-point. Here Gadamer takes his cue from Martin Heidegger. Heidegger provides a mode of apprehension different from the scientific model of a finite mind trying to grasp the world objectively, a mind aware of its own limitations but constantly trying to overcome them in the shape of historical prejudices (Gadamer 1989: 346). Heidegger wants to get round this subject/object opposition with a new mode of disclosing the world which will make the revelation of its being a function of its historicity. Gadamer's consequent question is: assuming Heidegger is right, how does a hermeneutics no longer in thrall to 'the scientific concept of objectivity . . . do justice to the historicity of understanding' (265)?

Briefly, we can try to get to the heart of Gadamer's Heideggerian premise as follows. What this 'being' is, over and above what it is known to be in science, is time – the dimension it shares with the subject trying to know it objectively in science. According to Heidegger, scientific knowledge is necessarily ignorant of this shared historicity. Because historicity is common to both, it cannot objectively be known by one. As a result, both he and Gadamer regard scientific modes of knowing, which neglect the authentic 'being' elusive to science, as subjectivizations: the world is objectified by scientific knowledge, certainly, but in a partial, instrumental fashion, tailored to the needs of the human subject, and so subjectivized. Subjectivizing and objectifying, like Romanticism and Enlightenment, are refractions of each other. By contrast, an understanding alive to 'being' is neither subjective nor objective; in Gadamer's words, 'it belongs to the being of that which is understood' (xxxi).

Subjectivization, with its correlative dividing up of the world into useful objects, characterizes modernity. Modernity, appearing here in the character of scientific technology, has been criticized both for its blindness to the ideological content of its claims to be objective and also, as here, for its exploitative, instrumental treatment of nature. My next chapter will deal with these historicizings of modernity – mostly as they lend themselves to the ideological critique of modernity; but when I consider the Lacanian outcome of psychoanalysis, I again refer to the latter, Heideggerian critical heritage.

Hermeneutics for Gadamer is thus 'a theory of the real experience that thinking is' (xxxvi). Its origins in Heidegger have as their main consequence that we interpret the past through a mutual dialogue which characterizes its and our existence. We are there in the world not to know it, but to see through the illusion of knowing it to our common historical existence (257). Gadamer defines this mutual construction as 'historically effective consciousness'. The 'effect' works both ways, constructing history simultaneously as it produces our typical 'being' in it. Historicism, therefore, has been right to the extent that it sees we are historical creatures through and through. It has been wrong where it used this insight as a licence for relativism. We gain knowledge of ourselves, of the truth, from the kind of history we construct. Why? Because to understand historically typifies our authentic 'being'.

Gadamer unpacks the tightly interlocking definitions at work in *Truth and Method* through his dialogue with his own hermeneutical tradition. He returns to the terrain made familiar by Schleiermacher's and Dilthey's hermeneutical confrontations with science, moving through critiques of aesthetic and historical consciousness and the questions they raise to his own typically contemporary answer in a theory of language. During this long process, he gradually formulates an influential theory of literary interpretation, whose historical nature is bound up with its capacity to tell the truth. At the same time, the highly wrought philosophical story he tells becomes eminently more comprehensible when applied to interpretative practice. The success or failure of Gadamer's philosophy is presented as hanging on the plausibility of his descriptions of how we read the literature (in the broadest sense of the word) of the past.

The scope of hermeneutics – art, tradition and language

Gadamer's method is to take two discourses typically differentiated from scientific truth-telling, those of aesthetic and historical consciousness, and restore to them a truth-telling function. This capacity turns out not to be the scientific one of objectifying a world but a case of a universal hermeneutical principle guiding all our uses of language. Gadamer fixes on two key concepts which he wishes to transvalue in the course of redirecting aesthetics and history away from the pure expressiveness prized by Schleiermacher and Dilthey and towards a hermeneutical version of the truth. In the case of aesthetics, the key concept is 'play'; in the case of history, it is 'tradition'. Both concepts, Gadamer believes, will help him demonstrate 'the ontological structure of understanding' at work in these two discourses (293). Their truth, in other words, will be recovered as the kind of being they produce, the kind of event they are, irrespective of their expressive felicities.

In the Kantian aesthetic tradition Gadamer wishes to revise, play epitomizes the expressive value of an art which has given up all claims to truth by differentiating itself from science. If we are at our most human when we are at play, as Schiller thought, then a playful art has ample recompense for its surrender of truth to science. Equally, though, scientific truth begins to look distinctly limited if the quintessentially human expressiveness of art lies outside its jurisdiction. Gadamer is concerned to show how both sides come out badly from this epistemological deal, if expressiveness is tied to art and truth shackled to science. Kant's 'leading insight' is that we expect our aesthetic judgements, if correct, to bind others to thinking the same way, to compel them to share our judgement that this is beautiful and that sublime (52). Yet if aesthetics has given up claims to tell the truth, the logic of this obligation is hard to demonstrate. Perhaps our aesthetic experience constitutes a common culture, automatically including us in a historical community of shared values? But this only postpones our awkward question, since Kant has shown that the *factual* descriptions of this culture can have nothing to do with the aesthetic judgements the culture generates. The independence or 'differentiation' of the aesthetic here eventually leaves it with nothing to talk about except itself (58). Yet, in the Kantian tradition, the aesthetic remains an ultimate power of expression. Gadamer puts the paradox of such aesthetic 'differentiation' this way:

> The work of art would seem almost by definition to be an aesthetic experience; that means, however, that the power of the work of art suddenly tears the person experiencing it out of the context of his life, and yet relates him back to the whole of his existence.
>
> (Gadamer 1976: 70)

Gadamer is effectively saying that however profound the Kantian and Romantic complements to scientific knowledge aspire to be (as devised, say, by Schiller, Schelling or Solger), provided they remain expressive rather than truth-telling, their meaning is limited to art (77, 83). To him, then, it is as cramping to confine discussion of the entire range of extra-scientific experience and insight to art criticism as it is to make truth subject to exclusively scientific criteria. Both are equally deceptive subjectivizations.

To some extent, Dilthey thought the same; but his harnessing of Romantic aesthetics to the task of founding the human sciences remained at heart expressivist, factually recording symbols which demanded empathy rather than a recognition of their truth. How, though, can Gadamer retrieve the question of artistic truth from the impossibility to which scientific truth has condemned it? Gadamer takes 'play' to be the clue to the being or ontology of the work of art which a subjectivized aesthetics and science ignore. Play, according to Gadamer's definition, ceases to describe our disengagement from the truth-content of experience in order to contemplate something else, something expressive. Play is the mode of being produced by art, as legitimate a truth as anything defined by science. Play places something in the world rather than abstracts something from it; it is a peculiarly effective form of self-presentation. In the case of painting, for example, the aptness of its playful presentation means that the thing represented 'experiences an increase in being' (153); and this enlargement of being is also the painting's ontological basis. Unlike a mere sign for something else, 'the picture does not disappear in pointing to something else but, in its own being, shares in what it represents' (153).

For Gadamer, 'all playing is a being played' (106). Part of what it is to be something is to be able to precipitate the further event of yourself in art. Conversely, the art which thus puts you into play by that action itself becomes existent. In structuring your being anew, art enjoys 'a transformation into the true', and the being of *its* presentation is revealed. In getting you right it shows what it is. Play works both ways ontologically (112, 155). Aesthetic consciousness is no longer adequate to describe art, because what happens in art is more than either side of the artistic relation, conscious representative or unconscious represented. Neither remains unchanged by the event, the play, that brings them both into being. By representation here Gadamer does not, therefore, mean copy, or anything necessarily verisimilitudinous; he looks for a better analogy in canon law, where the emphasis is on the mutually dependent existence of the delegated representative and the person whose essential interests he or she represents – on the power of attorney rather than on a mimetic likeness. Lawyers don't need to look like their clients (1976: 141 and n.; 1986: 34–5).

Gadamer is not immediately clear on the nature of the existence or being which art brings into play. Sometimes it seems not an enlargement but the sheer authenticity of things (1976: 5). We hear that 'in being presented in play, what is emerges' (1989: 112). This absolute verdict suggests that in art the genuine article is uncovered: artistic play 'produces and brings to light what is otherwise constantly hidden and withdrawn'. Predictably, matching this disclosure is art's corresponding authenticity 'in which play expresses itself fully in the unity of its course' (1989: 112–13). Gadamer cites the example of tragedy to persuade us of this mutual confirmation of art and being. In Greek tragedy – specifically Greek tragedy as understood by Aristotle – events are played in front of us so as to remove in a peculiarly effective way barriers between ourselves as spectators and the authentic. Gadamer draws attention to the fact that pity and fear, the emotions which Aristotle believes are definitive of the right response to tragedy, are opposed, disjunctive emotions, not normally evoked by the same object. Overall, the tragic spectacle is similarly fissured, inviting us to take pleasure in witnessing the painful. In overriding these normally divisive differences, tragedy, according to Gadamer, shows us the way to becoming 'free from everything that divides us from what is' (131).

Tragic representation brings into play responses to life which are usually mutually exclusive. In so doing, it lets things happen in a different, more intensified way than ordinarily. Presented to the audience is a reality unconstrained by the customary compartmentalization of life. Gadamer considers that a 'decisive' aspect of the Aristotelian view of tragedy or our understanding of the aesthetic is the fact that 'in defining tragedy [Aristotle] included its effect' (130). Here, though, Gadamer has no more become a believer in the aesthetics of reception than a believer in the existence of some essence of life which the tragic spectator knows as an object. The incidents in the Oedipus cycle are not proper objects of scientific observation; nor is the meaning of Sophocles' dramas equivalent to the history of different effects they have had on successive audiences. Gadamer argues instead that the extremity and inescapability of the fate represented in tragedy provokes in us an acceptance of 'the same for all' (131). At any historical moment, the spectator of a Greek tragedy understands it by crossing the historical divide between then and now, experiencing in him- or herself that overcoming of difference which the play had originally plotted. The play is neither a window on a remote past, nor is it discontinuous with the present. The understanding spectator of tragedy encounters in it his or her own story, and the difficulties overcome in experiencing this connection parallel the tragic plot's own reconciliation of opposites. In fact, the greater the differences between past and present conceded in viewing tragedy, the closer the nevertheless sympathetic audience will come to experiencing the overriding fate which tragedy represents.

Tragedy is therefore a particularly important aesthetic example for Gadamer, because of the kind of *tradition* revealed in the understanding of it. This tradition lets us see the 'common truth' represented in tragedy because of, not in spite of, differences of culture and environment. The opposite reactions of affiliating pity and estranging fear, which Aristotle claims that Greek tragedy provokes, reinforce emotionally the philosophical paradox that Gadamer identifies in traditional understanding. Our dramatic engagement in the play is a recognition of sameness through difference. Just because Oedipus and Jocasta, say, seem so remote from our experience, we can learn to what strangely distorted forms our shared human nature can grow in alien circumstances. We have this insight deepened for us by historical distance; but Aristotle's interpretation emphasizes that this was the story which Greek tragedy already told to its first audiences. Hence his emphasis on their divided response of pity and fear. The tradition we enter now, when we read or watch the play, began then. Tragedy shows how we can grasp a common being persisting behind otherwise mutually exclusive distinctions – pity and fear, sameness and difference, past and present. We understand the play by entering the tradition which makes this existential increase possible.

The tragic example discussed here has grown complex because it holds together in fruitful tension the concepts central to Gadamer's hermeneutics. It demonstrates that we understand the past by appreciating our historical distance from it; this difference, however, is only graspable by us through traditions linking us with the past. Tradition is thus neither blind authority nor outmoded prescription, neither the target of Enlightenment critique nor the source of Romantic expressiveness. Tradition is the process by which we both question the past and feel addressed by it (281–2). Just as 'genuine experience is the experience of one's own historicity', so tradition is 'a genuine partner in dialogue' (357–8). The fact that we don't find everything in the past cast in our own image enables us to understand it as part of a tradition out of which we have evolved precisely by understanding our differences from it. Gadamer hopes thus to have broken out of the methodological circle binding the hermeneutics of Schleiermacher and Dilthey (293, 297). Tradition is the mode in which our existence is historically differentiated and thus authenticated. This dialogue with the past is ongoing, just as our futures are open-ended. Both past and present have to remain separate so that one can question the other, and so that a 'fusion of horizons', making possible agreement and disagreement, can take place. Once more, this 'genuine' dialogue results not in a present subject conclusively circumscribing a past object in scientific knowledge but in a 'logical structure of openness' or readiness for more experience (362). The art of questioning is 'the art of questioning ever further – i.e. the art of thinking. It is called dialectic because it is the art of conducting a real dialogue' (367).

Like Schleiermacher and Dilthey before him, Gadamer has in *Truth and Method* plotted a course from aesthetics, through historical interpretation, towards a universal hermeneutic philosophy. His dialectical method first of all revises the notion of play central to the Kantian aesthetic tradition. He changes the meaning of play from an unrealistic going through the motions – a pleasurable, consciousness-raising semblance of action – to *the* authentic form of self-presentation. Understood in this sense, play is a 'playing along with', part of a larger dialogue out of which are constructed the identities of both players (1986: 22–5). This aesthetic play, in which art and its objects enhance each other's truth, is then used by Gadamer to model historical interpretation. To engage with another past voice in question-and-answer, the present-day player must participate in a tradition, a repository of common standards, but one by which our distance from the past can be measured. This dialectic of sameness and difference is open-ended. If to understand the past is to understand our difference from it, to understand the present must also be to actualize our potential to differ from it. Gadamer moves towards Foucault's project of a 'history of the present' because to understand, for Gadamer, is always to agree to differ – an ontological difference or event which typifies our existence as temporal, as historically effected consciousness.

Gadamer's conclusion tries to provide ultimate hermeneutical flexibility. He aims to clinch his argument by establishing that the dialogue out of which meaning emerges 'is actually the achievement of language' (378). This linguistic turn is characteristic of mid- to late 20th-century philosophy; it also differentiates Gadamer from Schleiermacher and Dilthey and further aligns him with Heidegger. For if language is to become the universal medium of Gadamer's hermeneutics, it must participate in the truth of being with which Gadamer hopes to have broken the scientific monopoly on truth. It must be the case for all language that 'being an event is a characteristic belonging to the meaning itself' (427). All understanding is a 'coming to an understanding' (446), a dialogue in which we realize further our own historical nature. In contrast to the expressive philology of Schleiermacher and Dilthey, Gadamer argues that language exhibits the elements common to thinking and being, periodically forgotten and recovered throughout the history of philosophy (460–1).

Eager to get beyond his forbears in the recovery of the 'being' he thinks excluded by subject/object science, Gadamer is happy to find supportive precedents in the Greeks and in Romantic philosophies of identity, but keen to describe our historical being in contemporary philosophical terms. This means that the prejudice and tradition he wishes to rehabilitate, in spite of Enlightenment dismissal and Romantic mystification, are deployed by language in this ontological sense. That original identity of people of all ages which allows us to compare like with like and so show how the present understandably differs from the past is linguistic through and through (1986: 46). However, an equal and opposite consequence of Gadamer's philosophy is, as his discussion of tragedy proved, that the interpretation of literature is of primary importance in demonstrating the historical character of hermeneutical understanding. If we want to show how language works, we should look at the way in which we understand art and, more specifically, the literary productions of the past. There the dialectic of question and answer underpinning all understanding traditionally incurs the enlargement of being typical of the projective, open-ended character of our existence. In dialogue, in the play of tradition, how we belong to the past is disclosed for us in our characteristic difference from it; and this, for Gadamer, models the workings of language, elaborating that linguistic structure by which difference is by definition meaningful, and individuality in usage therefore a common increase in resource.

Criticism or dialogue?

The most telling criticisms of Gadamer's hermeneutics take the form of accusing him of achieving too much. His method overcomes the subject/object structure of cognition, but only to lock us into an ontological model which is equally tyrannical and exclusive in its turn. His critics argue that if any interpretation of literary tradition is a kind of existential experience, it becomes impossible for that interpretation ever to be criticized. If understanding is our characteristic mode of being, all its acts are *faits accomplis*. Like the 'lifeworld' described in Husserl's later philosophy, understanding is the horizon we cannot look beyond. Gadamer's way of establishing the truth of art appears to make criticism impossible, for to criticize this kind of interpretation would amount to saying it hadn't happened. An understanding which can vindicate itself simply by having happened, justifying itself as an event, looks impregnable. As an 18th-century writer on hermeneutics before it gained philosophical prominence, Johann Martin Chladenius, had already argued, 'there is nothing contradictory in an event; the contradictions arise from the different conceptions of the same thing'; but it is this gap between event and concept which Gadamer has closed (Mueller-Vollmer 1985: 69). This hermeneutic creates its own facts. We cannot criticize a view of the past which establishes itself as a present reality. We seem, in Paul Ricoeur's words, to have to choose 'either a hermeneutical consciousness or a critical consciousness' (Ricoeur 1981: 63).

Criticism initially appears a casualty of Gadamer's rehabilitation of tradition and his restoration of truth to art. Yet an openness to criticism and competing interpretations surely characterizes the transmission of the past. Gadamer's dialogue with the past could indeed be critical, but that criticism then immediately hardens into contemporary fact: conversation with the past always perpetuates tradition. Gadamer's description of the 'conversation that we are' really means that we can never break with tradition because any dispute with it only exemplifies our self-defining projection of ourselves out of it. This is the other reading we can give of the openness Gadamer attributes to those learned in prejudice and tradition. The more their flexibility and existential possibility can be seen as a product of the sophistication with which they commune with tradition, the less important becomes the nature of that past, its rights and wrongs, its truths and falsities. Gadamer may have moved beyond the pure expressiveness he deplored in Schleiermacher's historicism, but his own ontology can look equally uncritical.

Gadamer has two quick answers to this kind of objection. The first is to repeat that the subject who comes into play through historically effective consciousness is a being characterized by its lack of fixity, by its increased faculty for self-development, in fact by its more acute sensibility to the force of criticism. All Gadamer claims to show is that our relation to tradition and the past is not of the same order as our scientific knowledge of objects: subject and object cannot be extricated from each other in our formative dialogue with tradition. But the result is not dogma but precisely a capacity for resistance and creative departure; entry into a language which we otherwise would not possess. In language we articulate ourselves and are understood in a continuously critical conversation.

To his answer we might reply with the supplementary question – how long has tradition been like *this*, open-ended, non-coercive, inherently self-critical? Is history really like a play, open to reinter-pretation, delivered to us as a phenomenological script in whose creative direction and animation we can make our self-defining choices? Is it not the nightmare from which we are trying, like Stephen Dedalus, to awake, the debilitating burden of the past, the anxiety of influence, even Henry Ford's 'bunk'? Gadamer's second answer could be to make the point that his central aesthetic example was tragedy; and that the hard-won acceptance of a traditional allegiance there was far from being complacent or straightforwardly edifying. In fact it was agonistic: a recognition of sameness heightened by the extremity of circumstance and the conflict of response through which this recognition of common humanity takes place. Gerald Bruns argues that to take on the full meaning of Gadamer's example implies that now 'we have this thought to chew on, that what comes down to us from the past says no to us, is not obsolete but refractory and resistant, excessive with respect to interpretation, satirical with respect to our allegories'. This inheritance liberates through damage: the enlightenment and initiative it stimulates are not utilitarian but, in a word, tragic: 'it will not serve at all except to draw us out of ourselves, leaving us, Oedipus-like, exposed and possibly horrified at our own image' (Bruns 1992: 211). At the end of Sophocles' play, the blindness Oedipus inflicts upon himself becomes the sign of his insight into what he has done. Certainly, if we can see an Oedipal structure in the question-and-answer of Gadamer's dialogue, then he can scarcely be accused of viewing complacently the tradition orches-trating the past and its outcome. This deplorable story maims the interpreter it makes heroic.

Nevertheless, it does seem somewhat perverse to defend Gadamer as a critic of tradition when his whole project is to rehabilitate it. Gadamer undoubtedly believes that authority and its twin pillars, tradition and prejudice, are, when genuine, essential to communication. Provoked by this conservatism, his critics have called him authoritarian, blind to traditions other than his own, and culturally prejudiced. The Oedipal structure of Gadamer's hermeneutics then does not explain a progressive, though tragic, emancipation but the preceding repression and forgotten violence. A critic like Habermas can agree with Gadamer on the story his philosophy tells, but not on its meaning. Misunderstanding, concedes Habermas, does presuppose agreement, the continuity of a tradition; the critical reading of literature or history does require a common basis in understanding. 'On the affirmative answer to this question we agree; not, however, on the way in which that prior consensus is to be defined' (Mueller-Vollmer 1985: 313).

Habermas's analysis proposes something much more like a hermeneutics of suspicion, one in which we must be vigilant in detecting the false consensus, an ideological construct imposed by those who have the power to make the rest of society think the way they do. To engage in critical dialogue with such an imposture makes a nonsense of criticism. Gadamer's model does not allow for the systematically distorted communication we frequently recognize at work in the transmission of the past. This can happen at both ends of the temporal continuum. The naive critic is peddled a line which he believes, and so he connives at the bland surface-meaning which represses a latent violence and censors the truth. Or else the critical manipulator tendentiously ignores the success of repression, the sublimation on which Freud thought culture flourished, and barefacedly uses culture as an ideological weapon. In both cases the dialectic of culture and barbarism clearly seen by Walter Benjamin collapses into one or the other. More optimistic than Benjamin and more sceptical than Gadamer, Habermas offers a contrasting 'depth' hermeneutic which, like psychoanalysis, will comprehend the distortions of prejudice and tradition, uncovering the truth they so deceptively package. Habermas, however, sees the current implication of culture in barbarism as inescapable and has to postpone his own corrective to Gadamer to a time when 'truth can be guaranteed only by that consensus which might be reached under the idealized conditions to be found in unrestrained and dominance free communication' (314).

Until that time, Gadamer can reasonably point out that an absolute scepticism regarding tradition is as implausible as uncritical obeisance to its authority. These two extremes replicate the condition Gadamer diagnoses for contemporary culture – 'the conflict between art as a "religion of culture" on the one hand [obeisance] and art as a provocation by the modern artist on the other [scepticism]' (1986: 7). Unquestioning endorsement and unremitting suspicion, Romanticism and Enlightenment revisited, are equally impracticable hermeneutic stances, regrettably characterizing the present inability of Gadamer's culture to get on productive terms with the past. The consensus basic to communicative competence is undermined just as much by distrust as by complacency. Gadamer turns the tables on Habermas by relativizing Habermas's psychoanalytical stance. How can Habermas know that his scepticism does not, sometimes at least, evidence his own historicity? Constantly to be seeing through the past's estimation of itself may prevent Habermas from taking it seriously. So to analyze the past may feel like taking an utterly objective approach, but of course from the past's point of view depth-hermeneutics is primarily expressive of Habermas's own special historical preoccupations. The way out would be to treat the past as more of an equal; less as a patient and more as a partner in the play by which both present and past understand each other by becoming increasingly different (1976: 41–2). To Habermas, this looks like the abandonment of any attempt theoretically to explain the past and thus plan rationally for the future. To Gadamer, though, total rejection of the structuring effect of the past is utopian and, ultimately, anarchistic. But then who is to say that the ideal society might not be one of anarchy?

4

HISTORICISM AND MODERNITY

MARX'S POETRY OF THE FUTURE

The thinkers featuring in this chapter are as keen as those in the hermeneutical tradition to define human beings as primarily historical creatures. Just like the hermeneuticists, they inherit unhelpful oppositions between science and expressivity, Enlightenment and Romanticism, and hope eventually to overcome them with new philosophical or theoretical alignments. Unlike the hermeneuticists they insist, in their different ways, on the primacy of the material circumstances of our lives over our ideas. The bodily conditions of our existence determine our consciousness of it, although we typically see things the other way round. Their materialism does not imply that they are less interested in interpretation. On the contrary, their elucidations of our ways of understanding the world grow more absorbing and demanding in proportion as they try to criticize interpretation. In doing so, they hope fundamentally to characterize our habitual disguising from ourselves of the true nature of things. Thus ideologies, values and repressions – properly understood – furnish revealing clues to, rather than successful distractions from, the truth. Nevertheless, Marx, Nietzsche and Freud all desire in some sense a future breaking-out of this inauthentic history, however culturally rich it might be in symbolic or mythical content – a new start which directly accepts our destiny and, as a consequence, estimates the world more justly.

This possibility, however, only concerns us as it shapes their critical interpretation of current historical expression. A communist society, a race of Nietzschean Supermen, or a completed psycho-analysis will be more or less attractive to different people, but each goal exists to save a critical method from relativism. Enlightenment, surfacing in a reworked form at the end of the interpretative process, stops it from being endless. The later 20th-century rereadings of Marx, Nietzsche and Freud that underpin so much contemporary critical theory strikingly abandon the scientific or philosophical goal but retain the critical process. Or else they criticize science in the way we have seen Gadamer do, and locate the 'being' it neglects in the shared historical reality of critical exchange between past and present. Both approaches emphasize textuality, an exclusive attention to the play and movement of the figurations, tropes and rhetorical strategies which the earlier thinkers had believed were motivated by the desire to hide the truth they themselves could lay bare.

'Motivation', after Saussure, has for us the added meaning of 'denoting', 'referring to' or 'representing'. See through motivation in this sense, therefore, and you leave the world behind for a self-sufficient sign system in which words exhibit only their relations with other words. The motivations Marx, Nietzsche and Freud thought they could interpret, though, described for them the historical character of all human expressions. History was to be rewritten as signifying people's interest in consolidating their present state of affairs against radical change. Existing cultures did not tap universal values but fraudulently universalized local fears and interests. Neo-Marxist, deconstructive and Lacanian criticism then 'unmotivated' this rhetoric, equating it with an ever-present textuality of history applying at any time because it held no final methodological end in view. Postmodern criticism was no less critical of ideology, but, as we will see in the final chapter, saw it less as a barrier to enlightenment and more as implicated in the construction of concepts thought to be definitively opposed to ideology – reality, progress, truth.

In his early *Economic and Philosophical Manuscripts* (1844), Marx sounds Kantian for a moment when he urges that 'History itself is a *real* part of *natural history* and of nature's becoming man' (Marx 1975: 355). In fact, while seeming to recall the Kantian ideal of nature fostering our distinctively human vocation, he turns this idea on its head to hope for the realization of human rationality and needs in sensuous form. Man ascends to nature, not vice versa. Marx plays the same trick on Kant in *The Communist Manifesto*, published four years later. There, again, he appears to describe the history of society as the assimilation of natural competitors by an increasingly sophisticated sociability. In fact, though, the final, proletarian candidate for victory in the class struggle entirely revolutionizes the terms of debate by abolishing classes altogether and so 'its own supremacy as a class' (1977: 238). Once more, society approximates to something more natural, not the other way round.

Marx's inversion, here, usually illustrated by his treatment of Hegel and Feuerbach, reveals his kind of revolutionary criticism in action. Already he has set about demonstrating that while in 'bourgeois society . . . the past dominates the present; in Communist society, the present dominates the past' (233). In anticipation, he aggressively reinterprets the past, eagerly seizing on inconsistency, contradiction or the unmanageability of the concepts it evokes to explain itself. The Marx of *The Communist Manifesto* is already looking for rhetorical overloading matching capitalism's loss of economic self-control; signs of 'the sorcerer who is no longer able to control the powers of the nether world which he has called up by his spells' (226). Here he echoes his contemporary Heine's critique in *The Romantic School* (1833) and elsewhere of the Romantic era's intuitive valorization of a nature beyond scientific management. The same relish for paradox and for sublimation wearing thin informs the picture Marx draws of a bourgeoisie disintegrating under the strains of its own expansionist logic.

Marx's historical understanding, however, is anything but formulaic. We will never find him dismissing current forms of expression as mistakes prior to full enlightenment. He never falls into that unproductive relationship with the past which we saw Gadamer attribute to Habermas's Marxian hermeneutics of suspicion. He remains Hegelian in his belief that the process by which we arrive at the truth is part of the truth. In keeping with this conviction, he elaborates on, rather than abandons, the hermeneutic tradition through his critical resistance to the past's attempts to prescribe the present. Given the theory fully expounded in *Capital*, this attempt must fail. Pretensions to historical explanations turn out to be of a rhetorical, figurative kind which demand all the resources of a critical sophistication to unmask them so as to produce the full text history expresses. And above all, for Marx, this critical effort is an historicizing one, one which exposes the temporal relativity of explanations which claim to be true for all time. Historicizing, therefore, in this way goes hand in hand with literary criticism. Historical continuity has a permanently rhetorical profile. Its proper literary analysis reveals the significant 'misconception' inducing a society 'to transform into eternal laws of nature and of reason the social forms springing from [its] present mode of production and form of property' (234). But again, this transformation is part of the historical truth that the analytic critic can tell about the society, just as in psychoanalysis the flight from the repressed experience, when knowledgeably retraced through its symbolic twists and turns, is as self-revealing as the trauma initiating it.

Marx can be seen here to repeat Herder's attacks on Enlightenment universals, except that Herder's intuition of a unified 'humanity' is exactly what is displaced by historicism. Marx anticipates Gadamer's belief that tradition must work; or else the mutually identifying dialogue of past and present cannot take place. He agrees that we understand ourselves historically, but he does not regard this understanding as vitiated if the open-endedness in the tradition facilitating it includes the possibility of a complete break – the unprecedented chance to start again. In this he is closer to Schleiermacher's divination of a miraculous alternative shadowing any historical fact. But let us look at Marx's kind of literary analysis of history at work.

The best and most popular example of Marx's extended literary criticism is his discussion not of a book but of an event, Louis Bonaparte's coup of 2 December 1851. Marx describes this as 'The Eighteenth Brumaire of Louis Bonaparte', immediately understanding it historically and textually. For in identifying the precedent (Napoleon's seizure of power from the Directory of 9 November 1799) by which Louis and his supporters justified their *putsch*, he also foregrounded the rhetoric by which they would hide from themselves the true content of their actions. Marx did not thereby dismiss these flourishes, but recognized in them the means of historicizing the actions they embroidered. As he explains in a letter of 1869, he had tried to 'show how . . . the *class struggle* in France created circumstances and conditions which allowed a mediocre and grotesque individual to play the hero's role' (1973: 144). In the same letter Marx criticizes Proudhon's account of the event for pretending to objectivity. By contrast, Marx argues that historical interpretation must not discount ideology but analyse the instructive angle at which it stands to truth, until we can see how it is in the nature of truth to have provoked just this ideological tangent. Accordingly, Marx immerses himself not just in attributable views of Louis Bonaparte's coup, but in all the rhetorical possibilities arising out of a historical comparison with the earlier Napoleon. The effect is a heightened sense of parody of the past by the present which attempts to dress itself up in borrowed historical clothing. Simultaneously, though, we are given an equal sense that the past itself parodied an earlier age for ideological purposes. By a kind of 'world-historical necromancy', as Marx calls it, the parody is missed and serious historical reenactment becomes credible.

> Camille Desmoulins, Danton, Robespierre, Saint-Just and Napoleon, the heroes of the old French Revolution, as well as its parties and masses, accomplished the task of their epoch, which was the emancipation and establishment of modern *bourgeois* society, in Roman costume and with Roman slogans . . . [bourgeois society's] gladiators found in the stern classical traditions of the Roman republic the ideals, art forms and self-deceptions they needed in order to hide from themselves the limited bourgeois content of their struggles and to maintain their enthusiasm at the high level appropriate to great historical tragedy.
>
> (Marx 1973: 147–8)

In each case, Napoleon's and Louis Bonaparte's, the limited nature of their political action is part and parcel of the inflated rhetoric, the necessary consequence of historicizing a history which, in its turn, had historicized the past.

There seems, at this point, no escape from historicism into a more objective mode. Marx appears to have anticipated his recent rereading by, for example, Jeffrey Mehlman, Edward Said and Christopher Norris. History has become textual. We never encounter the real thing, only the images and figurations by which it is repeatedly parodied. The 'political and literary representatives of a class' have become all but indistinguishable (177). Making the most of this dilemma, Marx indulges in a wealth of literary and historical comparisons, magnifying the parody wherever possible, enjoying the logic of ideological succession which his argument appears to establish. The dialogue between past and present, the hermeneutics by which one takes its colour from the other has become a farce. Or has it? Marx's *Eighteenth Brumaire* has indeed been seized on as evidence of the textuality of history, and its precociously postmodern farcical turn as an embarrassment to Marx's 'analytic grasp' elsewhere. Hayden White tells us that 19th-century historians like Ranke, Michelet, Burckhardt and Marx are committed to 'poetic insights' whose dominant rhetorical figures control their historical explanations and selectively define their 'possible object of mental perception'. For White, 'the historical field is constituted as a possible domain of analysis in a linguistic act which is tropological in nature' (White 1973: 430). As a description of Stendhal's Waterloo or Marx's *Eighteenth Brumaire*, this sounds too orderly; yet to exclude these historical narratives from 'history' would surely be to prescribe arbitrary limits to the literariness which textualists like White want to introduce into the critical appreciation of history.

I have been maintaining that, for Marx, an understanding of the past is shown to be historically relative by its textualizing of the events it describes. To the extent that we treat history as the object of literary criticism, we historicize it, detecting the limited perspective and partial interests which render its account tendentious. It is not invalidated as a result; but it is made to disclose the truth about its own version of the truth. In the *Eighteenth Brumaire*, Marx pictures an age incapable of escaping its own historicism. Its view of history resembles the continuity later ascribed by the Russian Formalists to literary history. 'In the evolution of each genre, there are times when its use for entirely serious or elevated objectives degenerates and produces a comic or parodic form' (Scholes 1974: 88). For the Formalists, this is the saving of the genre: ironic or parodic manipulation of the conventional fixtures of literary tradition restores them to that state of unfamiliarity essential to their vitality, thus extending their life-span. But, according to Tomashevsky, when the parody is 'noticed despite the author's attempt to conceal it, it produces a detrimentally comic effect' (95). And Marx's attack is on those who 'hide from themselves the limited bourgeois content of their struggles'. The repetitions and reenactments of the past in a comically diminished form sustain Marx's polemical rhetoric throughout the *Eighteenth Brumaire*. They are, however, used to show that *this* literary history is played out, and not to prolong or energize it in a revitalized, ironic version. You cannot, in any case, arrest the literary development of ideology in a desirably classical or tragic stage; but bourgeois history is also beyond the power of literary tradition to save by reading it as the ironic recuperation of an outworn form, like the fun and games *Tristram Shandy* has with our expectations of a novel. To recognize this, though, is to defeat the anxiety of influence, the nightmare weight 'of the dead generations', by appreciating that the 'social evolution of the nineteenth century can only create its poetry from the future, not from the past' (149).

How can we attach meaning to this poetry of the future? Marx writes of 'the indeterminate immensity' of the goals of proletarian revolution. While he can describe how he believes it must happen in theory, can he envisage it with the language at his disposal? Must he not, in all consistency, historicize his own understanding and concede the extent to which, on his own view, his conceptions, however revolutionary, are dominated by the idioms of the past? And in that case, do we not rehabilitate the deconstructive idea that the nearest Marx can come to expressing the truth is in his farcical disruptions of the narratives to which he is still confined? He homes in on 'the crying contradictions' (170) of his age which, like capital in the *Economic and Philosophical Manuscripts*, are the 'inversion and confusion of all human qualities', muddles he can only theoretically see beyond (Marx 1977: 110). At best, perhaps all we can hope for is what Terry Eagleton has called 'the Marxist sublime', in which the incoherence revealed by the Marxian social analysis of capitalism necessarily projects its opposite – a contrasting, bodily rather than ideological fulfilment of human needs (Eagleton 1990: ch. 8).

We should bear in mind several points before accepting Eagleton's image of Marxism as the aesthetic adumbration of what it cannot say more literally. The apparently unstoppable rhetorical displacements of historical period which Marx delights in exposing in the *Eighteenth Brumaire* describe a *specific* not a general case. The flux of 1851 is not universalizable, as is brutally emphasized by Marx's day-to-day account and tacit insistence on the propriety of a journalistic response to these supposedly momentous events. In other words, farce is the inevitable outcome of a unique situation, whose protagonists comically claim they have access to universal legitimacy because they are re-enacting an essentially heroic model of political action. The obvious Marxian counter is to point out the opportunism of all such use of precedent. Marx's refusal to dress up the proletarian revolution in comparable fashion keeps the poetry of the future free of the historicizing, rhetorical constructions into which we would especially not expect him, the author of the *Eighteenth Brumaire*, to let it collapse. Marx's historicism is therefore expressed by reticence, not volubility. Marx was steeped in literature and history to an extraordinary degree; S.S. Prawer's comprehensive study of his reading and allusions has him virtually fulfilling Goethe's prophecy of an age of *Weltliteratur* single-handed (Prawer 1978). His erudition was such that he could easily extend and not just record any ideological vociferousness, improving on, elaborating, and in the *Eighteenth Brumaire* deconstructing *avant la lettre* its governing allusions and tropes. Marx's literary reserve is therefore all the more striking. It implies that the proletarian revolution beggars all description, but not because of its sublimity: because of the unprecedented literalness which alone will do justice to its break from the literary historicizing of ideology – when it is heard in a 'new language ... without reference to the old' (Marx 1973: 147). Part of Marx's history of his own present describes a rhetorical circus in which the recovery of straightforward natural justice looks impossible. He knows this dilemma is symptomatic of the age in which he writes. The future holds a poetry once more, a bodily aesthetic, as Eagleton implies, in which the original sensuous meaning of *aisthesis* will be restored. The notion of a non-figurative poetry, a poetry arising out of the just estimation of things, seems impossible by definition because it cuts through the dominant Kantian view of art which separates art from true description. Unlike Gadamer, though, Marx thinks that we must first create the future it will be poetry to describe.

NIETZSCHE'S PRELUDE TO A PHILOSOPHY OF THE FUTURE

Although lacking substance, Marx's poetry of the future thus escapes ideological contamination. Its poverty of figurative content specifies the historical moment from which it is envisaged. His age exploits the ideological uses of literary alternatives to the literal – fictions which have been traditionally employed by poetry but which also comprise the rhetorical means by which an age, culture or society tries to get the norms of its ruling class accepted as universal. Historicizing critics drawing on Marx can therefore either develop his critique of ideology, showing up the literariness structuring historical legitimation, or continue to imagine this poetry of the future. We can epitomize this dialectical process by drawing on one of Walter Benjamin's so-called 'Theses on the Philosophy of History' where he describes how

> to Robespierre ancient Rome was a past charged with the time of the now which he blasted out of the continuum of history. The French Revolution viewed itself as Rome reincarnate. It evoked ancient Rome the way fashion evokes costumes of the past. Fashion has a flair for the topical, no matter where it stirs in the thicket of long ago; it is a tiger's leap into the past. This jump, though, takes place in an arena where the ruling class

gives the commands. The same leap in the open air of history
is the dialectical one, which is how Marx understood the
revolution.

(Benjamin 1973: 263)

We will look at Benjamin's ideas in more detail later on. For the
present we should note that the critic's definitive placing of
ideology is viewed from some outside, an 'open air' which again
radicalizes Gadamer's idea of an open-ended tradition to include a
criticism so severe as to envisage tradition's demise and a new
beginning. Marx's understanding of the revolution is dialectical
because, living in the ruling class's arena, he can only grasp
emancipation antithetically, as the outside of his own limitations.
Were he to jump outside himself and inaugurate a fresh tradition,
Benjamin's theses argue, were the revolution to take place, then
it would crystallize a Messianic moment, a last judgement, a
complete reshuffling of all the cards in the historical pack.
Benjamin's highly self-conscious theological language is meant to
be apt here precisely because it is *not* figurative, but literal. The
divination of a new heaven and a new earth would defeat all simile,
all likeness.

Dialectically, though, the space for theological description is
cleared by the ideological placing of existing rhetorical resources.
The 'open air of history' is glimpsed as the area beyond the
ideological coastline mapped by historicism. Benjamin's battle is
to get people to become aware of their ideology in this manner;
to get them to see the antithetical, revolutionary freedom it simultaneously describes. Other neo-Marxists, Gramsci in particular,
provide influential versions of this activism. Latter-day Marxists in
the tradition of Althusser retain the theology of an alternative to
ideology; but they see the recourse to theology as the sign that there
is no remedy at all and so are correspondingly defeatist about the
struggle within ideology to bring about its demise. For Gramsci,
though, to wrest the ideological consensus from the ruling class is

of paramount importance. Success here would eventually lead to the abolition of ideology altogether, just as the proletarian revolution in *The Communist Manifesto* would dissolve all classes, including the one it principally benefits. In the meantime, though, Gramsci claims that the criticism of those intellectuals 'organically' rooted in the processes of inevitable social change Marx predicts is to be distinguished from more peripheral commentary. Such 'organic' critics can, with conscious historicism, interpret the rhetorical strategies of ideology and so have an effective revolutionary role to play. Althusser, on the other hand, believes that ideology is ubiquitous: it shapes our supposed escapes from it and prescribes our critical resistance to it. Accordingly for Althusser, in a Gramscian struggle to reorientate ideological awareness, both sides must be equally deluded, their views equally symptomatic of a limited historical viewpoint. Historicism ceases to be dialectical. Criticism replaces one ideology with another; God is his way of describing a subject free of ideological illusions, certainly, but also one with no historical role to play in ideological struggle.

Althusser and his pupil Foucault leave us instead with a history composed of ideological perspectives. Ideological critique produces more ideology, generalizing the specific situation described in the *Eighteenth Brumaire*. A poetry of the future seems as far away as ever. Our understanding of the literature of a period changes in the light of present needs, but there is little sense that our apprehension of those needs is reciprocally altered by the past that reflects them. Nor are we inspired with a feeling for a history taking shape outside ideological negotiations. Foucault, as we shall see in the next chapter, squeezes the last radical possibility out of this dilemma for historicism. He thus assists a postmodern reformulation of Marxian reticence on several revolutionary fronts, postcolonial and feminist. But the way to that initiative lies through other thinkers as well.

Perspectivism is usually thought to originate in the ideas of Nietzsche and Freud. Althusser likens the pervasiveness of ideology to a history of the unconscious. Foucault's archaeology of knowledge revises Nietzsche's genealogies, in which historical systems of knowledge and value exhibit not truth but successive manifestations of the will to power, successive perspectives of interested parties. Modernity, or the belief from Descartes onwards that our knowledge of the world is dictated by our own capacities rather than by a being in excess of our objective uses of the world, is rumbled. Kant and Hegel had, as far as possible, made the sympathetic activity by which the human subject puts together a liveable world a matter of logic. The claim that the only world that we can know is tailored to our rationality becomes an incontrovertible proposition. Marx, Nietzsche and Freud revive historicist doubts as to whether there can be a general subject of history. In contrast to what they see as an outmoded form of natural law, they insist on the particular interests powering any generalization or any claim disinterestedly to tell the truth. The history of modernity becomes the histories of ideology, power and the unconscious – histories of the latent, selfish content of a culture's surface expostulations of honesty and good faith. The new histories clear the way for a critique of modernity, for an analysis of history which will be, in Foucault's words, 'freed from the anthropological theme' (Foucault 1972: 16).

The full plot is certainly more complex. We have seen that Marx's critique of ideology is intended to make possible a new, authentic subjective expression – the poetry of the future. Until that time, historicist critics of literature are obliged to look for its power to redirect their own sense of being historically located towards this new project, this new modernity. Does Nietzsche similarly transvalue rather than ditch the Enlightenment? We can get closer to Nietzsche by considering again Walter Benjamin's interpretation of the Marxist dialectic as a criticism exposing the historicism of the past in such a way as to imply a future redemption for the present. Radical rereading of past writings can rearticulate them in opposition to their own self-estimation. So we have new historicist critics now making Renaissance humanism trumpet a theatrical despotism, or Romanticists returning Romantic sublimities to the material conditions they sublimate, with a corresponding freeing of the voices these two rhetorics had repressed. Benjamin adds another dimension to this kind of criticism. He imagines it also refusing to corroborate the ideological certainties from which it set out, exciting instead the sense that they too could be beneficially reread. For these radical premises were the legacy of precisely those sorts of traditions which have just been reinterpreted. Present-day radicals may have opposed their ancestral traditions, but their criticism of those traditions was still framed by the agenda which has now been displaced. Benjamin's criticism thus saws off the branch he is sitting on; it falls into the 'open air' of history.

It does so, as Habermas stresses, by establishing a superior 'solidarity' with the past (Habermas 1987: 13–15): one that gets round those ideological barriers permitting only certain spokesmen – the victors – to speak up; but one which does not neglect to admire the genuine magnificence of the ideological architecture which stopped previous investigators in their tracks. We should, in other words, remember that Benjamin's famous statement that every document of civilization is also 'a document of barbarism' is not true in reverse. Benjamin's dialectical picture of tradition conceives of the possibility of correcting past civilizations' systematically misleading self-presentations. At a stroke, for example, it makes viable the projects of feminist and postcolonial criticism and theory familiar today. It opens up the opportunity of an undistorted communication with the past which we saw Habermas desire and find lacking in Gadamer's hermeneutic. But Habermas perhaps plays down the disconcerting effect on present understanding of a fundamental re-evaluation of its formative traditions. Marx and Benjamin do not.

Nor does Nietzsche. His early essay 'On the Uses and Disadvantages of History for Life', written just over twenty years after Marx's *Eighteenth Brumaire*, expresses a profound and revolutionary dissatisfaction with the present by calling for a radical re-evaluation of the past. He sees their interconnection, but deplores it as the source of present ills. Like Schopenhauer, under whose influence he is still writing, Nietzsche holds that 'the un-historical and the historical are necessary in equal measure for the health of an individual, of a people and of a culture' (Nietzsche 1983: 63). Given his present historical situation, though, Nietzsche thinks this an 'untimely' meditation, out of key with a prevailing dependence on history damming up those life energies Nietzsche wishes to liberate. History must, therefore, serve the present and see its task as supporting initiatives for living well. Schopenhauer, adapting Kant, had argued that 'what the faculty of reason is to the individual, history is to the human race' (Schopenhauer 1966: II, 445). History encourages a sense of integrity, instilling confidence that our actions can be well-founded, part of an ongoing tradition, worthy destiny or Kantian 'purpose'. Nietzsche calls this kind of history 'antiquarian'. Along with 'monumental' and 'critical' history it can, in just measure and in the right place, promote life; but not in his time, not in his place.

Already Nietzsche is beginning to plot the main outlines of a philosophy to assist people in coping with the loss of outmoded certainties in religion, ethics, science and history. Nietzsche approves the undermining of an inhibiting cultural inheritance, as he sees it, but he is equally opposed to the nihilism which is the usual consequence of such a massive loss of faith. In the case of history, the certainty under erosion is 'the demand that history should be a science'. Nietzsche presents scientific history as a Hegelian legacy, and, like Marx, understands it as the necessarily farcical repetition of an older idea. For a history to become scientific implies the possibility of a final judgement on the past, and this 'Last Judgement' is nothing but Christian eschatology 'in a new dress'. Such history is 'disguised theology' of a kind which 'condemns all who live to live in the fifth act of a tragedy' (Nietzsche 1983: 102). Unlike Schleiermacher's divinatory alternatives to written history, this dogmatic theology provides a script from which we cannot deviate. It also, Nietzsche believes, gives us an unjustifiable trust in our own capacity for justice. However, since people can remain neither as pessimistic nor as hubristic as the 'Last Judgement' scenario requires, they become instead ironic or even cynical. They know, that is, the pretensions of historical science to be unfounded, but go along with the ideological content it must really comprise. This kind of knowing bad faith, satirized in our time by Peter Sloterdijk's *Critique of Cynical Reason*, pleasantly bolsters the German nationalism of Nietzsche's age with a sense of cultural superiority or of historically having the last word. Contrary to popular belief, Nietzsche would have none of that.

Nevertheless, to abandon these false 'truths' could appear excessively traumatic. How does Nietzsche propose that we cope with this? First, he holds that we need the illusions which an all-encompassing history would destroy. Apt historical judgement devalues the ideological circumstances under which we can imagine that we act originally and effectively. Denied these illusions, we might never act at all. Secondly, we need from history not scientific generalizations, but examples. Where history is concerned, the scientific tendency is ridiculous, as Nietzsche intends to show by his Swiftian example of the fairground placard: 'Here can be seen the biggest elephant in the world except itself' (92). Life, he agrees with Schopenhauer again, 'exists complete in every present time' (Schopenhauer 1966: II, 441), and as a result Nietzsche can proclaim that 'the *goal of humanity* cannot lie in its end but only *in its highest exemplars*' (Nietzsche 1983: 111).

Nietzsche, therefore, takes features we have seen to be characteristic of historical explanation and gives to them a brilliant but extreme twist. The conclusion he draws is, if not to abolish history, then to render it oracular, full of a meaning with which it will discompose the present. To see beyond present standards is the 'prelude to a philosophy of the future', as he subtitles *Beyond Good and Evil*, but one to be divined from the past. 'When the past speaks it always speaks as an oracle; only if you are an architect of the future and know the present will you understand it' (94). This Delphic model of historical understanding, like the healthy stand-off he arranges between the unhistorical and the historical, figures a compromise between Nietzsche's enormous classical learning and his philosophical desire for a complete break with existing traditions. Like Benjamin, he tries to reread the past as a prophecy which will change the present, not as a justification or explanation of how the present came about. Unlike Benjamin, he does not link this prophetic activity to redemption or justice, but to 'life'. This 'life' is not the process we saw Dilthey assume as a kind of regulatory principle ensuring the uniformity which makes history possible. Life, for Nietzsche, is grasped in its intensities. Anticipating Benjamin, he thinks these stand in the 'open air' of history, part of an eternal 'now', but for entirely different reasons. Nietzsche's championing of the individual over generally accepted truths magnifies the voices of life's winners rather than discovers a solidarity with its unspoken losers. Nietzsche's 'life' intensifies to an exemplary degree in the character of the Superman.

> These individuals do not carry forward any kind of process but live contemporaneously with one another; thanks to history, which permits such a collaboration, they live as that republic of genius of which Schopenhauer once spoke; one giant calls to another across the desert intervals of time and, undisturbed by the excited, chattering dwarfs who creep about beneath them, the exalted spirit-dialogue goes on.
>
> (Nietzsche 1983: 111)

These great men communicate by overcoming 'historical justice' – which Nietzsche calls 'a dreadful virtue' (95) – not by means of it. Again, it seems that they need their illusion of supremacy to act at all, and historical rectitude would stop all that. But for Benjamin, here precisely reversing Nietzsche, historical rectitude

(*Gerechtigkeit*) is exactly what we are unable to achieve, except in prophetic, redemptive mode.

The acceptance of illusion is part of Nietzsche's breaking with metaphysical tradition. That line of thought thrived on the distinction between appearance and reality, or between the world as it looks, possibly fraudulently, to us, and as it exists in itself, essentially. An ascetic commitment to the reality behind appearances leads to a contempt for the world in which we live and act. The store we have seen Nietzsche set by life and action makes his reaction to this view predictable. But he believes that the modern loss of transcendental value returns us to a world which the ascetic tradition from Plato onwards has successfully downgraded. We are traditionally persuaded to see the world of illusion and appearance to which we are now, in Nietzsche's view, abandoned, as a departure from the truth, irrationally labouring under the sway of desire and passion. The result is nihilism, the loss of all values and certainties whatsoever. The cure is to embrace the only world we have, to esteem its expression of our will to power, and to relocate truth and value in that. We must accept this mixed result with such heroic commitment that we can approve the possibility, in some sense, of its eternal recurrence. Nietzsche's interpreters have long disputed the 'sense' in which we are to accept 'the eternal recurrence of the same'. Is it to be taken as a cosmological fact, or as a moral prescription to act out only those deeds with whose eternal recurrence we could be happy, or simply as expressive of a properly positive, unascetic disposition towards life?

At any rate, to accept illusion to this extent dissolves its illusory character and restores it to reality. Nihilism is thus defeated. There is no room left for ideological critique except by returning to the discredited dualism of appearance and reality. Nietzsche locates ideology there, in the philosophies and religions whose resentful hatred of appearances evidences their authors' pusillanimous failure to accept their mortal lot. The Nietzschean critic's task is then to unmask the will to power in the work of those who deny it, the ideologically deceived, while simultaneously hoping that his or her own writing demonstrates a healthy will to power. In Nietzsche's essay 'On Truth and Lie in an Extra-moral Sense', virtually a primer for deconstructive criticism, we find that truth as the will to power deploys itself in 'a mobile army' enlisting all the devices of rhetoric. The object of Nietzschean criticism, then, is not only to disclose this unavoidable state of affairs, but to take advantage of the new philosophical importance it imposes on stylistic panache and aesthetic success.

Nietzsche's attempt to lose all critical discrimination except as the measure of different intensities of power, different 'styles' as Derrida put it, has been immensely influential. Mediated by post-war French philosophy, especially Foucault's, it has underpinned much 'new historical' resistance to traditional historical narratives. However, as I have been stressing, it exists uneasily with Benjamin's Marxist counter-claim that to see through historical illusions need not be to negate action but to begin the formulation of a programme of political intervention. It might even be to see through the will to power itself to the infinitely more varied motives and interests which in justice we ought to be able to record; and the ideal, utopian impulse of that redemptive motive to justice is just what, for Benjamin, projects it beyond present critical practice into a better future. 'Remembrance', as Gillian Rose paraphrases Benjamin, is here '*both method and outcome* of the revolution' (Rose 1993: 76).

FREUD, LACAN AND THE ILLUSION OF A FUTURE

These discussions of Marx and Nietzsche let us see the degree to which modernity and historicism are interconnected. Modernity obliges theories to make themselves the object of their explanations. What lies outside a theory is still conceived of in its terms, as the reality which might typically provoke theoretical organization of this kind. Such reflexivity, though, means that Marx and

Nietzsche can legitimately be asked to answer the questions they pose of others. How can their theories escape from being a particular case of what they describe? Are they not bound to exhibit the deceptions on which they pass judgement? As we have noted, Marx and Nietzsche answer this interrogation by posing a future decidedly wise to the historical compromises of ideology they diagnose elsewhere. They aspire to an enlightenment not presented in history but to be gained from the effects on the present of reading that history against the grain. They do so, though, by acknowledging the historical circumstances cramping their own mode of expression, and by trying to mobilize their historical sense against historicism. Writing at the moment when historicism can become self-conscious, they postulate a poetry of, or philosophical prelude to, the future. While acknowledging the hermeneutical necessity of tradition, they call for a completely new tradition.

At this point we saw the two thinkers diverge. Nietzsche's 'future' is one in which illusions and reality are no longer distinguished. Reality is what great men make of it. It only looks illusory when eclipsed by a more powerful creation. It never stands in need of correction, but forces all things, including criticism, into alignment with the principle it embodies, the will to power. The philosopher George Santayana famously opined that 'those who cannot remember the past are condemned to repeat it' (Santayana 1905: 284). But Nietzsche's goal appears to be acceptance that the past repeats itself in every embodiment of the will to power. Neo-Marxists, though, envisage an emancipatory project for remembrance. To keep future traditions in an intelligible relation with the past they transform, that past has to be interpreted anew in a redemptive light. And until that 'future' dawns, it only exists as it is implied by the redemptive reading of the past.

When Freud wrote 'The Future of an Illusion', the illusion referred to, of which he was predictably sceptical, was religion. In the Marxist tradition as we have described it, illusion does seem to have a future, not the illusion of ideology but that of a hypothetical justice divined in the critical reading of the past. The religious idiom implicit here is, I have been suggesting, impossible to eliminate. Freud seems closer to Nietzsche in his desire to achieve enlightenment by embracing and accepting the past more knowledgeably than before. Freud appears to have resisted acknowledging his affinities with Nietzsche. In establishing the new science of psychoanalysis he thought it more important to state its central beliefs in an independent psychoanalytic language (Freud 1986: 15.244). 'It was plain', he wrote in a letter of 1931, 'that I would find insights in him very similar to psychoanalytical ones' (Gay 1988: 46n.). Like Nietzsche's genealogies of power, Freud's psychoanalytic method exposes the instrumentalism of history, its characteristic uses. Instead of innocently supplying us with an objective record of the past, history is caught up in the business of assuaging present feelings caused by our repression of the past. Nietzsche and Freud disagree over the nature of what our histories hide. They agree about the false guilt growing out of our fear of recognizing the basic dynamics of life, whether in the will to power or in sexuality. Furthermore, they confront the same problem over the status of 'illusion', sometimes seeing it as the target for their demystifying critique, at other times conceding that our need to have illusions in order to act makes them hard to divorce from reality in a meaningful sense. And to see its task as the unravelling of illusion, the rationale of action, picking an interpretative path through the rhetorical tricks of which it is composed, is for Freudian explanation to locate literary criticism at its heart.

Freud also revitalizes the Enlightenment and historicist traditions considered earlier in chapter 2 of this book and reaches his own distinctive compromise between them. He happily begins his anthropological speculations from the scenario repeatedly invoked by natural law theorists. In brief, civilization defends us 'against nature', against our vulnerability to the elements and to the selfish, unscrupulous desires of other people (1985: 12.194). Yet entrance into the civilized state brings its losses too. We have to surrender opportunities for the satisfactions of indulging the untrammelled instincts which so threaten us in other people. These instinctual drives are so powerful that civilized behaviour becomes as much about devising compensations for their renunciation as instituting prohibitions against them. Like Montesquieu and Kant, therefore, Freud believes that civilization generates tension and competition, and these discontents are finely balanced against the happiness it also brings.

Yet Freud 'scorned' to distinguish between civilization and culture (184). He joins the tradition extending from Aristotle's *Politics*, through Herder to Cliford Geertz, whose work supports the ethnological emphases of new historicism examined in chapter 5. This tradition argues, to different degrees, that our humanity is formed, not merely enhanced, by cultural activity. He therefore frequently draws analogies between the development of the individual and the development of society. Like Vico and Herder, he does not believe in an unproblematic linear progress in which we leave behind earlier, childish stages of our evolution to enter an unconnected modernity. Humanity is distinguished by its expressive integration of its past in its present, and we forget at our peril the extent to which the child is father of the adult.

In advancing an expressive theory of history, Freud clashes with the Enlightenment idea of science in his own day. He finds himself, as he humorously describes it, on the side of the writers of fictions and of ancient superstitions. The initial source of conflict, the embarrassment Freud laughs off, is the primary focus of psychoanalysis on dreams. This emphasis, he argues in his popularizing summary 'The Claims of Psychoanalysis to Scientific Interest', 'brought psychoanalysis for the first time into the conflict with official science which was to be its destiny' (1986: 15.34). Dreams assumed this centrality for Freud because they brought into play those acts of interpretation which could reveal bodily symptoms to have psychological meaning. Like neurotic symptoms, the apparently involuntary production of images in dreams turned out to tell a story which the practised analyst could explain. An analysis perfected through its application to dreams, though, sounded highly unscientific. Freud preferred, in this introduction to his work, to put forward first another 'triumph for the interpretative art of psychoanalysis' (136), the deciphering of slips of the tongue, misreading, forgetfulness, self-destructive mistakes and incoherences of ordinary life. These 'parapraxes', though, which he himself so brilliantly explained as stemming from a variety of unconscious motives, remained part of the 'psychopathology' of everyday life. Normal life, as opposed to pathological behaviour, was better illustrated by dreams. In 'A Short Account of Psychoanalysis' ten years later, the focus on dreams is no longer a scientific embarrassment but proof of the general validity of the psychoanalytical art of interpretation (15.177).

Nevertheless, this ultimate rapport with science, in which the interpreter's detection of a narrative threads together apparently disconnected images of the analysand's experience, looks more like a complement to orthodox scientific method, comparable to the 19th-century cultural sciences Dilthey had hoped to found. In a 1935 Postscript to 'An Autobiographical Study', Freud described how his 'interest, after making a lifelong *détour* through the natural sciences, medicine and psychotherapy, returned to the cultural problems which had fascinated me long before' (257). His discussions of these result in conclusions indicating 'not a material but a historical truth' (258). Historical truth for Freud contrasts with truth in the natural sciences by being learnt in the telling. Not detachable from historical circumstance, it requires the analyst to acknowledge the individuality and peculiarity of each personal recapitulation of the tensions of civilized life. The fact that each of us has a different story to tell is as important as the 'law, order and connection' each story exhibits to scientific analysis.

Which is why Freud's writings can be so interesting. Far from being reductive tracts, they exhibit great ingenuity in response to untold variety. For Freud, all history is case-history. To say this is to point up the individuality of the evidence; it is also to suggest that it is inexhaustible and uncontainable. Freud sees psychoanalytic applications across the whole range of culture – philological, anthropological, sociological, aesthetic, educational, philosophical and religious. 'Freud', as Peter Gay writes, 'has compelled us all, historians and others, to live in his world . . . the psychoanalytic vocabulary has become common coin in our time' (Gay 1985: 17–19).

Yet this wealth of relevance comes not from conclusion, doctrine or a celebrated thesis such as the 'Oedipus Complex'. Freud's contemporary ubiquity lies in a common interpretative idiom which understands historically. Like Marx and Nietzsche, he uses and problematizes hermeneutics; and his sophistication in the interpretative art has its own distinctive style, one later used by both Marxian and deconstructive critics to rearticulate their own insights. Freudian analysis identifies a difference between the manifest content and the latent content of a text, a dream, behaviour, a cultural institution or any phenomenon open to interpretation. In the historical difference between the apparent and the hidden substance of an expression resides its meaning; but the relation between the two may be far from coherent, The latent content is secreted, in Freud's view, because we have repressed something we cannot bear to acknowledge. While the form in which this primal disturbance is discharged *is* one that we find acceptable, to be so its derivation from what is repressed has to be 'unrecognizable'. The translation, reflection, imitation or other symbolizing of the repressed experience must be effected in ways which elude ordinary modes of representation and logical standards of coherence – consistency, freedom from contradiction, grammar.

This tallies with Marx's description of historical agents who hide from themselves the limited content of their supposedly emancipatory notions, misconstruing them to the point of farce.

It also applies to the masquerades disguising the will to power. The doctrinal fundamentals of Freudianism obviously compete with Marx's and Nietzsche's explanations. Ideological obscurity does not, for them, refer back to a prohibited desire for the mother and hatred of the father, or to the ambivalent struggle between erotic and aggressive instincts favoured by the later Freud as an explanation of the history of civilization. Freud, however, refines their common historicist understanding of meaning as the production of the present by the past. In addition, Freudian psychoanalysis performs again that disquieting *détour*, as he might call it, through which the re-evaluation of the past it makes available so reroutes our path back to the present that, approached now from an entirely unfamiliar angle, it looks uncannily different.

The most popular image of Freudianism, though, is the doctrinal one. Freudianism is most often identified with sensitivity, sometimes hypersensitivity, to the potential of objects to be sexual symbols, no matter how often or playfully Freud, a heavy smoker, might have insisted that 'Sometimes a cigar is only a cigar'. Freud is generally credited with a belief in the ubiquity of sexual meanings more readily than with a genius for historical interpretation. And of course his writings give good grounds for this view, even those in which the psychoanalytic investigation of historicism is uppermost. In his paper on 'The Uncanny', for example, Freud addresses what he thinks is a specifically aesthetic problem, arising from the reading and interpretation of Romantic literature, but one which he suspects has great significance for psychoanalysis. He corrects an earlier commentator's explanation of the uncanny in Hoffmann's tale, 'The Sandman', by elucidating the sexual meaning of the story's symbols and events, principally the projection by its hero, Nathaniel, of the horrible, fairy-tale threat of the Sandman (who, when children won't go to bed, 'throws handfuls of sand in their eyes so that they jump out of their heads all bleeding') on to characters in real life (Freud 1985: 14.359). Freud writes confidently that

I would not recommend any opponent of the psychoanalytic view to select this particular story of the Sandman with which to support his argument that anxiety about the eyes has nothing to do with the castration complex. For why does Hoffmann bring the anxiety about the eyes into such intimate connection with the father's death? And why does the Sandman always appear as a disturber of love? He separates the unfortunate Nathaniel from his betrothed and from her brother, his best friend; he destroys the second object of his love, Olympia, the lovely doll; and he drives him into suicide at the moment when he has won back his Clara and is about to be happily united to her. Elements in the story like these, and many others, seem arbitrary and meaningless so long as we deny all connection between fears about the eye and castration; but they become intelligible as soon as we replace the Sandman by the dreaded father at whose hands castration is expected.

(Freud 1985: 14.353)

But the experience of the uncanny supports 'the psychoanalytic view' by illuminating its historicism. Freud's own explanation goes on to invoke the Romantic literary topos of 'the double', and, developing Otto Rank's argument, to interpret it in a sense opposite to its earlier meaning in animistic ritual and superstition. There it connotes the prolongation of life, providing a shape in which an individuality can outgrow the boundaries of mortality. This manifest content, though, is interpreted by Freud as latently indicating the opposite. Like compulsive repetition, the double refers back to the repression of precisely the impossibility of achieving such longevity. The traumatic shock to an infant's self-esteem when it realizes that the world is not an extension of itself returns to haunt it in adult life. In an uncanny reversal of self-duplication, the double becomes the harbinger of death, and the adult re-experiences, in an acceptably aesthetic rendering of the uncanny, that primary childhood encounter with his or her mortal limits, too painful to remember directly.

In the Romantic literature Freud looks at here, the animation of objects comes to signify death, and death impinges on us by its uncanny interference in life. Such aesthetic examples are important for psychoanalysis because the dramatic convergence of opposite meanings they stage figures the capacity of psychoanalytic explanation to disrupt present understanding. Early in 'The Uncanny', Freud seems content to vindicate a psychoanalytic reading of 'The Sandman' by pointing out such a reading's power to dissolve the apparent arbitrariness of the story's symbolism and to relocate its central imagery in an Oedipal narrative. But perhaps such conventional success on the surface obscures the latent investment which psychoanalysis has in using the past to make arbitrary current standards of coherence and certainty, including its own? A succeeding, personal anecdote with which Freud continues the argument of 'The Uncanny' leans towards the latter emphasis.

> As I was walking, one hot summer afternoon, through the deserted streets of a provincial town in Italy which was unknown to me, I found myself in a quarter of whose character I could not long remain in doubt. Nothing but painted women were to be seen at the windows of the small houses, and I hastened to leave the narrow street at the next turning. But after having wandered about for a time without inquiring my way, I suddenly found myself back in the same street, where my presence was now beginning to attract attention. I hurried away once more, only to arrive by another *détour* at the same place yet a third time. Now, however, a feeling overcame me which I can only describe as uncanny, and I was glad enough to find myself back at the piazza I had left a short while before, without any further voyages of discovery.
>
> (Freud 1985: 14.359)

Here the sexual content is from the first the manifest, surface content and the latent content, in whose connection with the manifest content the meaning of the tale lies, is once more the repetition and doubling producing the uncanny effect. To accept a recurrence which, in the heat of the moment, feels as if it might go on for ever, would require perhaps the difficult Nietzschean willing of the eternal return of the same. But here, reduced from cosmic proportions to almost comical embarrassment, involuntary repetition personalizes the discomfiture precipitated by Freud's psychoanalytical method. The more we know it is the same place, our present, the less we feel at home in it, because more and more we are called to account for why we are there. In fact it seems not too strong to say that because it is the same, it is made especially questionable by the psychoanalytical 'voyage' or 'détour' which has even put itself under suspicion – 'my presence was now beginning to excite attention'.

The scientific method, as Freud wished to characterize it, of psychoanalysis lets us reinterpret the past in new ways which then necessitate a reappraisal of the present. Freud's essentially historicist procedures return us to a present now rendered uncanny in its mixture of sameness and difference, familiarity and strangeness. On the one hand, Freud's approach appears to achieve enlightenment. He can begin his article on 'The Uncanny' by listing the meanings of the German word for 'uncanny' given in Sanders' and Grimm's dictionaries so as to show how its ambivalence derives from the instability of the meaning of its opposite – canny or *heimlich*. As a psychoanalytic reader, he successfully constructs a privileged viewpoint from which he can stand back and watch this ambivalence in action. Nevertheless, as personalized illustrations like the one quoted above imply, this problematizing of present meaning by etymological research provides a model applying to psychoanalysis itself. The revaluation of psychoanalysis, prompted by its success, results in Freud's writings about psychoanalysis (metapsychoanalysis) and his return to cultural studies. In the former writings we find him arguing that in order to account adequately for its data, analytic explanation must move beyond the pleasure principle. The pleasure principle's relative successes in balancing individual satisfactions and social interest allowed Freud to differentiate aberrant from normal behaviour. Now he is also obliged to take notice of a death-instinct whose aggression, directed against the self as much as against others, leaves psychoanalysis identifying a continuing crisis in the human constitution rather than enlightening us in the practicalities of enjoying a better life. Suddenly it is as if there is no future, only the childish illusion of an escape from the ever-present struggle of Eros and Death, dramatically enacted in the individuals and cultures of Freud's own time (12.314). Freud's writings on the shock of the Great War contextualize developments in his thought. He laments not only the human casualties of war but also the loss of common, civilized standards whose disinterestedness had lent him confidence that his own project would have a fair hearing in the scientific community. At the same time he confidently condemns spurious uses of science by both sides in the war for propagandist and ideological purposes. A logic of conflict dominates Freud's polemic as his diagnosis is historically implicated in the divisions it describes (12.61–6). In its own way, Freud's historicism problematizes modernity as much as do the historicisms of Marx or Nietzsche. The subjective foundations of reality finally reveal 'the cunning of unreason', as Ernst Gellner dubs the psychoanalytic discovery, in contrast to the Hegelian 'cunning of reason' (Gellner 1985).

Such studious self-criticism on the part of psychoanalysis as we meet with frequently in Freud's writings can have the air of unequivocally undermining its own case. The charge that psychoanalysis, by its own lights, must be a repression of something, and so should first cure itself, only adds grist to its mill. Attacks of this kind must presuppose the applicability of psychoanalytic technique in proportion as they claim psychoanalysis is self-wounded by it. But Freud's sensitivity to the historical circumstances in which he wrote invites other kinds of explanation of his theories. A philologist like Sebastiano Timpanaro can ask, in his book *The Freudian Slip*, why Freud felt impelled to invent a new science to account for uses of language satisfactorily explained on the principles of textual criticism which Timpanaro, unlike Gadamer and the hermeneutic tradition, thinks of as already scientific. Timpanaro is also a Marxist, and so his answer to his own question concerns Freud's need to universalize the bourgeois psychology of his existence in a manner comparable to bourgeois economists' 'eternalization of capitalist relations of production' (Timpanaro 1976: 13n.). Less predictably, a Marxist approach might enlist Carl Schorske's interpretation of the meaning of Freud's publication of *The Interpretation of Dreams* in 1900 in an increasingly illiberal and anti-Semitic Vienna. 'By reducing his own political past and present to an epiphenomenal status in relation to the primal conflict between father and son, Freud gave his fellow liberals an ahistorical theory of man and society that could make bearable a political world spun out of orbit and beyond control' (Schorske 1981: 203). Schorske's essay is brilliantly documented and works by eliciting the historicist content of Freud's text in the service of its own explanation. Deconstructive critiques, such as Neil Hertz's reading of 'The Uncanny', also enlist their subject's help to describe psychoanalysis' strenuous repression of its own figurative status as only one more example of the uncanny it supposedly stood outside to explain, only one more fiction in that Nietzschean army of metaphors posing as theory or truth (Harari 1979: 296–321).

Readings like Hertz's rely on a more generally Lacanian recasting of Freudianism which has laid great stress on his theory's reflexivity. Lacan seizes on those opportunities Freud offers for his followers to understand subjectivity as something made in the process of dream-work, in the passage from latent to manifest content, rather than as a fixed identity expressed by one interpreted in the light of the other. Lacan's preference for a subject-in-process has thus taken psychoanalytic interest away from the formation of an ego and refocussed it on the mechanisms of displacement and condensation, whereby the subject defines itself through its movement between unconscious and conscious states without ever being reducible to either. Lacan thinks this describes how language signifies in any case, and so defines a condition in which psychoanalysis itself must participate. Psychoanalysis thus avoids having to claim the scientific objectivity Nietzsche criticizes, but its consequent reduction of its subjects to impersonal linguistic functions looks to be at the cost of being able to talk about historical individuals at all.

Recent reinterpretations of Lacanian theory, though, have pointed out the extent to which Lacan's suspicion of ego-formation, and, with it, psychoanalysis' theoretical independence of the processes it describes, diagnoses that destructive subject/object paradigm of knowledge we have already seen criticized by Heidegger and Gadamer. A contrasting immersion of the subject in the incomplete processes of self-interpretation renders it historical through and through. Understanding, as we recall from reading Gadamer, 'belongs to the being of that which is understood': the historical individual is recovered in the dialogue we can have with it once we abandon ambitions to make it an object of science. Abandoned is the delusion of technological mastery which had blinded us to the common historicity of the supposedly distinct subject and object of knowledge. As might have been expected from their common interpretative character, psychoanalysis comes to repeat the latest developments of the hermeneutic tradition.

More obviously in Heidegger's than in Gadamer's work, the undermining of the technological objectivization of the world by a subject intent on scientifically mastering that world furnishes a critique of mid- to late 20th-century culture. To be consistent, though, this disapproval cannot claim superiority to what it describes but must disclose what it condemns from within, from inside a shared dilemma. Lacan's theory famously privileges a mirror-stage in infant development in which the baby first gains a sense of its own integrity, but one founded on misrecognition, distortion and violent self-gratification, setting the pattern for all relations between ego and other, self and world (Weber 1991: 106–7).

Lacan, here, is constrained to expose, rather than objectively critique, a paradigm of knowledge blighted by aggressive and domineering impulses. He thus transposes Freud's later sense of a self-defeating conflict in the psyche's instincts, individual and cultural, back into Freud's original model of an ego emancipating itself through enlightenment as to its real motives. For it is precisely the ego's differentiation from a lower nature, equally personal, that it consequently dominates which is the source of the violence which Freud subsequently diagnoses: 'at every moment [man] constitutes his world by his suicide' (Lacan 1977: 6–7, 28). This reinterpretation, however, leaves Lacanians with some typically postmodern problems, such as describing experience adequately without invoking an ego. Subjectivity in egoistic form is all too historical, part of 'the ego's era', the increasingly discredited condition of modernity. But to break with egoistic language or critical positions looks as impossible as denying history. Teresa Brennan characterizes Lacan's 'theory of history' as describing 'a specific era in history – that of the ego'. But, she adds, 'the era he is describing is one that curtails historical thinking' (Brennan 1993: 28). Faced with this historical dilemma, the Lacanian must look to the 'future'. From his 'Report to the Rome Congress' of 1953, Lacan uses the idea that psychoanalysis of the past can project a new future uncontainable by present conventions as evidencing 'the little bit of freedom' required (Lacan 1977: 88).

Is this reflexivity disabling, or is it just worldly-wise? Do the 'difficulties' Lacanian theory generates for 'traditional logic', as Samuel Weber asserts, clear the way for a postmodern logic (Weber 1991: 16–17)? We can perhaps draw two relevant conclusions. One is, of course, to point out yet another instance of the historicist pattern this book has been tracing. The rereading of early Freud with Lacanian hindsight allows us to see a greater continuity in his work; the ego psychology was already riven with the conflicts of the later cultural studies. But this reinterpretation of the past creates the means to embarrass present understanding, dismantling any objective vantage-point to which it may have pretended, putting it in need of the same reassessment it set out to visit upon the past. Freud's historicism, that uncanny return to the present after a long détour, enjoys an afterlife in Lacanian theory. Weaving together past and present in a story which guarantees explanatory ascendancy to neither, placing neither as subject nor object, historicism figures something like the kind of knowledge the Lacanian wants. Lacan's words to the Rome Congress don't sound too far removed from ideas we have met in Benjamin and Habermas: 'Analysis can have for its goal only the advent of a true speech and the realization by the subject of its history in relation to a future' (Lacan 1977: 88).

The other consequence, again a recurrent topic in this book, is that literary interpretation and historical explanation are brought closer together. The inconclusiveness of a literary interpretation of a text, the fact that it never squeezes from the text a meaning rendering future interpretation redundant, derives from its historicity. Comparably, the avoidance of scientific mastery which Lacanian analysis hopes will typify its timely critique of technology finds model expression in a literary interpretation opened up by historicist dialectic. Critics popularly talk of providing a Shakespeare, a Milton, or, in Peter Gay's case, a Freud 'for our time'. Such ambitions are not usually meant to license the author's opportunistic distortion of the past. They indicate that changing standards of accuracy or shifting priorities of judgement characterize the development of the subject deploying them as much as the object to which they are applied. Historical dynamics account for the apparent endlessness of much psychoanalytical criticism after Lacan. Barbara Johnson's reading of Derrida's reading of Lacan's reading of Edgar Allan Poe's *The Purloined Letter*, itself a parable of interpretation, tries especially to avoid following a pattern of mastery in which a later interpretation always trumps an earlier. Instead, the critical difference she locates in each reading is an historical difference; Johnson dissolves critical ascendancy in historical descent. Criticism of this kind chooses conspicuously amenable texts. Gothic writing, such as some of Hoffmann, Melville, Poe and James, with its calculated anachronisms and affinities with detective fiction, almost by definition raises the question of the uncanny return of a repressed past, the question privileged in psychoanalysis. Is this special pleading? Perhaps, but we should note that the application of psychoanalytic criticism does not depend on this selective view of literature but on a more general premise. Disagreement between Johnson's readers is an expressive rather than a subject/object science, measuring changed circumstance or shifting perspective rather than recording error. The historical frame of reference is what changes as the criticism uncannily repeats the literary expression it interprets anew without establishing 'any ultimate analytical metalanguage' (Young 1981: 242, 164). And because of this isomorphism, this expressivity common to text and its interpretation, the process need never end. Criticism simply keeps pace with history, adding to the original story, bringing it up to date.

5

HISTORICISMS OF
THE PRESENT

FOUCAULT – FROM ANTI-HISTORICIST THEORY TO NEW HISTORICIST PRACTICE

In addressing the problems characteristic of modernity, historicism becomes still more flexible. It adapts the hermeneutical tradition to accommodate even more radical disruptions of tradition; the interpretative exchanges between past and present become sharper and more critical at both ends. But what happens after modernity? Classical critiques of modernity, as we might call those of Marx, Nietzsche and Freud, claim a wiser understanding of history. They feed severer examinations of historical continuity, inspired by their more radical dialectic between past and present. The question, though, is whether avowedly postmodern critiques of history still historicize history from their own vantage-point, or try to abolish it. As we have just seen, Lacan's return to Freud, as Samuel Weber emphasizes, shows a connection between postmodernism and a self-critical modernity; a repetition whose uncanniness Freud had already theorized but which Lacan can recast in the terms of a new historicism critical of Freud's scientific pretensions. But is such productive dialogue between the two eras always possible? Doesn't postmodernity typically protest a scepticism of any kind of narrative which might significantly join it to what went before? Don't we at last encounter thinkers not content to relativize history and science, but eager to discredit anything in relation to which they might be relativized?

Michel Foucault's work, for example, has had a considerable and often productive influence on criticism of an historicist kind. Yet his suspicion of hermeneutics looks directly opposed to the hermeneutics of suspicion, as Paul Ricoeur calls it, by which tradition and historical explanation are revalued, transformed and generally opened up to a more sophisticated critical practice, one taking its bearings from Marx, Nietzsche and Freud. Foucault appears fascinated by history, but only, it appears, in order to prove that there is no intellectually respectable continuity between past concerns and their modern transformations. A dialectic between the two is a deception. The only kind of history on Nietzsche's list for which Foucault has any time is 'critical' history, eventually dismissed by Nietzsche as too destructive of those illusions we need for effective action and life. Foucault, in his essay 'Nietzsche, Genealogy, History' (1971), reshapes the early Nietzsche of the *Untimely Meditations* from the perspective of his later writings, much as Lacan does with Freud, in order to engineer 'the sacrifice of the subject of knowledge' (Foucault 1984: 95). Again, a subject/object science is the target, but it is attacked here in order to show the illusoriness of both subject and object except as the effects of a will to power transcending both.

How can Foucault recognize these effects except as *historical* manifestations of power? A history based on any continuity is, for him, compromised by the subject unified across time which it serves. This subject, stationed at the end of the line, assumes all historical paths lead to him. In fact, his own secret synthetic activity is what confers on history its unerring and explanatory progress towards his own moment. In opposition to this subjective unification of history, Foucault produces a critique which weaves in and out of a historicist idiom. Historical explanation, Foucault asserts, is itself a historical characteristic of modernity. In the book which made him famous, translated as *The Order of Things* (1966), he sets out a series of periodizations of knowledge, distinct fields of discursive possibility – scientific, political, economic, ethical, religious, medical – to support his historicism. Like Althusser, and following the philosophers of science, Bachelard, Cavaillès and Canguilhem, Foucault defines history as much through its discontinuities as its continuities, as much through the differences between successive 'epistemes', as he calls them, or each period's discursive regulation of what it is possible to know, as through their similarities. As we shall discover, the discursive groupings themselves are similarly discontinuous, supporting rather than moderating Foucault's assault on the consistency of history. While Bachelard resorted to psychoanalysis to explain that epistemological breaks accelerate scientific progress beyond the epistemological obstacles of common sense, Foucault, doubting progress, is content to let such breaks speak for themselves; and what they 'say' is both encouraging and embarrassing for historicism.

Foucault's disagreement is not only with the 'anthropological' history composed by the modern subject. It extends to any historical view which stops short of excluding past epistemes from productive relations with the present. The stimulus he offers to historicist criticism, though, comes from his belief that his own and related work inaugurates yet another epistemological break, allowing another set of discursive functions to emerge. *The Order of Things* describes how a Renaissance mode of signification, founded on universal resemblances between things, gave way to a classical episteme detaching language from the things it represented. People no longer read the great book of nature, written in God's hand, but sought different skills in adequately representing nature as an object of knowledge. A difference in discipline, a redeployment of power, completely alters the philosophical agenda in keeping with its reorganization of the entire discursive sphere. Each new kind of knowledge creates its object rather than progressing to a rounder knowledge of the preceding one. The classical episteme, in which language functioned as an invisible and therefore totally successful medium of representation, was in turn replaced by an historical episteme. Then the means of representation grew opaque, and so visible, registering the emergence of 'man', the historical subject whose point of view they had come primarily to express rather than an objective world to which he had uncluttered access. In the classical episteme, representation remained transparent to what it represented, itself as elusive as the act of representing in Velasquez's painting *Las Meninas*, on whose power to tease us out of thought Foucault gives us an extended commentary at the start of *The Order of Things*. At the end of the 19th century, the foundations of knowledge mutate to reveal their historical bias. And in Foucault's own time, the evolutionary logic by which history predicts modernity and props up the modern subject is the crumbling episteme giving way to a new one.

We have already seen modernity 'rumbled', as I called it, by the work of Marx, Nietzsche and Freud. I argued that these thinkers found an historical character in all knowledge, a rhetoric with which people disguised from themselves the true content of their actions. Historical understanding deciphered this ideology with all the skills of literary interpretation and problematized the traditions which had handed down the past in the images by which it wanted to be remembered. But Foucault seems to be taking a more radical line. Throughout his career he continually reformulates a different discipline which will uncover the rules of discursive formation. In its most systematic presentation, he calls it 'archaeology', defining a mode of inquiry free of history's retrospective legislation. It allows him to ask:

> what in fact are *medicine, grammar* or *political economy*? Are they merely a retrospective grouping by which the contemporary

sciences deceive themselves as to their own past? Are they forms
that have become established once and for all and have gone on
developing through time? Do they conceal other unities?

(Foucault 1972: 31)

In his unearthing of 'other unities', Foucault looks committed to
a more genuinely historical recovery of the past than before. This
traditional ambition, though, is complicated for him by the shape,
highly problematic for historiography, in which he thinks the
past should appear. Foucault seeks the rules identifying both the
emergence and the dispersal of past objects. The objects themselves
(the staple of historical salvage, after all, whether empirical or intellectual), their connections, organizing concepts and recurrent
themes are secondary to the process of discursive formation. Yet, in
Foucault's slightly circular argument, a discursive formation only
certainly exists when it can produce objective effects. History
returns, though, when his description of the 'law of emergence' of
such objects aims to be sophisticated enough to account for the
contradictory variety of things which define any historical moment
in the writings and disciplines of the past.

Foucault, then, claims that he has defined a 'discursive formation', and thus historically located an 'episteme', when he 'can show
that it may give birth simultaneously or successively to mutually
exclusive objects, without having to modify itself' (44). This also
seems to hold true for science. Foucault's immediate examples
are from the histories of medicine, psychology, economics and
grammar. In 'What is an Author?', Cuvier and Saussure are as
much founders of biology and linguistics because they make
possible systems diametrically opposed to their own (1977: 133).
Contradictory positions do not disqualify these disciplines but
historicize them. Nor are contradictions evidence of an ideology
to be seen through or a repression to be psychoanalysed. There is
not, in Foucault's view, a unified truth, which people may disguise
from themselves and keep unconscious; and so the interpreter's task

is not to unearth this bedrock lying beneath its contradictory manifestations. Instead, Foucauldian archaeology takes cross-sections of the contradictory significance existing at any one time. The mapping of historical strata exposes the discursive formation whose tolerance of these contradictions keeps itself in power. In Hegel's phenomenology and Marx's dialectical materialism, contradiction is the motor-force of change. In Foucault it is the sign of an established discursive formation. Foucault, like his near-contemporary Marxist teacher Althusser, thinks that the power belying our sense of being autonomous individuals resides precisely *in* that sense, policing us through our ideas of emancipation, through our moments of imaginary resistance, expressed in the contradictory fullness of what is said, not in truths unsaid of which our words are the distortion. Like the purloined letter of Poe's tale, the explanation is hidden by being placed right under our noses, where we would never think of looking for it.

Foucault thus extends Nietzsche's attack on history to include in its targets ideology, repression, a subject/object science and hermeneutics. History must be contradictory to be adequate to the discursive effects characterizing an epoch. It is therefore neither systematic nor totalizing. Only that which keeps the episteme in place is intelligible to history. It records 'relations of power, not relations of meaning'. The new history is clearly not going to be very communicative. In an interview published in 1977, Foucault is quite frank about this:

> History has no meaning though this is not to say that it is absurd or incoherent. On the contrary, it is intelligible and should be susceptible of analysis down to the smallest detail – but this is in accordance with the intelligibility of struggles, of strategies and tactics. Neither the dialectic, as logic of contradictions, nor semiotics, as the structure of communication, can account for the intrinsic intelligibility of conflicts.
>
> (Foucault 1980: 115)

This conclusion has been construed as pessimistic by some, as enabling by others. Foucault resists 'history' as a retrospective projection on to the past of the coherence it needs to legitimate its own discipline. The alternative, though, seems to be to abandon explanation altogether and depict instead 'the exteriority of accidents' making up the past. Again in the essay on 'Nietzsche, Genealogy, History', Foucault advocates using the historical sense to 'construct a countermemory – a transformation of history into a totally different form of time' (1984: 93).

Superficially, this 'countermemory' sounds like an exercise in redemption, a remembering of all the voices conventionally dismissed by history, reminiscent of Walter Benjamin's exercises in salvage. The 'accidental' connections masquerading as historical, once their ruse is perceived by Foucault's 'new historian', will no longer stand in the way of an authentic recovery of the losers of history (93). But Foucault believes that a catastrophic unconnect-edness *is* exactly the authentic state of affairs, past and present. The accidental conjunction of objects paradoxically reflects the infinitely flexible design of the power whose effect they are and which they can therefore never escape. Foucault's is a philosophy directed against redemption. The idea of a past restored to life in the present, or of a present irradiated by the life of the past, is a pretence. Yet Foucault, according to a much-quoted passage from *Discipline and Punish*, still wants to write a 'history of the present' (1979: 31).

A less frequently quoted passage, though, also has him, like Benjamin, adapting Nietzsche to urge us to envisage a future: 'what must be produced is not man identical to himself, exactly as nature would have desired him or according to his essence'. That, Foucault thinks, would be to restore ideology and repression as barriers separating us from authenticity and enlightenment and not, as he had repeatedly argued, to see through this opposition. On the contrary, 'we must produce something that doesn't yet exist and about which we cannot know how and what it will be' (1991:

121). In the second volume of his last major work, *The History of Sexuality*, he describes the object of the studies there as being 'to learn to what extent the effort to think one's own history can free thought from what it silently thinks, and so enable it to think differently' (1992: II, 9). This is puzzling. The use of the past here to confound the present investigator and force him or her to imagine something new follows a dialectical pattern we have seen operating in the historicism Foucault repudiates. How else, though, could Foucauldian critique be expressed? Coherence would align it with the discursive norms of Foucault's own time. Yet contradiction of those norms could also have been discursively prescribed. Foucault's answer is his final return to Nietzsche, and, behind Nietzsche, the stylistics of Burckhardt's history. We should envisage this alteration to the present, which allows us to get the present into perspective and write its history, in terms of its use for life. Life can oppose truth with the prophetic intensities extolled by the philosophical contemporaries of Foucault, such as Gilles Deleuze, Felix Guattari and Jean Baudrillard. Or else what is useful for life can be understood, in Foucault's words, as 'techniques of the self', aesthetic arts by which existence becomes pleasurably well-made, to be lived in good style (II, 10–11). Resistance is no longer a theory, vulnerable to the Foucauldian reduction of truth to power. It takes the form of an irreducible imbalance *within* 'the strategic field of power relations' (I, 96). Disruptive local intensities of power escape the regimen of truth. They allow power to style itself in another character. Their potential is revolutionary because it is aesthetic, linked to the 'techniques of the self', the modes of production of that person 'that doesn't yet exist.'

This appears to reformulate Benjamin's messianism, but in stylistic or aesthetic rather than theological terms. In his preface to 'The Use of Pleasure', Foucault refers to Benjamin's book on Baudelaire (which prominently examines the *flâneur*'s politics of style), not his 'Theses . . . ', as well as Burckhardt and Stephen Greenblatt as having contributed work to this 'neglected' field (II,

11). Without the embarrassing religious formulation, though, there is the risk that Foucault's new self will simply be the old in different proportions, no more and no less authentic, its novel intensity becoming commonplace as it is legitimated by the new regime. There are few hints that Foucault expected anything else. But in that case isn't he torn between a residual wish for emancipation to be possible, and in thinking differently to be able to think more justly, and a Nietzschean acceptance of an eternal recurrence of the same – the same power maintaining itself through us from different perspectives and in different historical technologies? He does address the latter proposition in 'Theatricum Philosophicum', taking a Deleuzean view of Nietzsche's 'eternal return'. In keeping with the idea of the discontinuous redeployment of power in different discursive regimes, Foucault welcomes Deleuze's view that it is 'difference' which recurs eternally, 'and the analogous, the similar, and the identical never return' (1977: 194). This lets him rework the notion of epistemological break in Mallarméan vein: 'the present is a throw of the dice . . . in the same stroke, the dice and the rules are thrown'. On the emancipatory possibilities thus opened up, Foucault is notoriously cryptic. Otherwise he would have to agree with Adorno's 'finale', surely echoing Benjamin, that 'Knowledge has no light, but that shed on the world by redemption: all else is reconstruction, mere technique' (Adorno 1974: 247).

Foucault returns to a stylistics of history. To be consistent, he must deny himself the illusion of objective theorizing about his research. Acknowledging his own entrapment within a contemporary discursive regime, he must work out his differences with it in a practical way, from within. He gets on with his history, in other words, but through topics and from angles which decentre the received ideas of what is of major importance for the interpretation of culture. Thus, within the history of medicine, he will concentrate on marginalized patients and treatments, using his readers' initial prejudices against seeing a history of Bedlam, say, as something more than an example of ignorant inhumanity comfortably to be deplored, and eventually embarrassing their assumption of superiority. For once epistemic discontinuity between early modern and 20th-century medicine is properly conceded, Foucault forces us to admit the possibility of a new comparison: we haven't superseded an earlier stage of knowledge in an unbroken continuum of medical progress; we have broken into a new discursive practice in which, at some point, power is likely to be achieving the same ends. The example of punishment is one of Foucault's most striking. Our automatic revulsion at past sentencing, when 'every penalty of a certain seriousness had to involve an element of torture', grows more thoughtful when modern, supposedly more innocuous disciplines are shown by Foucault to belong to the same logic of power, and their changes from past practice to be due to new technologies or the 'state of the art' where power is concerned and not enlightenment or moral improvement.

'The extreme point of penal justice under the Ancien Régime was the infinite segmentation of the body of the regicide', writes Foucault; and he begins *Discipline and Punish* with gruesome eyewitness reports of such an *amende honorable* (1979: 227). 'The ideal point of penalty today', he continues, 'would be an indefinite discipline: an interrogation without end'. Then comes the shocking parallel, which I compress for effect. 'The public execution was the logical culmination of a procedure governed by the Inquisition . . . Is it surprising that prisons resemble factories, schools, barracks, hospitals, which all resemble prisons?' (227–8) If Foucault is right, then our moral superiority vanishes as putatively better practices turn out to be comparably Inquisitorial discharges of power and not a different kind of behaviour altogether. No interpretation can revive the Ancien Régime in a present form, but the intensity with which power is invested in different institutions, past and present, is the same.

Foucault's stylistics, then, embody his thought in practice rather than in theory. He uncovers the past in guises contrary to its own sovereign modes of self-justification. At the same time he writes a history of the present by getting us to recognize that he is writing outside the familiar and traditional frameworks of historical explanation, about former intensities of power identifiable now in different places and disciplines. The effect is not 'of emancipating truth from every system of power (which would be a chimera, for truth is already power) but of detaching the power of truth from the forms of hegemony, social, economic and cultural, within which it operates at the present time' (1980: 133). In intention, at least, Foucault makes no connection between past and present; the anti-hermeneutical stance is maintained. Here, as Robert Young explains, 'the *idea* of history cannot be taken further; rather it can only be addressed through a tension in the writing itself' (Young 1990: 85).

Foucault's descriptions of the past disrupt its hierarchies. Consequently, his writing must show continuity only through discontinuity, the difference which Deleuze claimed recurred eternally, articulating the power behind past discursive formations in the radically different idiom of his own episteme. Because we can never stand outside power and make it the object of our critique, we have to look after our philosophical interests in a different way. Foucault tries to do this by writing the history of how past and present are connected by the power responsible for their estrangement. He thus points to a future, possibly a freer future, but one which will be similarly discontinuous with its past (our present), and of which our grasp must therefore remain experimental. Again, this fastidiousness may amount to what Adorno despised as 'reconstruction, mere technique'. But its eschewal of theory for what may be gleaned from the tensions and paradoxes of historical writing is latterly given an existential locus by Foucault. In a late essay, 'What is Enlightenment?' Foucault sounds very much as if producing his own idea of the care and technique of the self, the use of history for life:

> The critical ontology of ourselves has to be considered not, certainly, as a theory, a doctrine, nor even as a permanent body of knowledge that is accumulating; it has to be conceived as an attitude, an ethos, a philosophical life in which the critique of what we are is at one and the same time the historical analysis of the limits that are imposed on us and an experiment with the possibilities of going beyond them.
>
> (Foucault 1984: 50)

The location of our being ('ontology') in criticism cannot help but recall Gadamer (the essay translation comes from a section of Paul Rabinow's *The Foucault Reader* called 'Truth and Method'); and the emergence of experimental novelty out of a decentred history surely revives the hermeneutical critique of modernity. It is hard, at any rate, not to view Foucault's final immersion in historical practice as yet another variant on the historicism with which he always tried to break.

DERRIDA'S POST CARDS

Foucault's influence on contemporary critical theory and practice has been immense, evident not only in the writings of actual devotees but also through its gaining of a general terminological currency, comparable to the widespread literacy in psychoanalytical idioms. Like Freudian and Lacanian language too, Foucault's key terms have been taken out of context, but in a manner of which he might have approved, to provide the means for the assimilation of postmodernity to popular philosophical and critical under-standing. Most students know that Foucault appears to be a structuralist but is in fact highly critical of all totalizing thinking. They know, too, that his articulation of his ideas through histori-ography, and finally through the practical writing of *The History of Sexuality*, problematizes the received wisdom on the ahistorical nature of poststructuralism. Less often invoked is his departure from hermeneutics. Yet that is the tradition which can provide an explanatory context for evaluating the authenticity of his break from a dialectical understanding of history. It also helps measure the extent to which, latterly, his endeavour to retain a liberating force for his historical practice still shadows the dialectical model. That model had been refined by the critics of modernity to allow them to formulate a theory of historical interpretation different from a narrative of progressive enlightenment. The hindsight with which they read the past no longer guaranteed them critical superiority. They no longer felt better or more knowledgeable than their predecessors, just differently organized by a different historical configuration, a different frame of reference. Foucault's further sophistication of the consequences of this view, though, has usually been understood as always stopping short of endorsing its value. That, after all, would be to fall back into the history of continuous progress which his new episteme discredits. Nor can Foucault proclaim the eternal recurrence of the same dilemma, but only the difference by which power eternally reconstitutes itself from one episteme to another, from one discursive formation to the next. Power is never a positive entity in Foucault's descriptions; it resides in the differences between different discourses, differences which both give these discourses their meanings in contrast to each other and place them in a hierarchy. A thinking different from *these* prescriptions becomes the only possible locus of value, and one whose concrete advantages Foucault never quite expounds, or which he has to rely on his writing of history to demonstrate.

This account of Foucault does, I think, show the affinities of his thought with the postmodern tail of psychoanalytic theory discussed at the end of the last chapter. It thus connects him with the postmodern critique of modernity but, crucially, recasts that as the problematic of historicist criticism. Derrida also sees this convergence of postmodernity and historicism. He sees it definitively in the Bodleian Library on a postcard reproducing a 13th-century drawing by Matthew Paris, frontispiece to a fortune-telling book, in which Plato is depicted dictating to Socrates. The book Derrida writes about the postcard ironically encloses his insight in that most manipulative of communicative forms, as keen as any historian to preempt the other's response, a love letter. The section about the postcard is a *récit*, a narrative with a strongly characterized narrator, not a treatise. Socrates, it transpires from the postcard, whose earlier wisdom Plato claimed to transcribe, was the writer all along:

> Have you seen this card, the image on the back [*dos*] of this card? I stumbled upon it yesterday, in the Bodleian (the famous Oxford library). I'll tell you about it. I stopped dead, with a feeling of hallucination (is he crazy or what? he has the names mixed up!) and of revelation at the same time, an apocalyptic revelation: Socrates writing, writing in front of Plato, I always knew it, it had remained like the negative of a photograph to be developed for twenty-five centuries – in me of course.
>
> (Derrida 1980: 9)

And the narrator's egoism here colludes expressively with the picture of historical fraud:

> What a couple. *Socrates* turns his *back* to Plato, who has made him write whatever he wanted while pretending to receive it from him. This reproduction is sold here as a *post card*, you have noticed, with *greetings* and *address*. . . . I wanted to address it to you right away . . . a kind of personal message, a secret between us, the secret of reproduction.
>
> (Derrida 1980: 12)

In fact the book he published is, in its English translation, 521 pages long, full of endless 'amorous transference' (218), shuttling between the lover's and the historian's desire.

What is the philosophical plot of this book? Derrida uses his postcard to confront psychoanalysis with postmodernity in the shape of a radical historicism. As a theory of historical understanding, psychoanalysis argues that the message the past sends to us is one we write ourselves. In Derrida's conceit, it is as though, like Plato on the postcard or the importunate lover–narrator, we get behind our supposed past and dictate what it hands down to us so that we hear what we want to hear, ensuring that the letter will always reach its destination. If so, our interpretations of past literature are circular. We bring certain techniques to our reading, and we know we have interpreted correctly when we unearth material to which those skills can be appropriately applied. Psychoanalysis 'finds itself' (413); but this, as Foucault might have said, is 'to make an answer of the question itself' (1992: II, 10). To validate the circle as the subjective but logical requirement for knowledge to be possible is a recurring characteristic of modernity, the target all postmodernity has in its sights. Nevertheless, as we have discovered, psychoanalysis can be more sophisticated than this simple hermeneutic sketch. Because of its therapeutic applications, the circle of self-justification could be broken by visible improvement in the well-being of the interpreter; for in psychoanalysis, the interpreter is also a patient. Yet treated simply as a mode of interpretation, psychoanalytic theory still need not be circular. We have written the letter the past sends back to us, but the message may have been so altered in the process that it has become unreadable. In effect, it may reread us or the tradition of understanding by which, as Gadamer argued, we exist. It may not, as in Derrida's apparent critique of Lacanian psychoanalysis, reach its destination. We would have to change the assumptions and presuppositions with which we embarked on our investigation of historical writing – our understanding, *we*, would have to change – for the letter still to be addressed to us after its rite of passage. And the revelation dazzling the narrator of *The Post Card* in the Bodleian Library certainly dramatizes that too. But if we can become adequate to this future which the letter has interpreted for us, then we are still its addressees, and it has reached its destination.

This dialectic engenders once more the 'funny' postmodern logic Samuel Weber saw to be the consequence of Lacanian critique.

Derrida rejoices in the double-takes that his complex historicist scenario throws up. In the book of the postcard, *The Post Card: From Socrates to Freud and Beyond*, the postman of historical truth conveys past writers' dictation to their successors, but not in the overweening, presumptuous manner resented by Marx and Nietzsche. The past only gets the message it so originally rewords from a present it is now empowered to bypass as it speaks to the future. Historical difference becomes *différance*, Derrida's famous coinage for a meaningful relation indefinitely deferred, like the photographic negative to be developed after twenty-five centuries. The past, a good Nietzschean, overcomes its own monumentality and tyranny 'so that', as John Forrester comments on Lacan's report to the Rome Congress, 'the future becomes (once again) an *open question*, instead of being specified by the fixity of the past' (Forrester 1990: 206). The originally therapeutic model of psychoanalysis is replaced by an ideal of emancipated interpretation, converging on the undistorted communication with the past desired by Benjamin and Habermas. But we need the therapeutic historicism arising out of this parallel to give the open air of history any outline or substance. Otherwise our conclusion will be as tentative and equivocal as those we drew from Foucault's *oeuvre*.

Let us try to rehearse Derrida's conceit. Leaning over his shoulder, Plato dictates a past for Socrates to write down. The supposed amanuensis of Socrates' spoken dialogues has in fact got his master to write them. But Socrates' trick is to send this writing, like a postcard, to Derrida. He leapfrogs Plato, confounding Plato's simple desire for mastery, and offers instead a subtle contribution to hermeneutical dialectics only intelligible much later on. Yet the significance of the postcard is also to decipher a present and open it up for future meanings. Socrates not only foils Plato's intentions for him; his writing also deciphers Derrida. By a kind of telepathy, the past sends messages disconcerting present understanding, and so tells a fortune, opens up a future, engaging in what Nick Royle calls 'a sort of reader-response criticism in reverse' (Royle 1991: 7). The arbitrariness of the postcard's source in Matthew Paris' book of divination contributes uncannily to its meaning.

On a personal level, Derrida's text exploits this confusion, reading meanings into everything in a happily anecdotal manner. More generally, though, the postcard represents the primacy of a voice – Plato's, though, rather than Socrates' – behind a written philosophical tradition. Derrida is famous for asserting the anteriority of writing to speech, in defiance of popular belief. Derrida's grammatology made Socrates' voice an effect of Plato's writing. It might seem that here the reverse happens and that Socrates' writing is only an effect of Plato's voice. Is Derrida willing, in his staging of a radical historicism, to risk even this cornerstone of his thought? Well, no – because Derrida would claim that the systematic quality making Plato's words significant is still writerly and has nothing to do with the presence betokened by his speaking. Furthermore, Derrida's reversal here is true to a further emphasis within postmodernity. In particular, postcolonial and feminist writings frequently present themselves as recovering an oral tradition opposed to a hegemonic written tradition, but an oral tradition whose writerly credentials are as implicitly valid as those of the tradition which actually has got published and printed. Afro-American criticism which addresses what H.L. Gates calls a 'speakerly text' and feminism which voices a 'parler femme' appear to set themselves against Derrida's and Foucault's emphasis on writing and discourse. In fact, though, they implement postmodern hermeneutics once more, setting up the tension between past and present as a tension within writing, but one self-critically created by confronting a largely oral heritage with the written archive, which may now want to preserve it but has previously been the means of excluding it, devaluing its oral status, adjudging it illiterate, the offspring of Herodotus and not of Thucydides.

We will go on later to consider this squaring-up of oral and written history within postmodernity. More often than not current historicism has been taken to involve simply a readjustment of the boundaries of history, to make them more inclusive, or an inversion of its hierarchies, moving issues of supposedly minor interest on to centre stage. Derrida is quoted on the back of Gates's *The Signifying Monkey* in this vein: 'it is rarely the case that work on a marginalised corpus makes such a contribution simultaneously to linguistics, rhetoric, and literary theory'. And, as just recognized, Derrida's deconstruction of marginal/central achieves its most radical expression in his exploitation of the paradoxes of historicism. As was the case with Foucault's work, however, the future for which it clears a space, the fortune it tells, remains indeterminate or deferred, an amorous propensity like Roland Barthes' futuristic *Fragments of a Lover's Discourse* (1977). Critical theories advancing feminism or attacking ethnocentrism can perhaps fill that space with questions of justice, critiques of power and therapeutic remedies. They should, though, be approached via a new historicism which has tried to learn, however incompletely, from this final twist of the hermeneutic tradition, even if its agenda does not press so obviously to be heard. Otherwise the new critical practices will simply repopulate without displacing the old configurations which radical historicist reinterpretation has taught us to target. Perhaps that is all they can do: postcolonialism is really neocolonialism, and feminism another bid for hegemony? But in that case they would not have taken full advantage of the innovatory possibilities which historicism has made available to them.

NEW HISTORICISM

'Being here and being there'

It is helpful to look at the most self-consciously historicist critical practice of the present day before examining the histories of the present told by postcolonial and feminist theory. Although postcolonial and feminist theorists more directly develop the argument we have been tracing throughout this book, self-styled 'new historicism' more ostensibly fits our subject. This itself must be historically symptomatic.

Since its acceptance as a respectable academic subject, English literary criticism has alternated between seeing itself as an historical or a formal discipline of thought. An early, professional insistence on the connection between the study of English literature and precise historical scholarship gave way to a more confident display of the challenges to understanding presented by good literature irrespective of context. In England, the foundational histories of the canon by George Saintsbury and others were superseded by the emphasis on practical criticism justified in a variety of ways, most influentially by I.A. Richards, F.R. Leavis and William Empson. American New Criticism also distinguished itself from contextual interpretation by, for example, identifying a host of 'fallacies' – intentional, affective, mimetic and so on – by which past critics had distracted readers from the essential being or rhetoric of literature itself. More recently, a return to history has polemically characterized its structuralist and poststructuralist predecessors as offshoots of the New-Critical formalism, although, as Brook Thomas argues, deconstructive methods might be more properly regarded as the logical consequence of 'the nihilism into which at least one version of historicism led' (Thomas 1991: 36).

The story each of these critical initiatives tells about itself is opportunistic and not answerable to an overall narrative. Nevertheless, the main disagreements always seem to be articulated through a broad contrast between historical and formal methods of literary criticism. Current new historicism distinguishes itself by its heightened consciousness of criticism's institutional past, and of how its methodological changes might have served particular cultural interests. Alteration of the American academic population as a result of a European flight from Nazi persecution can be matched by recent recruitment to higher education institutions of many more women and members of ethnic minorities. Each constituency has wrought its changes in critical practice, suggesting an underlying historicism which any critical theory endeavouring to understand itself is obliged to uncover. This is always a double-edged affair, as the critical establishment's accommodation of the new interests soon becomes the background *against* which new arrivals define themselves. Hence the concession that historical difference might incorporate cultural difference, and the view that old historicism might do enough by widening its agenda somewhat, is met by arguments for a distinctiveness of postcolonial or feminist theory necessitating yet another 'new' historicism.

'New historicism', though, is a label usually applied to a body of critical work on the English Renaissance, most conveniently and persuasively represented by the writings of Stephen Greenblatt. While this section will be 'led' by discussion of Greenblatt's work, other 'new' historicisms need to be acknowledged. The simultaneous historicizing of the Romantic period, led by Jerome McGann, relies more on hermeneutics than the anthropological and Foucauldian methods applied to the Renaissance by Greenblatt. The Romantic period, closer to our own, has arguably provided the tradition formative of current critical orthodoxy. Its strategic deformation *is* the same as critical innovation now, including, I hope to show, Greenblatt's. McGann's most effective theorizing points out, through the use of examples like Pound's *Cantos*, that:

> to the historicist imagination, history is the past, or perhaps the past seen in and through the present; and the historical task is to attempt a reconstruction of the past, including, perhaps, the present of that past. But the *Cantos* reminds us that history includes the future, and that the historical task involves as well the construction of what shall be possible.

> (McGann 1989: 105)

And Marjorie Levinson finds an appropriate epigraph for the collection in which McGann's piece appears in the words of Irving Wohlfarth: '"Chaque époque rêve la suivante." (Michelet. *Avenir*! *Avenir*!) To which Benjamin adds, by way of consummation, the all-important afterthought: "Not merely does each age dream the next one, but it aims, in so doing, to awaken."' By contrast, Greenblatt's historicizing of the Renaissance looks more like an updating of themes which have already loomed large in the history of historicism, 'the present of that past'. His work is divided between a liberal, pluralistic tolerance running against Enlightenment trends from Herder to Greenblatt's preferred ethnographical formulations by Clifford Geertz, and a more critical impulse complicated by its Foucauldian origins. The former receptivity to the past thickens historical description of its culture by attending to a greater range of contributory factors. The criticism emerges from the resulting portrait of an absolute power unscrupulously capitalizing on or colonizing all forms of cultural diversity. Greenblatt's resistance to this, however, given his Foucauldian scepticism of enlightened reason, can only be expressed by colonizing it on his own critical terms, showing a similar disrespect for *its* native interests, inhabiting it and articulating it without subscribing to its ends. His critical momentum takes him to the heart of the problem with which postcolonial theory begins.

Most attractive to a critic writing after Foucault and wishing to have no truck with universal, transhistorical humanism would be a kind of local knowledge of the past true to its own largely piecemeal self-awareness. The retrospective integrations and grand explanations given by later critics and historians would thus be avoided. To stay this close to the past is to keep its strangeness in focus; standing back to gloss its manoeuvres pretends to an implausible familiarity. In the formula of Geertz's ethnology, 'what is remote close up is, at a remove, near' (Geertz 1988: 48). Geertz believes that cultural and historical relativism are 'the same thing' (1993: 44). We get over the paradox of inevitably 'being here' while writing about 'being there' by fashioning a 'conversation' across the divide. To do this we do not create 'a universal Esperanto-like culture' in which we all share, but try to learn and to speak the different languages already in existence (1988:

144–7). To understand another's language, though, you need more than a dictionary, more than a grammar. To understand the use of words which gives them their meaning you require a thicker description of linguistic behaviour than is found in any conventional primer. In Geertz's ethnology, everything is the context for something else; nothing is the privileged repository of significance. The point is not to devise with hindsight a better explication of past events, but to enhance the way they are already 'scientifically eloquent' on their own (1993: 28).

Despite Geertz's cleverness over 'near' and 'remote' in interpretation, so that the closer and more local our acquaintance the more historical remoteness and otherness is respected, isn't the interpreter's enhancement of past eloquence still as likely to distort as before? But Geertz's point is that we should look 'through' our glosses on the past, not 'behind' them. The difference by which our rewriting of a Shakespeare play makes it more eloquent for us is also a measure of our historical distance from it. But we have no alternative. We cannot put our more informative reading aside to examine the bare original because our idea of what is authentic is also what our interpretation has created. In his essay on *The Tempest*, 'Learning to Curse', Greenblatt contextualizes the characters' ideas and use of language with reference to Cicero, not Geertz:

> Virtually every Renaissance schoolboy read in Cicero's *De Oratore* that only eloquence had been powerful enough 'to gather scattered mankind together in one place, to transplant human beings from a barbarous life in the wilderness to a civilized social system, to establish organized communities, to equip them with laws and judicial safeguards and civic rights.'
>
> (Greenblatt 1990: 20)

He then uses this resource of Renaissance education to sketch a colonialist mentality from his own position of postcolonial disapproval. The object of Greenblatt's criticism is constructed out of the ideological connections of Shakespeare's own day; yet these are only seen as ideological, and therefore for what they are and not as the eternal order of things, because of the historical difference between Shakespeare and Greenblatt. Greenblatt, it seems, hasn't the option of seeing things differently. He can't help being right; and were Shakespeare's play to see its own ideology, and to present things more realistically, it could only concur further with Greenblatt. The play does partly subvert colonialism, as Greenblatt shows, by allowing to the colonized Caliban an eloquence which eludes his civilized masters and so wins out on the Ciceronian standard. It is Greenblatt's present that seems incapable of self-criticism. Past subversions always prefigure his enlightened present. Remaining disagreements in outlook never reflect adversely on Greenblatt's present understanding but accurately describe historical difference. The hermeneutical circle is drawn tight.

Greenblatt famously worries about confining subversion to the past, and under the influence of Foucault his hermeneutical use of Geertz does put itself in question. As well as 'thick description', there is another concept driving Geertz's thought which new historicism appropriates. Geertz claims to have learned thick description from the Oxford philosopher, Gilbert Ryle. Thick description inspires interpretation and encourages the reader to look for meaningful exchanges where before there were only haphazard movements to be seen. Greater acuteness of historical perception is stimulated by the example of the coming to life of unreadable gestures in the alien culture whose vocabulary the investigative anthropologist learns to use. Extending Ryle's commonsensical applications, Geertz shows that thick description dissolves apparent contingency and arbitrariness by demonstrating that historico-cultural differences can be meaningfully at odds with our own related sign systems. In effect, we acquire more words: we learn what a 'wink' is as opposed to a blink; we distinguish circus tumbling from falling over; we confront the endless dissimulations complicating our decisions on how exactly a word or a gesture is being used. The wink is deceptive; the tumbler has an accident at which it is inappropriate to split our sides laughing; Iago's loyalty to Othello becomes vicarious possession, sexual or demonic. Any number of unforeseeable rituals are brought into our ken. But the other basic notion donated by Geertz to the new historians, and less explicitly acknowledged, is his cultural determinism.

In his essay 'The Growth of Culture and the Evolution of Mind', Geertz gives an explanation of cultural determinism which he describes as 'oddly two-headed'. He wants cultural materialism to achieve two notionally contradictory aims: to show that culture is a determinant of people's physical lives, and that in its current state it is not an absolute indicator of peoples' physical capacities. The paradox we now feel when we try to hold these beliefs simultaneously is, argues Geertz, the result of an 'antecedent error' (1993: 65). The error was to think that mental and cultural development could ever be separate processes. The fact that nowadays sociocultural change and refinement proceed apace, while the organic evolution of our brains does not, indicates that *homo sapiens* as a species the world over has the innate capacity for the cultural competence displayed by any individual groups or members. This pleasingly liberal position does not contradict the view that in the past 'tools, hunting, family organization, and, later, art, religion, and "science" moulded man somatically; and they are, therefore, necessary not merely to his survival but to his existential realization' (83). In other words, what was to be explained for Geertz was not some contemporary rupture of cerebral and cultural development, but contemporary disparities in the cultures emerging from and in different ways realizing the same potential. High technological expertise and supposedly less sophisticated forms of social organization can still be equally expressive of a common human nature, or, in the idiom of Geertz's cultural materialism, comparable methods for its completion.

Geertz's argument here serves an ethnology which wishes to distinguish cultural differences, but without prejudice. His suspension of value-judgements on, say, Balinese cock-fighting, is therefore not morally irresponsible. His job is to show the varieties of cultural behaviour emanating from a recognizably human source – that is, one which we can interpret. The differences between social practices are of interest to him only as they reveal different realizations of the subject his science studies, the human. In a nutshell, he has achieved his purpose if he has interpreted the Javanese claim that 'To be human is to be Javanese'. For the foreigner to accept that paradoxical statement is just to understand the conclusion above: only because we share a certain level of development as a species can our humanity be realized or 'fashioned' in such exclusive ways.

If we now return now to Greenblatt's worries about subversion, we can see better how his argument works. In *Shakespearean Negotiations*, Greenblatt compares the culture of Shakespeare's time with the liberal-humanist, first-world culture he and most of his readers share. His main interest is in showing how a striking energy accrues to Shakespeare's drama through its appropriation or symbolic acquisition of materials normally belonging to cultural stock-in-trade other than the theatre's. The novel, theatrical presentation of ceremony, dance, emblem, ritual and language stemming from a non-theatrical provenance amplifies and profits dramatically from the energy ordinarily concentrated around them. The theatrical shift, too, can imply a subversive disrespect for propriety. Utilized by the theatre, the display of absolutist power and religion, for example, might appear undermined by its new make-believe and secularized context. The 'negotiations' which preoccupy Greenblatt when he reads Shakespeare are those by which Shakespearean theatre's potential critique of its sources is contained, its subversions tolerated. The standard of understanding Shakespeare's discourse here seems to be the Foucauldian one of being able to appreciate how it can produce mutually exclusive effects. The match between theatrical make-believe and the fictions grounding successful monarchy can make a play expose as fantasy what is presented as immutable, or, in its pomp and circumstance, simply add to Royalist propaganda. That price, at any rate, might be worth negotiating as the cost to be paid, say, in *Richard II* for undermining Richard's sense of his divine right to rule and exposing Bolingbroke's pragmatism. Richard's weak character suggests that the institution of monarchy remains uncriticized by his personal confusions. On the other hand, Richard seems rightly confused by the genuine contradiction of assuming that a king favoured by God will necessarily be one favoured by the times. The audience who attended a performance of the play in the 1590s and then issued forth to support the rebellion of the Earl of Essex would thus have been both condemned and supported by *Richard II*. Which way the audience swings, though, seems less a question of cultural diversity and more the expression of a political choice with which we agree or disagree.

Greenblatt's main point *is* that we, now, are also negotiating and containing Shakespeare's subversive possibilities for our own times when we read and watch his plays. We identify as being formerly subversive the truth and reality we accept now – the divine right of kings to rule is untenable; Bolingbroke's kind of *Realpolitik* may work but is unprincipled and no substitute for monarchy. We could only undermine our present, argues Greenblatt, with just those ideas of order and morality which we believe could only have commanded genuine assent then. In this way we use the historical difference between Shakespeare's time and ours to invalidate any of Shakespeare's ideas which might depose our current certainties. Ruled out of court are any beliefs, modes of conduct, cultural attitudes which would contravene our own liberal-humanist pieties and nostrums. In reading Shakespeare we can find subversion anywhere, except that what we pick out in this way are those elements anachronistically converging on our own world-view. As we saw in the case of Greenblatt's reading of *The Tempest*, those not prefiguring our present remain, to our eyes, outmoded, of aesthetic and historical interest, perhaps, but unchallenging. Thus we 'complacently', to use Greenblatt's word, define subversion out of existence, containing it as effectively as we would the idea of an absolutist monarchy. For contemporary readers of Shakespeare, there is 'no end of subversion, only not for us' (38, 65).

Greenblatt does not fully explain his disquiet here. Many of his critics have taken him to be expressing pessimism concerning both our ability to be historical and to escape from ideology. We are, they object, unreasonably confined to writing an unchallenged history of the present, incapable of seeing round our ideological blinkers. If we bear in mind, though, the cocktail of Geertz and Foucault that Greenblatt is putting together, his conclusion looks rather different. We certainly encounter a Geertzian investigation of different historical and cultural groupings' characteristic universalizing and naturalizing of their own personal interests; and the difference between them and us, here, testifies to the diversity of human understanding. But instead of taking this habit as that which gives rise to a unified ideology, Greenblatt's readings imply the need to have a Foucauldian sensitivity to the already existing oppositions and contradictions within past cultures. And our judgements of the relative merits of these opposed positions cannot once more be forestalled by the need to acknowledge cultural difference and diversity between them and us. This time the disagreements are between them and them; and the onus is now surely on us to show *our* human diversity and demonstrate that a comparable difference of political principle survives in our own time as divisively.

A more critical dialectic than envisaged by Geertz is set in motion. Like Geertz, Greenblatt assumes a material human base responsible for differences in culture, characterized rather than invalidated by this power to produce diversity. Like Gadamer, Geertz and Greenblatt also assume that to understand our difference from the past is by definition to understand how this difference is significant. And translated into Foucault's terms, this suggests that we cannot distance the acts of subversion and containment within Shakespeare's culture. We necessarily replicate them in our own idiom. We may believe that idiom to be less gullible or manipulative, but the fit with Shakespearean negotiation means that the same basic issues of power, oppression and resistance are indeed at stake, however much we may like to claim the advantages of our post-absolutist savvy or liberalism. In reality, our superior sublimations of the power-struggle at the heart of cultural behaviour meets a useful corrective in a Shakespearean discourse which makes so incomparably available the energies at work in its own. When we accept that Shakespearean discourse is a version of the same dynamic at work now, then Shakespearean criticism can become more like a Geertzian comparison of different ways of being human, but one with a Foucauldian difference which dissolves the history of the human in the history of power. We cannot be Elizabethan or Jacobean, any more than we can be Javanese. But Shakespeare's writings express the specific historical realization of a human nature which is individualized now by our own very different cultural inflections. We may not find in Shakespeare's particular political, social or moral options subversive possibilities for us in the present, but the idea that the same selfish, power-ridden creature is catered for by our own norms, however high-minded their expression, *is* subversive of too easy humanist assumptions of emancipation and progress. Equally, the fact that we think this uncomfortable thought through the comparative interpretations of other cultures and times attests a critical dialectic at work, a hermeneutic that has recovered its teeth.

When Greenblatt tries to detail the process at work here, his explanation can sound strikingly like Gadamer. Above all, the work of art is an event. Although Greenblatt emphasizes the social character of the artistic event, he is as keen as Gadamer to find a way of describing art's power to present its object as a further event in the object's being, a happening in its existence important to our truthful estimation of it. The final chapter of *Learning to Curse* describes the kind of attention which new historicist criticism can pay to art as one especially alert to its 'resonance and wonder'. The 'uniqueness' at which we wonder is tied to a play's power 'to reach out beyond its formal boundaries' (170). Its singularity historicizes it and makes it exemplary; but the Kantian aesthetic here is over-ridden by Greenblatt's insistence that the occasion of, say, a Shakespeare play is one in which it negotiates the energies of its culture so as to present their truth as never before. It contributes, *Shakespearean Negotiations* fundamentally argues, to a circulation of social energies which require this propulsion if they are to be fully deployed. 'Artistic expression', Greenblatt argues, 'is never perfectly self-contained' (1990: 89). It helps transmit the social practices on whose energies it draws by returning them to the general cultural fold, but amplified, their momentum increased. Thus, historical relations between parents and children are magni-fied in Shakespeare's dramatization of King Lear's anxiety. *Othello* precipitates an event in the history of the Christian management of sexual mores. The death of Jack Cade in *Henry VI, Part ii* clarifies the Renaissance discourses of social status and rebellion as the moment of their transition into the discourse of property relations. In each case, the source of contemporary concern and energy from which the play borrows is returned to its cultural setting with interest.

Furthermore, as I have been stressing, Greenblatt's work of art reaches beyond its present to ours. Its failure to subvert our norms should not breed complacency but shock us into a more Foucauldian awareness of the kind of beings we are, creatures whose needs and ideals could have been realized in practices we now disapprove of but which our own behaviour now must somehow sublimate or shadow. This dialogue then adds to our understanding of the past when we reread into its expressions the concerns we now recognize so well from our own translations. In one of his most suggestive essays, 'Marlowe, Marx and Anti-Semitism', Greenblatt pits two examples of 'play' against each other. As with Gadamer, 'play' turns out to be truthful self-presentation, but with different resonances. For Marx, generally speaking, play retains a romantic fulsomeness, critical of a capitalist world in which all our activities are by contrast alienated from that true nature we reveal in play. Greenblatt focuses on Marx's reliance on the anti-Semitism of his readers in his essay *On the Jewish Question* to generate disapproval of the capitalist essence of their own society. Marlowe, on the other hand, has the same use for anti-Semitism, but not for play. The hero of *The Jew of Malta*, Barabas, plays the capitalist game with such consummate artistry that his aesthetics of villainy freezes the audience in admiring complicity, incapable of thinking a way out of this absolute, all-embracing truth. Both Marx and Marlowe use the figure of the alien to figure also the inmost workings of their society. But Marlowe, unlike Marx, makes play serve the same figurative function, standing both for entrapment and freedom: the most outrageous of deceptions can show an artist at play. And Greenblatt concludes with Marlowe that, if fraud and freedom are interchangeable, then Marlowe's drama demolishes the illusion 'that human emancipation can be achieved' (1990: 55).

Irrespective of the accuracy of his readings, especially of Marx, we can clearly see the tactics consistently at work in Greenblatt's writing. His final opting for Marlowe and not Marx on 'play' is decisive. Why shouldn't the hermeneutical strain detectable in Greenblatt's thought prevail, letting him think of his criticism as an emancipatory project which opens up different possibilities for the future by rethinking the past? Instead, Geertz's ideas about the diversity of the human are equated with Foucault's pessimistic understanding of the repetition of power through different epistemes. After so absolute an indictment of emancipation as Marlowe's, Greenblatt's own criticism can only replicate Marlowe's: at best, it can aspire to a disabused understanding of itself as the replaying of power in a deceptively emancipatory formation. Criticism does not free us from the power it criticizes, but recycles that power for its own purposes. For Greenblatt's reading of Marlowe turns both the Kantian association of play with disinterested free activity, and Gadamer's rejoining of play to the task of enlarging its object's truth, into a colonizing activity: detached from native interests and ideologies, artists and critics exploit the full potential of their material as unscrupulously as any Nabob.

Textual colonialism

We can understand the evolution of this 'textual colonialism' better from reviewing more generally the varieties and methods of contemporary new historicist criticism. American new historicism profited especially from the visits of Foucault to the University of California at Berkeley during the last years of his life. Along with Greenblatt, Louis Montrose, Catherine Gallagher and other editors and contributors to the journal *Representations* helped place an American new historicism in productive relations with historiographers like Hayden White and Dominick La Capra, theorists of postcolonialism such as Edward Said and Tzvetan Todorov, and, as we have seen, critical ethnologists like Geertz. Under a series title, 'The New Historicism: Studies in Cultural Poetics', the University of California published monographs on American naturalism, Irish nationalism and minor literature, Herodotus, literary practice and social change between 1380 and 1530, as well as on the Renaissance. And of course many new historicists published elsewhere too. Because of its traditional investments in idealism and transcendentalism, Romanticism promised to be a spectacular and particularly controversial annexation for the materialist relativism of new historicism. The criticism of McGann, Levinson, Kurt Heinzelmann, Jon Klancher, Alan Liu and many others in the same mould distinguished itself from Renaissance historicism, attributing to the Renaissance critics a more definite affiliation to Foucault, and to Romanticism an 'ideology' demanding its own kind of oppositional history.

In Britain, the new historicist scene on which recent anthologies draw is still less unified. Their common ground is a view of the

Renaissance as the field on which to test the varieties of materialist criticism available to the English tradition. David Norbrook, close to the great English historians Christopher Hill and Edward Thompson and looking towards new histories of political thought such as J.G.A. Pocock's, is interested, like the American Annabel Patterson, in a history of English republicanism, a tangible movement of political dissidence to be read between the lines of apparently orthodox literary productions. Other critics are still more detailed in their materialism, finding their texts, in Richard Wilson's words, 'imbricated in specific material contexts such as buildings, regions, customs, professions and laws (Wilson 1994: 15). The originally Sussex-based critics – Jonathan Dollimore, Alan Sinfield, Peter Stallybrass and the late Allon White – have been most directly linked to Greenblatt. Their cultural materialism, though, happily acknowledges larger debts to Raymond Williams, and in particular to his efforts to demonstrate that history is not literature's background but an extension of the same plane of action on which literature makes sense. To proclaim the cultural activism of literature in this way creates practical influence for literature at the expense of transhistorical certainties. A timeless, essential humanism for which Shakespeare's plays have often been credited founders on a new historical sensitivity to the play's active participation in and revelation of the ideological mechanisms by which the illusion of that transcendent value is constructed. On Jonathan Dollimore's materialist reading of *King Lear*, for example, the regenerative pity which he thinks a 'humanist' critic sees emanating from Lear's character to cross all boundaries of class and time actually reveals the political conservatism such sympathy requires and has to keep in place. Or, in the words of Blake's 'The Human Abstract', 'Pity would be no more,/If we did not make somebody poor'. For Dollimore, this scandalous revelation can only possess a 'potential' for subversion; it all depends on 'articulation, context and reception' (Dollimore and Sinfield 1985: 13). We are as likely, in other words, to conclude 'So much the worse for pity', as to hear the play's implicit call for a new social order in which pity will recover its virtue. It all depends on what we want to do with the text.

Terence Hawkes believes that this uncertainty of literary resistance opposes Foucauldian pessimism and clarifies 'a continuous process of meaning-making' (Hawkes 1992: 7). Once perceived, the variability of what people have successively meant by Shakespeare works against their declared use of his work as an incontestable cultural imprimatur. The only critical sin is positivism, and there is perhaps inherent virtue in historicizing because it sharpens our contrary awareness of the part which our interpretations play in 'the construction and reconstruction of our own world' (139). Hawkes is one of the funniest debunkers of contemporary pretensions to critical disinterestedness. Absent from his excoriations, though, is any sense of himself being discomposed by the texts he studies. He always finds what he wants; others have done the same, but their bad faith was not to acknowledge that ideological purpose. The sufficiency of Hawkes's disabused poststucturalism may, however, disguise the incompleteness of his historicism. Historicist aims to go 'back to the future' (Levinson) or to 'prefigure' a past which clarifies for us needs still to enjoy fulfilment (Ryan), must be deluded. The ambition of the (formerly) East German critic Robert Weimann to 'have as much as possible of the past significance and as much as possible of the present meaning merged into a new unity' must seem illusory to Hawkes just when it claims to depart from present interests (Weimann 1984: 187). But his own methods cannot, as a result, tolerate the full force of postmodern critical discomfiture. By contrast, Kate Belsey's study of identity and difference in Renaissance drama, more Lacanian in outlook, hopes 'to begin the struggle for change', unforeseen up till now but made possible by the pre-history of that female misrecognition central to patriarchy which her work recounts (Belsey 1985: 221).

In the English tradition, materialism and empiricism are much more closely associated than on the continent or in the USA. Many British critics who would characterize themselves as historicist, and who would certainly think of their own methods as up-to-date and 'new', are still less likely to have theorized their arguments or to be automatically interested in the position their writings might occupy in ongoing debates about critical methodology. The most influential English romanticists, John Barrell and Marilyn Butler, clearly share a historicism, more alive in Butler's case to its institutional past and present, and in Barrell's to the increased visibility lent to historical circumstance by contemporary theory. But neither is reflexive in Greenblatt's anecdotal but disciplined way. Although in Britain the greater emphasis has been, in Louis Montrose's words, 'upon the uses to which the present has put its versions of the past' (Veeser 1989: 183), this includes books on tradition by historians like those of many persuasions contributing to Hobsbawm's and Ranger's collection, *The Invention of Tradition* (Hobsbawm and Ranger 1993), unfashionably void of method-ological self-consciousness. The habit of scrutinizing the present with its own archive, doubling back on its techniques of self-understanding with the past it characteristically makes available, is far less integrated with historicist method.

Yet, if we move on to the next obvious question to ask – what is the new historicism exemplified in this canon? – reflexivity quickly becomes the key concept. Again and again, critics stage and confront an unavoidable mirroring of the present in the past and the dialectical struggle for objectivity which ensues. Attitudes towards the struggle vary. For some, it represents the chance to take political initiatives, to appropriate polemically classical texts from the repressive ideologies they have been used to bolster in the past. Here it is *Kulturkampf* which turns historians into historicists. Caught between mirrors, mutually reflective time-zones, the historicists abandon objectivity and try explicitly to make their own politically desirable assumptions loom larger in reflections from the past, thus magnifying their contemporary force and significance. And, provided you share the politics, there is perhaps a kind of emancipation to be experienced here as the past enlarges our power to articulate present concerns. Feminist and post-colonial readings here take the initiative in current debate. Renaissance 'others', historicists typically argue, are made up: savage projections, they show the mechanics by which contrary moral values serve the state. Because feminist and postcolonial theories make us better able to demystify the supposed aliens around which crystallize our own society's construction of the subject, they, as we shall see, become the historicist vanguard rather than new historicism itself.

For the less optimistic critics, not to be able to step through the looking-glass remains a diminishing experience. Loss of objectivity leads not to political initiative but political pessimism. If 'Mirror on mirror mirrored is all the show', and 'knowledge increases unreality', then we share the dilemma of Yeats's subject in 'The Statues'. We are caught in Greenblatt's postmodern perspectivism, in which history becomes nothing but the stories people tell to keep themselves in power. 'Always historicize', writes Frederic Jameson, expounding, as the historicist is quick to point out, a critical certainty his relativism simultaneously denies, telling us his critical story as though it wasn't fiction in order better to persuade us.

Greenblatt's Marlovian allegiance argued that, although literary historians may feel free of the particular constraints they describe, their historical objects only reflect back to them a relative difference of subjection, the new ways in which they are constrained, not an absolute difference from tyranny. We may not be subject to the severities with which the Renaissance institutions of Church and State enforced social conformity, but the represssive tolerance of the first-world democratic state is potentially more restrictive. No doubt many of us have shared the experience described by Gerald Graff:

> A friend of mine once remarked that on reading the opening
> pages of *Discipline and Punish*, an account of a hideous feudal-

style drawing and quartering, he almost threw up. 'Then I read
further', he said, 'and realized that for Foucault those had been
the *good old days*.'

(Veeser 1989: 172)

This is a bit unfair to new historicism and a simplification of
Foucault. We surely know that violence as nauseating is still going
on, but the moral economy of Western politics is most effective at
safeguarding us from the thought that, in relation to contemporary
exterminations, we might occupy a position comparable to those
early spectators whose company makes us want to throw up. The
relativism of new historicism shows us in what new disguises we
might still make up that obscenely goggling crowd. Our spectacle,
it might be said, is the third world, and the new historicist use of
Foucault's conflation of aesthetics and power shows that it is a
financial as well as a moral difference which puts us in the stalls and
other countries on the stage. Theatricality identifies spectators and
actors alike within a contemporary power game, whose rules the
new historicist claims to have learned from the past.

On this description, new historicists are wise to the power-play
underlying any historical pretension to be free of past or outlandish
formations of power. Hence their use of anecdote to attempt a
critical stylistics of the kind we have seen Foucault practise. By
anecdote is meant something precisely unrepresentative, non-
mimetic, juxtaposed to rather than figurative of the thing to which
it is illustratively adjacent. The new historicists endeavour to resist
power's descriptions of itself, hegemonic descriptions. They do this
not by privileging emancipatory discourses or liberationist
rhetoric, where the stories a discursive regime tells against itself
may be its most effective ploy. Instead, by decentring any master
narrative, by looking everywhere for the means to disturb its self-
presentation, they usurp the given hierarchy of meaning and set up
a retrospective, artificial democracy. They characteristically draw
together a wide variety of discourses from unlikely provenances

and involve them in the interpretation of a literary work whose genre and rhetorical designs on its readers had seemed unambiguous and exclusive. Discourses of the body, of medicine, exorcism, conduct and other archives of a purely anthropological character provide anecdotally interpretative moments with which to skew the reading a tragedy, comedy or epic ostensibly demands. The more anecdotal the critical intervention, the more likely its chances of evoking the arbitrariness which history disguises in the uniformity of narrative.

Nevertheless, and this is the crucial doubling-back typical of the historicist reflexivity, this retrospective liberalism is not allowed itself to go unquestioned. Its exemplary resistance to the authoritarian protocols of past texts is weighed against the powerful figure it may cut in the present. Decentring, in other words, can begin to look like deregulation. The right of any discourse or interpretation to undermine a received hegemony colludes with market economics. The ingenious exchange and articulations of power recorded by new historicists must, by their own argument, operate within their own work as it writes contemporary history as well as that of their chosen period or research. Greenblatt's work on Shakespeare removes the difference which privileges Renaissance art over its economic base. Nevertheless, this democratizing gesture, which rejects the Elizabethan and Jacobean use of art to mystify power, can be seen to mime the hegemonies contemporary with Greenblatt's own writing, Reagonomics and Thatcherism. Stanley Fish echoes this right libertarianism in his relish for the new historicism. 'In the words of the old Alka-Selzer commercial, "try it, you'll like it"' (Veeser 1989: 315). Fish thinks that to worry about being the flavour of the month shows professional naivety and a lack of realism about the way in which critics are obliged to work within one interpretative community rather than another more politically efficacious one – one in which it might count politically if Reaganomics prevailed in its critical forum.

By contrast, Frank Lentricchia, in a hostile article in the same anthology, finds such new historicist mirroring of the present reprehensible. Greenblatt moots the idea that there is some reserve in new historicist collaboration, some saving grace in the honest dismay with which a new historicist contemplates his or her reflexivity, a kind of Beckettian 'I can't go on, I must go on'. At the end of *Renaissance Self-Fashioning*, after a final anecdote, we hear that Greenblatt wants 'to bear witness at the close to my overwhelming need to sustain the illusion that I am the principal maker of my own identity' (1980: 257). Lentricchia is contemptuous of this: 'a paranoid fantasy, one especially characteristic of the recent literary mind', which, with characteristic passivity, assumes it cannot 'touch the structure of power which denies us such freedom' (Veeser: 242). The trouble with Lentricchia's professed disaffiliation is that he seems bound to add to, not detract from, the new historicist argument. Even if we agree with him, especially if we do, aren't we simply thickening our historicist description of the present?

Earlier I suggested that British new historicism, with its closer relation to empiricism (i.e. giving precise information about a work's historical context), tended to be too various to be dragooned into theoretical line. Nevertheless, the anecdotalism practised on the other side of the Atlantic does imply a rationale applicable to British untidiness. Historicism, to put it another way, is to some extent an incorrigible term. Like autobiography, it makes all things, including the subject's self-deception, material evidence. For example, one new historicist may read Shakespeare as a conservative ideologue undone by the transgressive or oppositional quality of his imagery, characters or plot. Overall, though, the plays, containing such resistance, reinforce his conservatism even if they do so in embarrassingly conflictual ways. The dialogic richness of a Shakespeare play, therefore, lets new historicists cast its implied author in the role of the Duke in *Measure for Measure*, returning at the end to endorse a status quo renewed by highly questionable, problematic means which he could only have employed in another character.

New historicism recasts history as a battle over fictions, a battle of communication. The organizing tropes which, as Hayden White has argued, direct any historical narrative, do battle with each other outside the archive as well. The winners in historical conflicts are those whose version of events is accepted. Any method, however, which argues that all historical transactions should be understood at the level of signs is approaching Gadamer's idea that hermeneutics describes our way of being, or Foucault's belief that discourse prescribes existential possibility. Renaissance new historicists frequently return (as in Greenblatt's *Shakespearean Negotiations* and *Marvellous Possessions*) to selected scenes from the West's discovery of the New World, principally the confrontation between the European colonists and the Amerindians, as a kind of paradigm. These incidents are picked to show how the Christian invaders understand all they need to of the Amerindian cultural codes; the baffled indigenous peoples succumb to imperialism because they lose a textual war of communications, a hermeneutical defeat indistinguishable from their physical submission. Language here is described as undeniably material. Whether or not it represents something becomes irrelevant. It constitutes the reality the conquistadors go on to enjoy a continent which God enjoined them to convert to Christian use. All descriptions are self-fulfilling prophecies when they replace a native world-description with their own model.

Two points need to be made about this paradigm, though. First of all it is, in a sense, old hat; or, what postcolonial theory is interested in now is exactly the reverse. We know that hermeneutical battle was won, but now, as the empire strikes back, we want to know the viable modes of opposition to colonialism which do not mirror its oppression or repeat its scenario with a new cast. Secondly, new historicism also colonizes; it colonizes other discourses, proclaiming its sceptical activism, neglecting native protocols for its own ends while still observing the overall power-structure of the discourse. It exhibits power without taking responsibility for it, saying it is only telling a story about power, yet impugning that fictional distance in its concurrent claim that power is nothing but the stories it tells about itself.

The colonial battle of communication is joined in Greenblatt's climactic essay on *Othello* in *Renaissance Self-Fashioning*, 'the supreme symbolic expression of the cultural model I have been describing' (Greenblatt 1980: 232). The opportunist entry into the power-structure is described as operating at three levels – Iago, Shakespeare and Greenblatt himself. Iago, we hear, is a master of 'what we have been calling the process of fictionalization that transforms a fixed symbolic structure into a flexible construct ripe for improvisational entry' (234). This glosses Iago's meditation at I.3.390–402:

> Cassio's a proper man, let me see now,
> To get this place, and to make up my will,
> A double knavery . . . how, how? . . . let me see,
> After some time, to abuse Othello's ear,
> That he is too familiar with his wife:
> He has a person and a smooth dispose,
> To be suspected, fram'd to make women false:
> The Moor a free and open nature too,
> That thinks men honest that but seems to be so:
> And will as tenderly be led by the nose . . .
> As asses are.
> I ha't, it is engender'd; Hell and night
> Must bring this monstrous birth to the world's light.

Characters' virtues make them readable, predictable and manageable as Amerindians. Stepping outside their codes, Iago retains the power that comes with knowledge of them, but his externality makes him irresponsible and unintelligible. He represents 'the principle of narrativity itself', rather than any single narrative; when asked for his own story, the teller of everyone else's story remains silent, as does the author of the play. Greenblatt in turn characterizes Shakespeare as possessing 'a limitless talent for entering into the consciousness of another, perceiving its deepest structures as a manipulable fiction, reinscribing it into its own narrative form' (252). Greenblatt, the critic, though, is just as much a colonizer of Shakespeare's discourse. Contrary to appearances, *Othello* manifests 'the colonial power of Christian doctrine over sexuality, a power visible at this point precisely in its limitation' (242). But this colonialism, which Terence Hawkes has helped Greenblatt to see, has been detected through the strategic contextualizing of *Othello* in writings on sexuality from Augustine to Sidney. Hence the critic's entry into Shakespeare's text is an improvisation making the power it is its purpose to reveal lose its original point and legitimacy under critical enlightenment. Greenblatt does not show his hand, no more than Iago or Shakespeare, except in his sceptical manipulation for his professional ends of discursive power. Power reappears, but to enable a critical discourse – 'nothing, if not critical' – founded on scepticism concerning this power's legitimacy.

Power without responsibility for it, an entry into its structures which bypasses the interests sustaining them – this sounds first of all like the Kantian aesthetic: a disinterested sense of the structure of human understanding beyond its utilitarian and scientific uses. But the new historicist critics' enhancement of their originals by showing how the power structuring them can be put to new use or regroup elsewhere moves towards Gadamer's hermeneutic revision of Romanticism. It is then a short step to Foucault's pessimistic reading of enhancement as the perpetual recurrence of power in different forms. If this genealogy holds good, Renaissance and Romantic new historicism are significantly linked. Romantic new historicists tend now to see Romantic claims for self-sufficiency as typically invoking images of a creative and autonomous self which have hitherto been understood by critics in too schematic and politically bowdlerized a manner, too much in line with the Romantics' own estimation of their culture. Resisting this self-image, Romanticists now increasingly try to join issues of feminism and race together to show how Romantic creativity, however ostensibly libertarian and revolutionary it appears, actually formulates itself in figures and designs which further the causes of patriarchy and colonialism. The self-production prized by Romantic poets and artists frequently images itself as a kind of imperialist annexation of an object of desire. Its gendering and exoticizing of objects of Romantic quest remind us that Romanticism was situated at the start of a period of unparalleled imperialist expansion. Mystification makes the prime area of that expansion, the East, more legible. Studies of Romantic Orientalism can quote Friedrich Schlegel's injunction that:

> in the Orient we must look for the most sublime form of the Romantic, and only when we can draw from the source, perhaps will the semblance of southern passion which we find so charming in Spanish poetry appear to us occidental and sparse.
>
> (Kabbani 1986: 29)

A continuity is to be set up between European writing and the Orient, the true sublime, identified as an enriched European legibility. What might be genuinely other or mysterious in the East is not allowed to produce discontinuity with this aggrandizing Western culture interested only in its own replenishment. Again, in Romantic fashion, failure to conceptualize the Orient is rewritten as symbolic expression of the Orient. Colonialism and the Romantic aesthetic of Orientalism share the same logic: their mystifications appropriate another discursive structure in contempt of its power and interest. Nevertheless, the truth remains that the Romantic new historicists of today, although for reasons we may find much more morally congenial, do the same to those colonizing, Romantic mystifiers. To expound this in more detail would also be to redescribe the Foucauldian strategies at work in Renaissance new historicism. Neither Romantic nor Renaissance new historicism stands outside discursive constraints, but both rewrite past discourses with a critical difference. To find the critical potential of this difference most fully articulated, though, we have to look at postcolonial and feminist theories which so often seem to begin where explicit historicist initiatives, like the ones looked at in this section, leave off.

POSTCOLONIAL STYLISTICS AND POSTMODERN LOGIC

In discussing historicism it becomes more and more natural to equate historical difference with cultural difference. The problems faced by the interpreter crossing historical boundaries are so similar to those of the cultural anthropologist that no apology for this conflation looks necessary. Both hermeneutical acts are so closely allied in procedure and intent that we easily forget their differences, or that one must, in some sense, be a metaphor for the other. Or perhaps 'metonym' for the other is more accurate, if assumption of that continuity with our past enabling dialogue is *extended* or reinforced by the parallel of interpreting other cultures. Since other cultures are frequently contemporaneous with our own, they can, if allowed, talk back in a more straightforward manner than the past. Equally, renderers of historical difference maintain the parallel at their end by understanding as a kind of translation the effort by which they try to register the other voices in which the past replies to their questions, a translation which may involve alterations to the language into which the translation passes. A.D. Nuttall, for example, writing of Pope's classicism, finds he has to distinguish Pope as 'translator' from Pope as (Dilthey's word) 'transposer':

> when Pope entered the altered landscape of another culture, he chose not only to translate classical meanings into English meanings but also to transpose certain alien habits of speech and thought. He did this because, like all great poets, he cared about language and form, and knew that the language of

> English poetry itself would be strengthened and enriched by the
> minor violations to which he was willing to subject it. He also
> found that the ancient world itself was far from being a uniform
> field.
>
> (Nuttall 1989: 134)

Pope risks distorting the English language under the pressure of
translating into it an alien form. But the reward for confronting
difficulty is a strengthening and enriching of the poet's language.
This increase in English, though, has departed from the strict
canons of translation and is licensed instead as transposition, as
classicism in an English key. This outcome is not necessarily built
into descriptions of the task of the translator and is characteristic,
for Nuttall, of the work of a great poet. Finally, the freedom of
transposition, it is hinted, might still reflect earlier freedoms and so
be truer to the variety of past uses to which the translator's text
might have been put.

Postcolonialism calls the bluff of this subtle historicism.
Historical difference is not the same as cultural difference, it states,
and the accommodations demanded of the interpreter of the latter
cannot be appropriated by historians as a sign of their good faith,
nor of a Diltheyan confidence that they can 're-live' the past.
Colonialism, the once imperial and now industrial and economic
hegemony of the West, has typically pirated cultural differences for
its own historical purposes. The histories of why one country
was able to lord it over another have too frequently used cultural
disparities as a justification. Explanations of the relations between
the two fields of historical ascendancy and cultural difference are
never innocent. All sorts of historical narratives – progressive,
altruistic, fatalistic – have employed the full range of associated
discriminations – race, colour, gender, religion, social practice,
primitivism – to justify almost any behaviour of one group of
people towards another. The discontinuities between the interests
of colonizer and colonized make a coherent history of their
exchanges virtually impossible.

With its emphasis on an epistemological break between colonizer and colonized, postcolonialism renews the postmodern questioning of historicism. But don't the difficulties recorded by postcolonialism apply only to texts written about colonized cultures? Hegemonic texts, texts belonging to the colonizing culture, surely remain free of this embarrassment? Postcolonial theorists from Franz Fanon to the present day have consistently refused to accept this compartmentalization by which the problems of the colonized are made peripheral to those of the central power. That set of priorities defines the colonialism under critique. Obviously the failure to treat subject peoples equally reflects on the ideals of justice possessed by the ruling society. If, on the other hand, justice is abandoned and the colonized are defined as inferior or irredeemably 'other', the effects on the colonizers can still be disconcerting.

From Hegel onwards, the domestication of the 'other' has become a paradigm of knowledge. To understand postcolonial, and much feminist theory, it is vital to understand the ruling colonial metaphor implicitly guiding the Hegelian exposition we have already looked at briefly (see pp. 47–8). Hegel contrasts with Kant in his use of Rousseau by refiguring the latter's tragic view of our understanding of nature – the more we grasp its value the more we must have become abstracted and estranged from it – in the self-defeating logic of his *Phenomenology of Mind*. From Bacon onwards, knowledge of nature is represented in the scientific tradition as power over another. But the more complete our scientific mastery over nature, Hegel shows, the more abject the thing enslaved. And the more abject the slave, the more hollow is the epistemological success and the value and significance attaching to the possession of the object of knowledge. Also vital for postcolonial thinking is the consequence that the more unjust our domineering estimation of the slave, the more his or her existence will remain unknowable. The other may slavishly conform to our expectations, but only in 'self-ignorance', as the feminist Luce Irigaray describes it (Irigaray 1985: 136). We get the knowledge we deserve, but what still lies outside it can enjoy alternative identities and modes of agency we can only guess at or demonize. The 'other' is the outline of the familiar, viewed as the boundary of its outside, sharing its definition, symbiotically related. When that circumference wobbles, the inside is disturbed as well as the outside. The false fixing of a subject-group as inferior is an act of coercion, damaging to the knower as well as to the known. The monstering of the 'other' both leaves its true nature to stalk potently beyond the reaches of the colonizer's knowledge, and leaves the colonizing mind disintegrating under the distorting force of its own warped vision. 'The White man's eyes', writes Homi Bhabha in a preface to Fanon, 'break up the Black man's body and in that act of epistemic violence its own frame of reference is transgressed, its field of vision disturbed' (Williams and Chrisman 1993: 115). Hegel thought that the contradictions in any particular mastery of nature show its historical limitations and propel us towards the next stage in universalizing our knowledge. A tradition of commentary from Alexander Kojève onwards, more congenially to postcolonialism, argues that the contradictions explode the entire epistemological project.

Postcolonial theory, therefore, rehearses major questions raised by the rise of historicism, giving them new edge and application. Historicism's apparent advance beyond the Eurocentric uniformity of natural-law theory can begin, in Hegel's thought, to look like opportunistic adjustments by the centre of power to accommodate changes of circumstance without loss of authority. Against that suspicion, we can note historicism's unarguable emphasis on relativism, on the singularity of historical events and the individuality of different cultures. Historicism here converges on that 'eventalization' which Foucault found so desirable, according to a late interview:

> What do I mean by this term? First of all, a breach of self-evidence. It means making visible a *singularity* at places where

> there is a temptation to invoke a historical constant, an imme-
> diate anthropological trait, or an obviousness that imposes
> itself uniformly on all. To show that things 'weren't as necessary
> as all that'; it wasn't a matter of course that mad people came to
> be regarded as mentally ill; it wasn't self-evident that the only
> thing to be done with a criminal was to lock him up; it wasn't
> self-evident that the causes of illnesses were to be sought
> through the individual examination of bodies; and so on.
>
> (Foucault 1991: 76)

Here the peculiarity to be preserved belongs to the dominant
culture, not the marginal ones to which it may gracefully concede
an eccentric life of their own. J.-P. Sartre's famous preface to
Fanon's *The Wretched of the Earth*, unlike Bhabha's preface quoted
above, notably lacks that self-critical grasp of postcolonialism. For
Sartre, the force of the postcolonial reversal is 'simply . . . that in
the past we made history and now it is being made of us' (Fanon
1967: 23). The solution, by an equally simple symmetry, is to join
the other side and so become a maker of history once more. There
is no sense in Sartre's piece that Fanon has discredited the making
of history itself rather than a particular historical agency. Yet Fanon
is very clear about the importance of seeing that colonial rule is
secured not only by force but through the writing of a history
which culturally estranges its subjects from their past. That past
is not allowed to count as history except as it can be transposed
into present colonial significance. That flexible dialectic which
allowed for the past's critical revision of present assumptions looks
oppressive and cynical from Fanon's perspective. 'Colonialism', he
claims:

> is not satisfied merely with holding a people in its grip and
> emptying the native's brain of all form and content. By a kind of
> perverted logic it turns to the past of the oppressed people, and
> distorts, disfigures and destroys it. . . . The effect consciously
> sought by colonialism was to drive into the natives' heads the

idea that if the settlers were to leave, they would at once fall back into barbarism, degradation and bestiality.

(Fanon 1967: 169)

Successful resistance to colonialism, therefore, means that 'the past is given back its value' (170). Again we should note that it is not just history as a narrative of enlightenment that is coercive here, but the dialectical assimilation of native traditions to the colonial ideology of progress. This ideology can be boosted or clarified by pronouncing these traditions to be monstrous or barbaric pre-history, although with the consequences mentioned above. Alternatively, they can be neatly excluded from serious historical interaction with the present by being respectfully placed in an anthropological, archaeological or comparative ethnological archive. To take one's model for cultural resistance to the colonizers from a museum then looks like the attempt to revive a mummy. We can usefully recall here Gadamer's disbelief in the galvanized corpse of Schleiermacher's New Testament beliefs, hermeneutically resuscitated. The epistemological break Fanon has to urge against his colonial masters is a comparably radical conversion. We are talking of 'quite simply the replacing of a certain "species" of men by another "species" of men' (27). The injustices of colonialism are not to be resolved by making it possible for both parties to acknowledge a common humanity.

After the conflict there is not only the disappearance of colonialism but also the disappearance of the colonized man. This new humanity cannot do otherwise than define a new humanism both for itself and for others.

(Fanon 1967: 198)

This new episteme, this new humanism, will so change the terms of historical reference that the revival of the histories repressed by colonialism will no longer look frightful or anachronistic, but normal. Although, as Bhabha points out, Fanon can repose in the existentialist humanism of his day, his final rallying-cry at the end of *The Wretched of the Earth* is a call to 'work out new concepts, and try to set afoot a new man' (255), a project anticipating more postmodernist reorientations.

Following Fanon, postcolonial theory claims that Western writing has been tailored as much to certain assumptions of its opposite as to notions of its own cultural integrity. Thematically, this can be easily demonstrated. It is plausible to argue that the following pieces of English literature are determined and distinguished from each other as much by the opposition they obliquely conjure up as by the England they extol – John of Gaunt's 'This royal throne of kings . . .' in *Richard II*, Andrew Marvell's 'To Holland', John Dryden's 'Annus Mirabilis', Pope's 'Windsor Forest', Gray's 'The Bard', Wordsworth's sonnet 'Milton! thou should'st be living at this hour', Tennyson's 'Locksley Hall' and T.S. Eliot's 'Little Gidding'. Each asserts, but through the concerns of its own period, that 'History is now and England'. The postmodern reader's task is not in some sense to disprove these avowals, but to show that, given a certain construction of 'History', 'now' and 'England', they are true.

Postcolonial theory is therefore much preoccupied with the methods whereby a culture co-opts others to its own point of view. Typically this appropriation produces a discrepancy of styles. The colonial subjects don't quite fit their subaltern uniforms, and while this maladroitness can add a subversive 'slyness' to their 'civility', as Bhabha describes, it also keeps a suitable distance between them and their masters and mistresses. Fear of miscegenation and hybridity make the grotesqueries involved in Westernization redouble the epistemological problems of the domineering culture and question its authority. Dismissed or repressed, the native culture floats free of scientific regulation; the simulated Westernism supposedly replacing it subversively mimics the domineering culture, fitting the bill all too well and thus making indistinguishable from *masquerade* its alleged supremacy. Edward Said's controversial but massively influential *Orientalism* fixes on this question of style.

The representative figures of the West's colonial management of the East 'are to the actual Orient . . . as stylized costumes are to characters in a play'. They simultaneously 'characterize the Orient as alien and . . . incorporate it schematically on a theatrical stage whose audience, managers, and actors are *for* Europe, and only for Europe' (Said 1985: 71–2). Said especially resents the shrouding or 'covering' of the machinery actually producing the object which much academic and political discourse on Arabs and Islam treats, he argues, with spurious objectivity. Although their rhetoric is geared to make us forget it, they, as much as any other form of Orientalism, are on the stage, flattering an audience. 'Verbs like "demonstrate", "reveal", "show", are used without an indirect object: to whom are the Arabs revealing, demonstrating, showing?' (310). Homi Bhabha illuminates the inadvertent self-critique of colonialism inherent in the stagy conformity Said shows, categorically this time, that it demands. The 'ambivalent' mimicry asked of Indian civil servants during the Raj created the loyal subaltern class ordered by Macaulay but maintained crucial moments of apartheid. An Indian always 'styled' himself a Western Oriental gentleman, hence its use as *the* racist epithet by Western colonialism. On the other hand, his inauthenticity is what, in Bhabha's words, 'produces another knowledge of [colonial] norms' (Bhabha 1994: 86). Through the stylistic ambivalence of mimicry is registered the fraud of the emancipatory story the West has told itself about its imperial mission as one to enlighten and further the progress of its subjects.

Postcolonial theory's emphasis on the critical potential of mimicry reflects a postmodern scepticism regarding our access to genuinely liberating programmes for action. Caught in the contemporary episteme, our thoughts of escape must have inbuilt limitations. Fanon described the 'colonial world' as a 'Manichaean world' (1967: 31). His successors tend to detect many more forms of colonialism, imposed internally as well as externally; the break-through into Fanon's new 'humanism' can seem as far away as ever.

Bhabha, Gayatri Spivak and others, confronted by the reverse colonialist treatment meted out to immigrant communities and a growing underclass, opt for forms of theoretical hybridity and miscegenation intended to reinforce in their very form of intellectual presentation their opposition to the neocolonial purpose. Like Foucault's late writings, they give us 'philosophical fragments put to work in a historical field of problems' rather than single-minded, clear-cut solutions (1991: 74). Maybe, as Foucault thought, these possibilities already evoke a new episteme? Cultural margins move to occupy the centre; the discarded empire resurfaces within. All the devices by which we can conjure 'imagined communities', as described in Benedict Anderson's frequently cited book on nationalism, are brought to bear in opposition to the prevailing concept of a monolithic state, creating an antithetical, multicultural audience keen to historicize past writing from its own point of view.

Traditional bids for the discursive power with which to inaugurate a new episteme are thus repeated by postcolonial theory. It would be 'a racialist fiction', writes the Afro-American critic H.L. Gates, to think that, for example, the institutionalizing of Afro-American studies at universities did not intend 'a vision of America, a refracted image in the American looking-glass' (Gates 1992: 151). In the case of Britain, Robert Young writes, postcolonial critical practice has demonstrated 'the extent to which colonialism . . . was not simply a marginal activity on the edges of English civilization, but fundamental to its own cultural representation' (1990: 174). The struggle to empower a postcolonial view is nevertheless distinguished by its attack on the very idea of a cultural centre with a single legitimate history in need of supplementation or revision. The argument works rather through a difference in language. The earlier bids for the power to rewrite history are repeated, but with a calculated stylistic difference, a subversively obvious mimicry which puts in question the usual aims and expected goals of cultural controversy. The symbiotic connection binding the controlling culture to its 'other' has the effect that to reverse their roles is to change the definition of neither. The previously oppressed would still mirror their oppressors, although this time, gratifyingly, from the position of power. But their identity would still be prescribed as before. To escape this Hegelian master/slave cycle, the postcolonial project must produce 'another knowledge' of both positions stylistically, through parodic distance not scientific mastery.

Clearly this Foucauldian conclusion offers solutions from the tail end of that Western hermeneutic tradition which had been the target in postcolonialism's sights all along. Foucault's unspecific ideal of 'thinking differently' receives welcome content and examples from postcolonial resistance. Consequently, though, some theorists are wary that such convenient dovetailing has the effect 'once again to make the rest of the world a peripheral term in Europe's self-questioning' (Ashcroft *et al.* 1989: 173). The empire can surely write back on independent terms. Still more specifically, the temptation for those representing a Western tradition hopelessly incriminated by its power is to hand over responsibility for imagining an emancipated future or authentic identity to its former dependencies. But doesn't this apparently expansive gesture abdicate too much? Aren't the relinquishers of power like embarrassed male whites in a class on Afro-American women writers who feel too guilty to contribute their criticisms. Their fastidious silence then, bel hooks claims, 'places black people once again in a service position, meeting the needs of whites' (hooks 1989: 47).

On the other hand, when Homi Bhabha approves of Heidegger's recasting of 'the boundary' as 'that from which *something begins its presencing*' (Bhabha 1994: 1), the way out of Hegel's colonial oppositions looks as indeterminate as before. Spivak is concerned lest Foucault's final commitment to historiographical practice rather than theory, criticism through a difference of writing and style not a philosophical confrontation, amounts to a 'functional abdication':

It is a curious fact of Michel Foucault's career that, in a certain phase of his influential last period, he performed something like an abdication, refused to 'represent' (as if such a refusal were possible), and privileged the oppressed subject, who could seemingly speak for himself.

(Spivak 1987: 208)

The life of Foucault's writer of *The History of Sexuality*, like that of Barthes' late *Fragments of a Lover's Discourse*, is just not an existential option for the subaltern consciousness, according to Spivak. Still more sweepingly, Aijaz Ahmad condemns a hermeneutical ontology he attributes to Said, by which, because of their Western episteme or way of knowing, 'Europeans were *ontologically* incapable of producing true knowledge (sic) about non-Europe' (Ahmad 1992: 178). This, argues Ahmad, is to take a fashionably 'cosmopolitan' view owing more to postmodernism than to a *contrasting* 'global' perspective genuinely free of colonialist prejudice.

Historically, it has seemed possible to distinguish between Orientalist exoticizing and more self-critical imaging of the East by Western writing. In the course of a summary of the rise of British Orientalism at the end of the 18th century and through the Romantic period in English literature, Marilyn Butler is able to distinguish the fetishizing of Eastern otherness from oppositional uses: either as a tool of comparative critical demystifying of a hitherto unqualified Christian hegemony, or as a poetic field for 'highly allegorized, defamiliarized versions of the British state' (Butler 1994: 396–9). Of course it is debatable how far this critical licence in fact only represents the slack or play in the overall discursive regime which is firmly in control all the time. If, as Paul Gilroy thinks, race is 'a distinct order of social phenomena *sui generis*' (Gilroy 1987: 27) and not just an epistemological aid to a knowledge of global power-struggles, as Ahmad believes, then the enlightened critique of Orientalism will always be missing something crucial. It will always be significant that, in the memorable title of Gilroy's book, 'there ain't no black in the Union Jack'. The British nation–state's self-criticism is here precisely beside the point. But it surely also remains relevant that only at some periods and in some constituencies does the colonial perspective of litera-ture attract critical attention. Critics like Ahmad are perhaps closer than they think to postmodernism in attacking the essentialism and prescription of both East and West that goes on within what Ahmad himself can call an 'episteme' (188).

In any case, subaltern literature, literature not consolidated by the national 'other' but adopting its position, seems to have little difficulty in staking out a critical position by fitting antagonisti-cally to authoritarian norms. The stylistic resistance we have seen developed by postmodern argumentation, producing a writerly rather than a theoretical opposition, receives support here. From Jean Rhys's *Wide Sargasso Sea* to Spivak's translation of Mahasweta Devi's *Draupadi*, postcolonial writing is able happily to invade classic story and myth through unconventional entrances because it has, as it were, the key to the back door. The authority of *Jane Eyre* and the tale of Draupadi from the *Mahabharata* is under-mined by being supplemented by obedient co-workers in the field. Rhys elaborates the story of Rochester's wife, Devi gruesomely mimes the triumph of Draupadi over her intended violator. The originals now look top-heavy from what they strategically excluded. They seem to garble their unitary message, because, after reading their postmodern sequels, we cannot help hearing scraps of the stories they chose not to tell. To the postmodern reader, perhaps perversely, they sound like official versions, implausible euphemisms. After *Wide Sargasso Sea*, *Jane Eyre* is patently about more subjects than it can manage and requires, to be recuperated, the postmodern critical latitude demanded from *Wide Sargasso Sea* from the outset.

A novel such as E.M. Forster's *A Passage to India* can thematize the funny mirrors that the colonizers and their subjects hold up to each other. Fundamentally, the echo which precipitates the 'rape' of Adela Quested reflects back the British violation of Indian integrity, and Adela acts out this aggression upon herself throughout the story, even to the extent of inconsistently retracting her accusation against Aziz and losing all credibility. After hearing the echo, her companion Mrs Moore does not entertain 'one large thought' (Forster 1961: 203). But Indian integrity is an invention of the British anyway; its 'other' identity lies in such excesses as the ecstasy of Professor Godbole and the apotheosis of Mrs Moore as the chanting crowd magnifies her name outside the courthouse with its own echo. What Forster cannot do is to send up or parody the entrapment by this Hegelian cycle of same and other, this hall of mirrors, this episteme he uses to understand the Raj. Not yet, at any rate, not there. Writing such as Chinua Achebe's *African Trilogy* can take that further step.

The titles of the first two novels – *Things Fall Apart* and *Ill At Ease* – are quotations from Yeats's 'The Second Coming' and T.S. Eliot's 'Journey of The Magi'. These two poems of 'annunciation' contain their own ironies and reversals of a dominant Christian tradition. Without too much imaginative effort, emigrés like Yeats and Eliot can themselves be styled postcolonial. Achebe, though, does not merely write about pre-colonial, colonized and post-colonial Nigerian cultures in order to show that their texture is rich enough to support the constructions of canonically Western values signified by their titles. He also implies that it is just his writing's success in meeting those standards that accounts for the destruction he describes. The canonical vindication the titles give to the African oral tradition recorded in the novels is also its displacement by the colonizers' written dispensation. This paradox, like that of the archival preservation extinguishing a living oral tradition, comes, as we have learned from Derrida to argue, from not accepting that speech is already a kind of writing no more nor less systematic and encyclopedic than the literally written word. As a result, Achebe does not let his readers make sense of his work as a successful appropriation of Western cultural value for African purposes, because such success is pictured as destroying the means by which it is achieved. It is the British who can only approach the tradition from which Achebe writes in a kind of pidgin, although, given its canonization, it is their tradition as much as his. Achebe writes their fumbling approaches to indigenous African languages in English. He thus exposes the barbarism and ignorance belonging to colonial culture by paradoxically writing the views of its victims from a position deeper inside and more learned in that culture's own language. The novel's argument is to turn 'Things fall apart' into a performative utterance completely apposite to itself. The encroaching British culture implodes along with the epistemological distinction between same and other on which it is founded. The Africans are already acculturated, otherwise, as Geertz argues, they would not be human. To try, then, to cultivate them, ostensibly with a view to furthering their humanity must actually be to do something else – to dehumanize them by violating the shape of their already existing humanity. The classic excuses of colonialism become a nonsense.

Traditional literary history evidently deforms under the pressure of this kind of writing. Historicism is still its essence, and a reordering of the present its goal, but readers have to revise their notions of influence, continuity and priority – which is original and which a copy – in keeping with the postmodern logic of the postcolonial script. H.L. Gates' theory of African/American literary criticism, *The Signifying Monkey*, similarly reaches into a black oral tradition for the concept of 'Signifyin(g)', his 'metaphor for literary history' – the parenthesis around the 'g' reminding the reader of its transliteration of orality (Gates 1988: 107). Again, the troping of literary precedents achieved by 'Signifyin(g)' is understood through a non-literary medium, like jazz, creating disjunctive parallels (transpositions again) rather than neat oppositions or mirror images. Along with his partner in interpretation, Esu, the signifying monkey – 'figure of figures' (xxi) or a kind of postcolonial Hermes – is a trickster who thrives on orthodox critical expectations which enable him to lead his victims by the nose. Always already double-voiced and hybrid, the African/American tradition, with its precedents in canonical writing and oral heritage, finds out the reader not prepared to acknowledge all the signifyin(g) possibilities thrown up by the revisioning of history. In this regard Gates quotes Ishmael Reed's poem 'Dualism: in ralph ellison's invisible man'.

> i am outside of
> history. i wish
> i had some peanuts, it
> looks hungry there in
> its cage.
>
> i am inside of
> history. its
> hungrier than i
> thot.
>   (Gates 1988: 238)

Fix on one figure to represent history, as Gates tells the moral here, and you make it literal, forgetting that it could always be different, oral perhaps, and you inside its mouth!

HERSTORY

Feminism and postcolonialism share most notably a distrust of the authority of historical narratives. They frequently collaborate in critiques of the scope, content and methodology behind the writing of histories. Women's studies is now a vast academic study-area. Its bearing on the uses of historicism for critical theory point-edly redirects the questions which have recurred in this book. Principally, feminist theory makes the case for the particularity of various women's histories in opposition to an Enlightened, general account supposedly applicable and accessible to all human beings. It also, in some forms, questions its own mode of representing the past, seeing the conceptual tools it inherits as part of the oppression it aims to resist. These two projects do not necessarily sit happily together. The attempt to resolve their differences, to establish for women a history and literature of their own while revising the very idea of history, provokes controversy, usually expressed as a disagreement over political tactics. Some more empirically-minded critics argue for the value of inaugurating a women's history which, ignored and repressed by male history, now stands alongside it, a different story on equal terms. Others object that parity of this kind leaves intact the exclusionary methods facilitating sexist history in the first place.

Put summarily, the former critics can claim victories in the canon-wars, the latter can point to distinct advances in the theory-wars. Both parties have achieved influential representation in academic institutions, canonical innovators more in America and theorists more on the continent. To those expounding a once systematically obscured female canon, theoretical emphasis on imagining a female writing free of previously culpable standards of historical scholarship makes it appear, in Janet Todd's words, 'that theory can substitute for reading female writers of the past' (Todd 1988: 78). The main problem is one of gaining representation, and that problem is left signally unaddressed by theoretical critiques of historical representation. On the other hand, theorists can argue that too much may be taken for granted by the new archivists: women have been successfully repressed in the past particularly because they were discursively produced as that homogeneous social group whose essential experience new feminist history now uncovers. For the editors of *m/f*, anthologized under the telling title *The Woman in Question*, 'how women are produced as a category . . . determines the subordinate position of women'. The 'reinstatement' of a suppressed history is therefore not 'a sufficient political practice' (Adams and Cowie 1990: 21).

A book on critical theory might reasonably be expected to support this last approach; but I hope that the self-critical hermeneutic tradition traced by historicism rather encourages the reader to see both approaches as requiring each other. Like postcolonialism, feminist theory reorientates received critical traditions so as to make them take notice of the unjustly neglected text. The moot point, though, is whether or not the new visibility leaves intact a coherent idea of tradition. Critics, for example, working in the Romantic period of English literature, and surveying a mass of 'new' women's poetry now anthologized as a matter of course, wonder if they are equipped by the ruling literary traditions to read it. The revaluation of Romanticism by modernism, and their common distrust of sentimentalism and personification have combined to disqualify the idiom of much women's poetry of the period, immensely popular at the time, from critical approval. Canons of critical theory, in other words, are as much put in question by feminist scholarship as the composition of 'literature'. To take women's writing in the Romantic period as valuable in its own right is, philosophically, to refuse to see it as the mirror image of male success. Again we find ourselves in the business of justification by means other than those we inherit and from which our researches started out. Yet at the same time, an otherwise utopian postmodern disaffection with existing norms is now given a content which is validated by its readability. And from our reading of this *stylistic* difference, new critical principles may eventually be deduced. Masculinist theory, unable to cope with a recognizable cultural alternative to its 'literature', ought to be suitably embarrassed, and its objective pretensions dismantled. But this victory need not by any means have to 'reinstate' its unified mirror-image; it can alternatively settle for accepting its own continual disconcertment by such writerly variety. This theoretical point is clearly put by Elaine Showalter, whose work has almost always been connected with the project of establishing the female canon:

> a few years ago feminist critics thought we were on a pilgrimage to the promised land in which gender would lose its power, in

> which all texts would be sexless and equal, like angels. But the more precisely we understand the specificity of women's writing not as a transient by-product of sexism but as a fundamental and continuing determining reality, the more clearly we realize that we have misperceived our destination. We may never reach the promised land at all: for when feminist critics see our task as the study of women's writing, we realize that the land promised to us is not the serenely undifferentiated universality of texts but the tumultuous and intriguing wilderness of difference itself.
>
> (Showalter 1986: 267)

Showalter's trust in the critical sufficiency of difference sets new feminist criticism fairly in the domain of postmodernity. Her historicism works by critical recalcitrance; not by posing a more comprehensive theory of what is historically significant, but by voicing writing traditionally excluded from such theories. She cites Geertz on the usefulness of the concept of 'thick description' (266), behind which, as we have seen, lies the ideal of getting to know by speaking a language, of becoming literally conversant with local differences, relieved of the compulsion to generalize anthropological conclusions. Needless to say, it is not the case that in the past difference has not been acknowledged. Usually to proclaim the integrity of one realm of difference has been to presume over another. Carol Gilligan recalls that female delegatees were only allowed observer-status at the 1840 World Anti-Slavery Conference in London. Yet, some time before that, Euripides had no difficulty in seeing connections between racism and sexism. In *Medea*, Jason asserts that the Asiatic Medea only receives proper recognition thanks to his twin conferment of wifehood and Greek citizenship. Medea, though, knows that the exoticism and magic which characterize her 'otherness' also shape the role in which she actually fits the society into which Jason has introduced her. She resents the fact that her femaleness and her foreignness require her to be the obverse of Greek virtue, the voiceless object of its policing, its inferior, consolidating mirror-image. The Chorus longs with her for a time 'when the female sex is honoured . . . [when] Male poets of past ages, with their ballads/Of faithless women shall go out of fashion' (Euripides 1963: 29–30). And the plot also implies that a comparable reversal of Athenian chauvinism (*Medea* dates from 431 BC, the first year of the disastrous war between Athens and Sparta) would be timely.

Even earlier than *Medea*, Sophocles' *Antigone* had provided the most influential paradigm of what can be at stake in sexual difference. It can be no accident that *Antigone* is so readily adapted to voice the protests of the colonized and co-opted of history, whether, to cite two recent, very different examples, under German occupation (Jean Anouilh's *Antigone*) or British (Tom Paulin's *The Riot Act*). Hegel famously uses *Antigone* to formulate the same/other dialectic with which, as we saw, postcolonialism has primarily to engage. On Hegel's interpretation, the peculiarly female obligations felt by Antigone, embodied in the absolute requirement that she bury her brother, represent 'the highest *intuitive* awareness of what is ethical' (Hegel 1977: 274). This divine law thus reflects back to the legislator, Creon, an image he desires for the human laws of his *polis*; principally, the law requiring that the body of an enemy of the state remain exposed to the elements. However, Antigone's female duty arises from the making of a family tie into a universal obligation. The male, with his additional access to a public, political sphere can see the limitations of the female view, although he is still unable to gainsay its rectitude. Hence the tragedy unfolds: both Antigone and Creon are right. The male's greater self-consciousness aligns him with Hegel's own history of philosophical progress beyond the accidents of particular circumstances and towards necessary, universal truth. But this lofty disinterestedness is perpetually brought down to earth and mocked by the example of the woman – 'the everlasting irony in the life of the community' (288) – who holds up the mirror to such supposedly high-minded progress, rewriting it as successive examples of male self-interest. 'Better to fall from power, if fall we must,/ at the hands of a man', Creon tells his son Haemon (Sophocles 1984: 94). Hegelian progress is only possible because each of its stages is exposed as having in fact universalized a particular 'family interest' in the way that Antigone intuitively did. The woman thus 'changes by intrigue the universal end of government into a private end, transforms its universal activity into a work of some particular individual, and perverts the universal property of the state into a possession and ornament of the Family' (288).

The woman is the historicizer here. She contextualizes and relativizes each male attempt to promulgate natural law or have legislation accepted as universally valid in relation to local historical interests. To that extent she is a much an impetus to progress as he, albeit an ironic one. From Milton's Eve, with her proleptic dreams, to the women of D.H. Lawrence's *The Rainbow*, she activates male dissatisfaction from her subordinate position because she sees the *particular* advantages of a progress he can only idealize and spiritualize. Hegel's loaded language shows where his sympathies lie, which form of progress he favours. Only through an increase in self-consciousness can we escape the master/slave positions of Creon and Antigone and emancipate both from their obsessive mirroring of each other. But the ironic power Hegel has conceded to the female figure of Antigone suggests that his philosophy tells the history of the same power-struggle, repeated over and over in different disguises until there is nothing further to master, nothing left to colonize, no conceivable freedom not finally tailored to a hegemonic purpose. Long before the Foucauldian characterization of this regime, Hegel's ironizing woman learned to call freedom slavery, tolerance repression, knowledge discipline. She expresses what Derrida, following Bataille, describes as the 'restricted economy' of the same/other dialectic and challenges us to imagine what might lie outside it (Derrida 1978: 251–278).

Herstory is history with a difference. While this difference is addressed here as primarily one authenticating feminist initiatives in theory, the corresponding advantages for all forms of sexual unorthodoxy or 'dissidence' are obvious. Gay theory utilizes the same kinds of resistance as feminist theory where it sees 'forms of homosexual subjectivity' residing, in John Fletcher's words, 'within the normative matrix in and against which they are constituted' (Shepherd and Wallis 1989: 92). Once more, resistance takes the form of trying to step out of the place of 'otherness' in which the deviant may be stigmatized but in which he or she definitely finds a social niche. Resistance of this kind entails political reconfiguration. In Jonathan Dollimore's lucid and many-sided survey, *Sexual Dissidence: Augustine to Wilde, Freud to Foucault* (1991), this activism insistently works at the level of theory as well as practice, and it does so through historicism. Theory uncovers new histories, but those histories then return the compliment: 'it is also necessary that we use the history recovered to read, question and modify theory itself' (Dollimore 1991: 25). It is therefore obvious to Dollimore that a stand-off between empirical and theoretical gender-studies is counter-productive and illogical. 'Theory alone does not rescue the subordinate from the repressive and exploitative representations of the dominant', not only for practical reasons but because theory needs the other knowledge of those it would rescue in order itself to see more clearly 'the way that dominant ideologies are typically structured so as to override contradictory evidence' (194).

Perhaps, breaking conclusively with Hegel's patriarchal economy, such unreserved utterance is what is already longed for by Medea and her Chorus. They inaugurate a tradition of such imaginings, stretching to Showalter's 'wilderness of difference'. In each case, to insist on the sexual politics at work in any discourse is to historicize it. When a French feminist theorist like Hélène Cixous asks the question of what lies outside a patriarchal discourse, she thinks first of Medea as representative of a singular richness abandoned as an episode in history.

> Where to stand? Who to be? Who, in the long continuing
> episodes of their misfortune – woman's abundance always

repaid by abandonment? Beginning Medea's story all over
again . . .

(Cixous and Clément 1986: 75)

She is one of a list of victims – Ariadne, Antigone, Hippolyta,
Phaedra, Helen – in a Hegelian history of men's surpassing of their
individual circumstances in the name of progress. The list extends
to the present day. The trouble with Hegel, for Cixous, is that
he 'isn't inventing things' (78). Other feminist thinkers state the
dilemma more baldly. Catharine MacKinnon is sceptical of the
value of post-modern historicism for feminism. 'Post-Lacan, actually
post-Foucault, it has become customary to affirm that sexuality
is socially constructed. Seldom specified is what, socially, it is constructed out of, far less who does the constructing' (MacKinnon
1991: 131). To a lawyer and feminist theorist whose feminism
draws inspiration from Andrea Dworkin, the answer must be
unambiguous. 'Male power is systemic. Coercive, legitimated, and
epistemic, it is the regime' (170). Presumably, therefore, all history
should be read as the transhistorical manifestation of this power.
But in thus conceding to men the universal jurisdiction they want,
but may in some embarrassment camouflage with *Antigones*,
MacKinnon leaves little room for the protests or ironies by
which the ubiquitous male regime might be mocked or sent up. Yet
genuinely universal injustices in the Western treatment of women,
such as unequal expectations regarding childcare, can, as Lorenne
Clark and Lynda Lange assert, give 'ample reason for concluding
that traditional political theory is utterly bankrupt in the light of
present perspectives' (Clark and Lange 1979: xi). Genevieve Lloyd
can similarly conclude that ruling metaphors for rationality in the
Western tradition – the imposition of form on content, the control
of passion, the subjugation of nature – valorize an aggressive, male
stance. Feminizing, by contrast, tends to be defined as what is
annexed in such acts of knowledge as opposed to what does the
knowing. Again, the female role is one of necessary subordination;
but Lloyd believes that although philosophy 'has defined ideals of

Reason through exclusions of the feminine . . . it also contains within it the resources for critical reflection on those ideals and on its own aspirations' (Lloyd 1984: 109). The rereading of philosophy so as to foreground its gendered standpoint involves, argues Lloyd, 'taking seriously the temporal distance that separates us from past thinkers' (110). We are thereby returned to the historical specifics of the woman's point of view, which Hegel, using *Antigone*, outlined too persuasively for his transcending of it to be convincing. Instead of taking his road, we engage, says Lloyd, 'in a form of cultural critique' (109).

Lloyd's resting-place in historicism, though, like that of Janet Radcliffe Richards' 'sceptical feminist', does not explain how the repressive regime might be critically reflected upon without mirroring its own incriminating methods. MacKinnon's, Clark's and Lange's positions imply that only after significant material and economic changes rectifying injustice will we begin to evolve a just view of things uncontaminated by the sexism of existing values. In the meantime, faced with such a blanket critique of history, it is difficult to see how we might do anything other than reiterate the patriarchal view. Postmodern thinking, as I have been emphasizing, tries to get what it wants by other means and is therefore more attuned to the power of parody, mimicry and stylistic difference to open up to criticism a tradition to which it is otherwise subservient. MacKinnon seems to end where Foucault begins, rather than, as she thinks, the other way round. But feminist thinkers have been more effective in devising ways of thinking differently within the discursive restraints he thought inescapable. Cixous's childhood experiences as a Jewish girl brought up in French Algeria are formative of her postcolonial feminism. She 'learned everything from this first spectacle'. She could not have 'imagined' it, but it made her an historicist for life, devoted to exposing 'the paradox of otherness . . . at no moment in History is it tolerated or possible as such' (Cixous and Clément 1986: 70). The 'other' co-opted by history cannot be theorized, but it can be written about in a style discomfiting to history's purpose, exceeding its economy and elaborating its expository figures and metaphors beyond their stated uses.

> So all the history, all the stories would be there to retell differ-
> ently; the future would be incalculable. . . . We are living in an
> age where the conceptual foundation of an ancient culture is in
> the process of being undermined by millions of a species of
> mole (Topoi, ground mines) never known before.
>
> (Cixous and Clément 1986: 65)

The book she wrote with Catherine Clément, *La jeune née* (*The New-Born Woman*), puns on the male gay writer, Jean Genet, and her criticism generally, insistent on all the particulars of language in opposition to the exclusions of universal grammar and narra-tive, reveals that 'History is always in several places at once, there are always several histories underway', concluding that 'this is a high point in the history of women' (Cixous and Clément 1975: 160).

Feminist reading, then, privileges the individual example. Like history, it avoids scientific generalizations based on the events it describes. In the role of Antigone, it treats the individual case with a respect for its otherness to and difference from anything else. But this degree of individual attention may well disrupt the historical narrative in which its subject has traditionally appeared, exposing the need for as many histories as there are events which challenge present understanding and ask to be retold differently. Julia Kristeva similarly valorizes the meanings which lie adjacent to official stories, those traces of an unconscious, prior to sexual differentiation, which physically transgress in rhythm and impulse the strict demarcations of standard uses of language. This results in the same consciousness of the specificity of words, one which encourages a strikingly revisionary response to historical images (her essay on the Virgin Mary, 'Stabat Mater', is perhaps the best-known example) to replace the historical narrative in which they were found. Cixous was content to affirm what 'the poets suspected' (85), and Kristeva's work starts from a study of the revolution in poetic language achieved by a male avant-garde. Kristeva thinks her 'semiotic' alternatives to standard historical interpretation carve out a reading position neither masculine nor feminine, while Cixous could perhaps describe Kristeva's feminist appropriation of the male vanguard as another 'high point' in feminist history. Their common emphasis is on readerly rather than canonical revolution, but they give us no reason for thinking that the two may not collaborate.

Luce Irigaray, another French contemporary, makes her own distinctive and controversial contribution to the project of feminist historicization. In *Speculum of the Other Woman*, she rewrites major contributions to the Western philosophical tradition through a mixture of ironic quotation and parodic colonization. In effect pitting Hegel's Antigone against the rest of his philosophy of history, she reads the male desire for progressive self-production in ever more rational forms as a version of the female's roles he leaves by the wayside – 'a search for equivalents to woman's function in maternity' (Irigaray 1985: 23). This already suggests a novel way of thinking historical texts differently. But Irigaray's main gambit is to send up the male reasoner's traditional quest for his own reflection in everything by turning his mirror into a speculum. His texts are thus probed for their hidden femininity. But Irigaray's definition of femaleness is of so varied a series of attributes that this apparently scientific project is bound to founder, revealing the irony behind Irigaray's proposal. She not only posits a new object of knowledge for the reader, historical versions of men's desire for a maternal function; she also embarrasses this scientific quest with its own history – one of disqualifying female experience from serious consideration. Now in pursuit of an object it has always ruled out of court, science can only mime its own project, becoming a rhetoric rather than a knowledge, or, like postcolonial subalterns, making the distinction of authority from its masquerades increasingly dodgy.

To be taken seriously in the past, Irigaray reminds us, women have had to mime men. Now, in pursuit of the maternal, male thinkers are put through their paces. Toril Moi disentangles Irigaray's complex plot. 'Hers is a theatrical staging of the mime: miming the miming imposed on woman, Irigaray's subtle specular move (her mimicry *mirrors* that of all women) intends to *undo* the effects of phallocentric discourse simply by *overdoing* them' (Moi 1985: 140). The result is readings of texts from Plato to Hegel whose ironic quotation and exposition, given our expectations of a feminist content, show the artificial lengths to which philosophers have gone to exclude all such content from the 'matrix' or womb they desire for their thought. Irigaray hasn't Lloyd's confidence in philosophy's power to reform itself and so reflect critically on this past exclusion. She is a postmodern to the extent that she makes her point stylistically, through a writing-practice which implicitly asks us to draw conclusions from her juxtaposition of a past text and present consciousness and thus formulate the historicism involved.

As much as postcolonial theory, feminist theory questions the desire motivating every text's bid for authority. Its insistence on the necessarily gendered expression of this desire concentrates the reader's attention on a particular interest latent in the most universal and abstract claims to logical priority. What it claims is true of philosophy it also claims is true of art, if they can ever be conclusively separated. Structurally as well as imagistically, every novel repeats the opening words of Beckett's *Molloy*, which parody an originary male creativity typical of the high modernism of Proust and Joyce: 'I am in my mother's room. It is I who live there now. I don't know how I got there'. Not only a thematics of femininity but the assimilation of a female generative principle allows the writer, like Mary Shelley's Frankenstein, both to supplant another sex's distinctive contribution to authoring and to find reasons for destroying his competitor. In the plot of *Frankenstein*, Frankenstein cannot create a female who is productive on her own account because that would visibly redouble the monstrousness of his own original usurpation of a female role in procreation. And this allegory, however sensational, is not easy to avoid when describing the problems of writing feminist cultural history within a more general patriarchal plot. Germaine Greer's account of 'the fortunes of women painters and their work' lists the series of obstacles faced by women who excelled or strove for careers in the visual arts. In so doing she has to explain two factors which, on the surface, are different.

> Western art is in large measure neurotic, for the concept of personality which it demonstrates is in many ways anti-social, even psychotic, but the neurosis of the artist is of a very different kind from the carefully cultured self-destructiveness of women. In our own time we have seen both art and women changing in ways that, if we do not lose them, will bring both close together.
>
> (Greer 1979: 327)

Read in the light of Irigaray's theory, this suggests that male art is neurotic in its suppression of what it owes to a female creativity, and that women engaging with this dominant aesthetic mode have to collude in their own destruction, the psychotic effacement of gender which bids to be as much a feature of their success as of their failure.

Greer's more hopeful conclusion envisages a mutual promotion of the interests of women and of art. This can happen in various ways. A willingness, like Greer's, to allow the critical interpretation of a painting or text to hang on the particulars of female experience, however marginalized, helps establish a facilitating tradition – 'another spring of hope and self-esteem for women working now, a fresher understanding of the difficulties and a better chance of solving them' (150). Simply to *have* a past provides an historicist resource for changing the present. Equally, as Lilian Robinson argues in a Showalter anthology, feminist theory can go 'beyond insistence on representation to consider precisely how inclusion of women's writing alters our view of the tradition' (Showalter 1986: 112). Readers thus attuned to the patriarchal dilemma will, *pace* Greer, have the possibility of evolving new critical norms, values and priorities for the same reason that masculinity will have the chance to refigure itself if its mirror is taken away. Readers will become more healthily sensitive to those versions of maternity really powering claims to vision and authority premissed on the exclusion of the womanly. Too often these claims are set within a silent Freudian narrative. Male authority is achieved through a relinquishing of any idea of maternal connection, when the 'reproduction of mothering', as Nancy Chodorow describes it, is more likely what is at stake. Such valorizing of female creativity on its own terms would clearly make the male troping of it a different thing from the repressive colonialism typical of the past. And the resulting seriousness accorded female initiatives generally could show a way out of the neurotic sexual agenda at present confronting any self-respecting design on critical justness. Historicizing *Frankenstein* a little further, for example, as Marilyn Butler's new edition does, we can conceive of it as a serious and detailed discussion of contemporary scientific debate about the nature of life and not exclusively an allegory of the necessary elimination of women from such debates. Zeal to identify its allegorical feminism can blind us to the novel's literal feminism. If we neglect to work through the implications of Frankenstein's injustice, we fail to take seriously Mary Shelley's own scientific understanding.

In conclusion, it can be seen that feminist theory's emphasis on particular interests and circumstances first historicizes our understanding of the claims to authority in writing and cultural production, and then helps us reconceive what they were trying to say anyway. The comedy, for example, controlling Virginia Woolf's *To the Lighthouse* opposes a powerful but hopelessly insecure male use of words to a complementary female idiom. The latter oscillates between, on the one hand, achieving fulfilment, and thereby losing distinctiveness, in its power to restore male security, and, on the other hand, reconfiguring the ends of life through just this success. The novel shows that the female characters' activities already possess alternative and less neurotic versions of the satisfactions proposed by Mr Ramsey's dominating projects. The voyage to the lighthouse, gently parodic of male initiation and the colonial effort, is repeatedly forestalled in Ramsey's mind by the real nurturing of Mrs Ramsey to which he and others owe so much but cannot possess or acknowledge except on impoverished, allegorical terms – 'Filled with her words, like a child who drops off satisfied' (Woolf 1975: 33). Lily Briscoe's climactic achievement of finishing her painting simultaneously clinches the novel's refutation of Charles Tansley's slander – 'Women can't write, women can't paint' – and reconceives Mr Ramsey's desperate attempts to get beyond Q on an alphabetical scale of philosophical importance through an artistic, open-ended, non-mimetic closing on the truth. Patriarchy is given the chance to see its own redundancy. The tragedy of the novel is that Mr Ramsey can acknowledge this in a way, but only after Mrs Ramsey's death, when she is figuratively but not literally redeemed for him. Historicism, sadly, has its limits.

Similarly sent up or subversively mimicked in Woolf's *Orlando* are great male modernist novels' pretensions to be exhaustively adequate to modernity. Woolf's simple device of incorporating, literally, a female experience of historical change comically exposes the inhibitions behind the self-advertising repertoire of formal innovation typical of Proust, Mann, Broch, Joyce, Musil and many others. Their efforts formally to meet the challenge of organizing novelistically the modern subject's arbitrarily constructed world can sound bombastic beside the provocatively whimsical tone of a novel whose switches of gender immediately speak the subaltern experience which this mastery excludes. Of course Woolf is a major contributor to the English modernist movement too, and Cixous's praise of Joyce's feminization of language recalls Kristeva's use of the avant-garde. But if a feminist stylistic difference thus helps to reconfigure modernist and postmodernist projects common to both sexes, this is because it initially refused to get in line, declared a particular interest and maintained its assymetry rather than compatibility with prevailing authority. Its everlasting irony can only be defused if male discourse disperses under the force of such historicist critique.

CONCLUSION

Reception-theory might seem to merit an extended discussion in a book on historicism. It does, but only in the shape of particular receptions. As was seen in the cases of postcolonialism and feminism, the preservation of reception-theory as an abstract model rather than the description of specific interventions in literary or cultural traditions encapsulates what these interventions are opposing.

Theories of reader- and audience-response claim that the meaning of a piece of writing depends on the community within which it is read or performed. Each interpretative community, as Stanley Fish has often pointed out, validates a particular reading, and, more provocatively, it is at least conceivable that the reverse is true and that no reading is a false one: every reading implicitly prescribes the interpretative community in which it makes sense. At such a level of abstraction, this theory remains studiously tautologous. It only denotes a practical concern when we ask if it is possible to belong to different interpretative communities at the same time. Historicism negotiates just such conflicts of interest and shows them to be the rule in interpretation and not just a hypothetical difficulty. In its most rigorous forms, it defines itself against a successful reconciliation of past and present, dividing itself as a result of dialogue with the past, revising the protocols by which it revealed that past and so refuting the idea that its interpretative community was ever self-identical. The attempt to rescue Fish from triviality by saying that this is still an integrated community which has agreed on conventions for change is somewhat embarrassed by the unforeseeable quality of change – its changeability – in historicism's stronger versions.

Reception-theory highlights the ways in which textual meaning changes through time. It lets us see more sharply the indeterminacy of the text, the potential for different appropriations by different interests, and the competing canons which result. It also reflexively critiques its own relativism by showing that certain 'great' texts recur in opposed canons or remain crucial points of orientation for surrounding changes in canonical composition. And if Bakhtin's ideas are employed, even individual interpretations become fissured when they are perceived to respond to the contrary and disunified voices already implying different audiences from within a single text. In his classic discussion of the phenomenology of reading, *The Implied Reader*, Wolfgang Iser's 'implied reader' is at liberty to join up the fixed points of a literary zodiac, as he describes a novel, in his or her own ways. After Bakhtin, though, we want to know how this can be done in different ways at the same time. Comparably uniformitarian, H.R. Jauss measures a work's aesthetic value by its power to widen its original audience's horizon of expectations, assuming that this disruption is always future-looking, if not progressive, and dovetails with subsequent sensibilities. Yet, as Franco Moretti argues, literary history is littered with the malformed, unevolved, attenuated relics of writings we can see no means of developing, or played-out traditions whose unfamiliarity neither critically energizes us nor allows them to leap into exotic life (Moretti 1988: 268). There is, unfortunately, a certain contingency about what is redeemable and what is not.

Some voices extinguished by ideology may, in fact, have had nothing further to say. All we can do is to give them the chance without prejudging the issue.

The idea that writing receives its meaning from reception is true in particular cases and meaningless as a generalization. A Victorian bowdlerization of Shakespeare will hardly charge our present with unforeseen significance; or, again to avoid prejudgment, it is especially hard to reconceive present critical norms so as to produce an interpretation 'saving' a happy *King Lear* from past enjoyment and present indifference. Equally, a flop then can be a flop now, and past and present may remain unrevised by this coincidence as much as by the previous disparity. As Benjamin saw, historicism eventually requires a concept like redemption, which works on the analogy of the salvage of an individual irreducible both to the past ideology which had obscured it and to the process of its retrieval. The new significance of the redeemed event revises present modes of understanding, empowering them to make still further historical discoveries. And so the dialectical historicity of past and present generates its own momentum.

Expressed in this way, though, change in present historical procedures is sufficient evidence of redemption. Theological notions of future transformation inspired by a newly significant and so prophetic past are then avoided. Historicism remains the secular record of changes in historiography, not the rainbow promising a new heaven and a new earth. Nevertheless, we can still ask why we attach value to acts of historical salvage. To call them progress is to subscribe to one version of Enlightenment historiography. It may, after all, have been in the interests of progress that objects now salvaged were first allowed to sink into forgetfulness. If redemptive historicism is to escape the ideologies of past and present, something embarrassingly apocalyptic seems called for, hence Walter Benjamin's wizened figure of theology hides under the table but pulls the strings. His parable needs quotation in full.

The story is told of an automaton constructed in such a way that it could play a winning game of chess, answering each move of an opponent with a countermove. A puppet in Turkish attire and with a hookah in its mouth sat before a chessboard placed on a large table. A system of mirrors created the illusion that this table was transparent from all sides. Actually, a little hunchback who was an expert chess player sat inside and guided the puppet's hand by means of strings. One can imagine a philosophical counterpart to this device. The puppet called 'historical materialism' is to win all the time. It can easily be a match for anyone if it enlists the services of theology, which today, as we know, is wizened and has to keep out of sight.

(Benjamin 1973: 255)

Some commentators, like Julian Roberts, historicize Benjamin's thesis and see it as an attack on 'the false leaders of Social Democracy, which in this context now meant all those, including the Soviet government, who had capitulated before Fascism' (Roberts 1982: 208). Their false radicalism could best be satirised by showing how effective was a supposedly discredited theological language in satisfying their belief in progress. In other words, they couldn't have the progress except in a language they thought reactionary, and they could not recuperate its theological idiom without completely rethinking their idea of progress.

Benjamin's work is certainly of its time. His historicism is notably similar to the collage practised by his artistic contemporaries, the 'essence of modernist artistic production', Helga Geyer-Ryan calls it, 'the deconstruction of questionable totalities and the remounting of the fragments into artefacts, the meaning of which has no resemblance to their former function' (Geyer-Ryan 1994: 21). But he modernizes a tension which above all others characterizes the historicism this book has analysed, that between continuity and communication. Each seems to need the other, for how can we communicate without lines of communication. But

the purpose of communication can be to reveal the unjust estimation of the past perpetrated on it by the traditions and heritages
through which we have access to it. Both natural law theorists and
historicists believed that community enhanced the personhood of
the solitary individual, whether as a general rule or in specific cases
which always demand to be taken on their own merits. Yet a strain
in both approaches registers the increased conflict resulting from
socialization and its accompanying politics or distribution of
power. Opening the lines of social communication may mean
closing down others, but it is extremely difficult to find a language
for this censored, unconscious expressiveness. All language is
social; Benjamin's act of remembrance has already projected us
into a future state in which such justice is possible. An alternative
history has to imagine an alternative society as well: a solidarity
which can only be constructed across the ages; a conversation so
innovatory that it might as well be discussed as happening outside
the tradition it had started by radicalizing from within; voices
of an unconscious community, modelling a juster society, whose
discovery must confuse the discovering intellect whose coherence
had depended on its repression. Disaffection with continuity,
tradition and accredited forms of transmitting the past stretches
through the critics of modernity to become the main source of
postmodern discontent, its formal problematic fleshed out by the
futures predicted by postcolonial and feminist theory. But the
awkwardness in trying to improve communication by disrupting
continuity shows that the claim the past has on its would-be
redeemers 'cannot', in Benjamin's words, 'be settled cheaply' (256).

BIBLIOGRAPHY

Achebe, Chinua (1988) *The African Trilogy*, London, Pan Books.

Adams, Parveen and Cowie, Elizabeth (1990) *The Woman in Question*, London, Verso.

Adorno, Theodor (1974) *Minima Moralia*, translated by E. Jephcott, London, Verso.

Ahmad, Aijaz (1992) *In Theory: Classes, Nations, Literatures*, London, Verso.

Althusser, L. (1984) *Essays on Ideology*, London, Verso.

Anderson, Benedict (1991) *Imagined Communities*, London, Verso.

Aristotle (1920) *Aristotle on the Art of Poetry*, translated by Ingram Bywater, preface by Gilbert Murray, Oxford, Clarendon Press.

—— (1988) *The Politics*, translated by B. Jowett, revised by J. Barnes, edited by Stephen Everson, Cambridge, Cambridge University Press.

Ashcroft, B., Griffiths, G. and Tiffin, H. (1989) *The Empire Writes Back*, London, Routledge.

Attridge, Derek and Ferrar, Daniel, eds (1984) *Post-structuralist Joyce: Essays from the French*, Cambridge, Cambridge University Press.

Bann, Stephen (1984) *The Clothing of Clio*, Cambridge, Cambridge University Press.

Barthes, Roland (1987) *Michelet* (1954), translated by Richard Howard, Oxford, Blackwell.

Belsey, Catherine (1985) *The Subject of Tragedy: Identity and Difference in Renaissance Drama*, London, Methuen.

Benjamin, Walter (1973) *Illuminations*, edited with an introduction by Hannah Arendt, translated by Harry Zohn, London, Fontana.

Carr, E.H. (1986) *What is History?*, London, Macmillan.

Cicero, Marcus Tullius (1928) *De Re Publica, De Legibus*, translated by C.W. Keynes, London and New York, Loeb Classical Library, William Heinemann.

Cixous, Hélène and Clément, Catherine (1986) *The New-Born Woman*, translated by Betsy Wing, introduction by Sandra Gilbert, Manchester, Manchester University Press.

Clark, L. and Lange, L. (1979) *The Sexism of Social and Political Theory: Women and Reproduction from Plato to Nietzsche*, Toronto, Buffalo and London, University of Toronto Press.

Clark, Maudmarie (1990) *Nietzsche on Truth and Philosophy*, Cambridge, Cambridge University Press.

Collingwood, R.J. (1994) *The Idea of History*, edited with an introduction by Jan Van Der Dussen, New York and Oxford, Oxford University Press.

Condorcet, Marie-Jean-Antoine-Nicolas Caritat, Marquis de (1955) *Sketch for a Historical Picture of the Progress of the Human Mind* (1795), translated by J. Barraclough with an introduction by Stuart Hampshire, London, Wiedenfeld and Nicolson.

Croce, Benedetto (1941) *History as the Story of Liberty*, translated by Sylvia Sprigge, London, George Allen and Unwin.

Curtius, Ernst Robert (1979) *European Literature and the Latin Middle Ages*, translated by Willard R. Trask, London, Routledge and Kegan Paul.

Deleuze, Gilles (1986) *Foucault*, Paris, Les éditions de minuit.

Derrida, Jacques (1978) *Writing the Difference*, translated by Alan Bass, London, Routledge.

——(1979) *Spurs: Nietzsche's Styles*, translated by Barbara Harlow, Chicago, University of Chicago Press.

—— (1980) *The Post Card: From Socrates to Freud and Beyond*, translated by Alan Bass, Chicago, Ill., University of Chicago Press.

Descartes, René (1967) *The Philosophical Works of Descartes*, translated by Elizabeth Haldane and G.R.T. Ross, Cambridge, Cambridge University Press.

Diderot, Denis (1968) *Les bijoux indiscrets* (1748), Paris, Garnier-Flammarion.

Dilthey, Wilhelm (1976) *Selected Writings*, edited, translated and introduced by H.P. Rickman, Cambridge, Cambridge University Press.

Dollimore, Jonathan (1989) *Radical Tragedy: Ideology, Religion and Power in the Drama of Shakespeare and His Contemporaries*, Hemel Hempstead, Harvester.

—— (1991) *Sexual Dissidence: Augustine to Wilde, Freud to Foucault*, Oxford, Clarendon Press.

Dollimore, Jonathan and Sinfield, Alan, eds (1985) *Political Shakespeare: New Essays in Cultural Materialism*, Manshester, Manchester University Press.

Drakakis, John, ed. (1985) *Alternative Shakespeares*, London, Methuen.

—— ed. (1992) , *Shakespearean Tragedy*, London and New York, Longman.

Eagleton, Terry (1990) *The Ideology of the Aesthetic*, Oxford, Blackwell.

Eliot, T.S. (1932) *Selected Essays, 1917–1932*, London, Faber and Faber.

—— (1963) *Collected Poems, 1909–1962*, London, Faber and Faber.

Engel-Janos, Friedrich (1944) *The Growth of German Historicism*, Baltimore, The Johns Hopkins University Studies in Historical and Political Science, Series LXII.

Euripides (1963) *Medea*, translated by P. Vellacott, Harmondsworth, Penguin.

Fanon, Frantz (1967) *The Wretched of the Earth* (1961), translated by Constance Farrington, Harmondsworth, Penguin.

Feuerbach, Ludwig (1983) 'Chapter One, Introduction' to *The Essence of Christianity* (1841), translated by George Eliot, in *The Young Hegelians: An Anthology*, edited by Lawrence S. Stepelevich, Cambridge, Cambridge University Press.

Fish, Stanley (1980) *Is There a Text in this Class? The Authority of Interpretative Communities*, Cambridge, Mass., Harvard University Press.

Forrester, John (1990) *The Seductions of Psychoanalysis: Freud, Lacan, Derrida*, Cambridge, Cambridge University Press.

Forster, E.M. (1961) *A Passage to India* (1924), Harmondsworth, Penguin.

Foucault, Michel (1970) *The Order of Things*, translated by Alan Sheridan, London, Tavistock.

—— (1971) *Madness and Civilization*, translated by R. Howard, London, Tavistock.

—— (1972) *The Archaeology of Knowledge*, translated by Alan Sheridan, London, Tavistock.

—— (1977) *Language, Counter-Memory, Practice: Selected Essays and Interviews*, edited with an introduction by D. Bouchard, Oxford, Blackwell.

—— (1979) *Discipline and Punish*, translated by Alan Sheridan, London, Allen Lane.

—— (1980) *Power/Knowledge: Selected Interviews and Other Writings 1972–1977*, translated by Colin Gordon, Leo Marshall, John Mepham and Kate Soper, edited by Colin Gordon, Brighton, Harvester.

—— (1984) *The Foucault Reader*, edited by Paul Rabinow, Harmondsworth, Penguin.

—— (1991) *Remarks on Marx, Conversations with Duccio Trombadori*, translated by R.J. Goldstein and J. Cascaito, New York, Semiotext(e).

—— (1991a) 'Questions of Method', translated by Colin Gordon in *The Foucault Effect, Studies in Governmentality*, edited by G. Burchell, C. Gordon and P. Miller, Hemel Hempstead, Harvester Wheatsheaf.

—— (1992) *The History of Sexuality*, 3 vols, translated by Robert Hurley, Harmondsworth, Penguin.

Fox, Matthew (1993) 'History and Rhetoric in Dionysios of Halicarnassus', *Journal of Roman Studies*, LXXXIII: 31–47.

Freud, Sigmund (1973–86) *The Penguin Freud Library*, 15 vols, edited by Angela Richards (1973–82) and Albert Dickson (1982–86), Harmondsworth, Penguin.

Gadamer, Hans-Georg (1976) *Philosophical Hermeneutics*, translated and edited by David E. Linge, Los Angeles, Calif., University of California Press.

—— (1986) *The Relevance of the Beautiful and Other Essays*, translated by Robert Bernasconi, Cambridge, Cambridge University Press.

—— (1989) *Truth and Method*, translated by Joel Weinsheimer and Donald G. Marshall, London, Sheed and Ward.

Gates, Henry Louis, Jr (1988) *The Signifying Monkey: A Theory of African–American Criticism*, New York and Oxford, Oxford University Press.

—— (1992) *Loose Canons: Notes on the Culture Wars*, New York and Oxford, Oxford University Press.

Gay, Peter (1974) *Style in History*, New York and London, W.W. Norton and Co.

——— (1985) *Freud for Historians*, New York and Oxford, Oxford University Press.

——— (1988) *Freud: A Life for Our Time*, London, J.M. Dent and Sons.

Geertz, Clifford (1973) *The Interpretation of Cultures*, New York, Basic Books.

——— (1988) *Works and Lives: The Anthropolgist as Author*, Cambridge, Polity Press.

——— (1993) *Local Knowledge*, London, Fontana.

Gellner, Ernst (1983) *Nations and Nationalism*, Oxford, Blackwell.

——— (1985) *The Psychoanalytic Movement*, London, Paladin.

Geyer-Ryan, Helga (1994) *Fables of Desire: Studies in the Ethics of Art and Gender*, Cambridge, Polity Press.

Gilligan, Carol (1982) *In A Different Voice: Psychological Theory and Women's Development*, Cambridge, Mass., Harvard University Press.

Gilroy, Paul (1987) *There Ain't no Black in the Union Jack*, London, Hutchinson.

Gombrich, E.H. (1965) *In Search of Cultural History*, Oxford, Clarendon Press.

Gramsci, Antonio (1971) *Selections from the Prison Notebooks*, edited and translated by Q. Hoare and G. Nowell-Smith, London, Lawrence and Wishart.

Greenblatt, Stephen J. (1980) *Renaissance Self-Fashioning, from More to Shakespeare*, Chicago, Ill., University of Chicago Press.

——— (1988) *Shakespearean Negotiations: The Circulation of Social Energy in Renaissance England*, Berkeley, Calif., University of California Press.

—— (1990) *Learning to Curse: Essays in Modern Culture*, New York and London, Routledge.

—— (1991) *Marvellous Possessions*, Oxford, Clarendon Press.

Greenblatt, Stephen J. and Giles Dunn, eds (1992), *Redrawing the Boundaries: The Transformation of English and American Literary Studies*, New York, Modern Languages Association of America.

Greer, Germaine (1979) *The Obstacle Race: The Fortunes of Women Painters and their Work*, London, Secker and Warburg.

Habermas, Jurgen (1972) *Knowledge and Human Interests*, translated by Jeremy Shapiro, London, Heinemann.

—— (1984) *The Theory of Communicative Action*, 2 vols, translated by Thomas McCarthy, London, Heinemann.

—— (1987) *The Philosophical Discourse of Modernity*, translated by Frederick Lawson, Cambridge, Polity Press.

Harari, J. ed. (1979) *Textual Strategies*, Ithaca, NY, Cornell University Press.

Harris, Horton (1973) *David Friedrich Strauss and his Theology*, Cambridge, Cambridge Unversity Press.

Hartog, François (1988) *The Mirror of Herodotus: The Representation of the Other in the Writing of History*, translated by Janet Lloyd, Berkeley, Calif., University of California Press.

Hawkes, Terence (1992) *Meaning by Shakespeare*, London and New York, Routledge.

Hegel, G.W.F. (1975) *Lecures on the Philosophy of World History: Introduction (1822–30)*, edited by J. Hoffmeister, translated by H.B. Nisbet, Cambridge, Cambridge University Press.

—— (1977) *Phenomenology of Spirit (1807)*, translated by A.V. Miller, foreword by J.N. Findlay, New York and Oxford, Oxford University Press.

Heidegger, Martin (1962) *Being and Time*, translated John MacQuarrie and Edward Robinson, New York, Harper and Row.

Herder, J.G. (1891) *Sämmtliche Werke*, edited by B.Suphan, Berlin.

—— (1968) *Reflections on the Philosophy of History of Mankind* (1784–91), translated by T.O. Churchill, abridged by F. Manuel, Chicago, Ill., University of Chicago Press.

—— (1969) *J.G. Herder on Social and Political Culture*, translated, edited and introduced by F.M. Bernard, Cambridge, Cambridge University Press.

Herodotus (1972) *The Histories*, translated by A. de Selincourt with an introduction by A.R. Burn, Harmondsworth, Penguin.

Hobbes, Thomas (1991) *Leviathan* (1651), edited by Richard Tuck, Cambridge, Cambridge University Press.

Holstun, James (1989) 'Ranting at the New Historicism', *English Literary Renaissance*, vol. 19, no. 2: 189–226.

hooks, bel (1989) *Talking Back: Thinking Feminist, Thinking Black*, London, Sheba Feminist Publishers.

—— (1990) *YEARNING: Race, gender and cultural politics*, Boston, Mass., South End Press.

Irigaray, Luce (1985) *Speculum of the Other Woman*, translated by Gillian C. Gill, Ithaca, NY, Cornell University Press.

Iser, Wolfgang (1974) *The Implied Reader: Patterns of Communication in Prose Fiction from Bunyan to Beckett*, Baltimore, Md., Johns Hopkins University Press.

Jauss, H.R. (1982) *Towards an Aesthetic of Reception*, translated by T. Bahti, Minneapolis, Minn., University of Minnesota Press.

Kabbani, Rana (1986) *Europe's Myths of Orient*, London, Macmillan.

Kant, I. (1928) *Critique of Judgement*, translated J.C. Meredith, Oxford, Clarendon Press.

—— (1933) *Critique of Pure Reason*, translated N. Kemp-Smith, London, Macmillan.

—— (1970) *Kant's Political Writings*, edited with an introduction and notes by Hans Reiss, translated by H.B. Nisbet, Cambridge, Cambridge University Press.

Kojève, Alexandre (1980) *Introduction to the Reading of Hegel*, translated by J.H. Nichols Jr, Ithaca, NY, Cornell University Press.

Kott, Jan (1967) *Shakespeare our Contemporary*, 2nd edn, London, Methuen.

Kristeva, Julia (1980) *Desire in Language: A Semiotic Approach to Literature and Art*, edited by Leon Roudiez, translated by T. Gora, A. Jardine and L. Roudiez, Oxford, Blackwell.

—— (1984) *Revolution in Poetic Language*, translated by Margaret Waller, introduced by Leon Roudiez, New York, Columbia University Press.

Kuhn, Thomas (1962) *The Structure of Scientific Revolutions*, Chicago, Ill., University of Chicago Press.

Lacan, Jacques (1977) *Ecrits: A Selection*, translated by Alan Sheridan, London, Tavistock Publications.

Lateiner, Donald (1989) *The Historical Method of Herodotus*, Toronto, University of Toronto Press.

Lemprière, J. (1984) *A Classical Dictionary* (1788), London, Routledge and Kegan Paul.

Levinson, Marjorie, *et al.* (1989) *Rethinking Historicism: Critical Readings in Romantic History*, Oxford, Blackwell.

Lloyd, Genevieve (1984) *The Man of Reason: 'Male' and 'Female' in Western Philosophy*, London, Methuen.

McGann, Jerome J. (1983) *The Romantic Ideology: A Critical Investigation*, Chicago, Ill., Chicago University Press.

Macherey, Pierre (1978) *A Theory of Literary Production*, translated by G. Wall, London, Routledge and Kegan Paul.

MacKinnon, Catherine (1991) *Towards a Feminist Theory of The State*, Cambridge, Mass., Harvard University Press.

Marx, Karl (1973) *Surveys from Exile: Political Writings*, vol. 2, edited and introduced by D. Fernbach, Harmondsworth, Penguin.

—— (1975) *Early Writings*, translated R. Livingstone and G. Benton, introduction by Lucio Colletti, Harmondsworth, Penguin.

—— (1977) *Selected Writings*, edited by D. McLellan, Oxford, Oxford University Press.

Mehlman, Jeffrey (1977) *Revolution and Repetition*, Berkeley and Los Angeles, Calif., University of California Press.

Meinecke, Friedrich (1972) *Historicism: The Rise of a New Historical Outlook*, translated by J.E. Anderson with a foreword by Sir Isaiah Berlin.

Moi, Toril (1985) *Sexual/Textual Politics, Feminist Critical Theory*, London, Methuen.

Momigliano, A. (1966) *Studies in Historiography*, London, Wiedenfeld and Nicolson.

—— (1977) *Essays in Ancient and Modern Historiography*, Oxford, Blackwell.

Montesquieu, Charles de Secondat, Baron de (1973) *Persian Letters* (1721), translated with an introduction by C.J. Betts, Harmondsworth, Penguin.

—— (1989) *The Spirit of the Laws* (1748), translated and edited by Anne M.Cohler, Basia C. Miller and Harold S. Stone, Cambridge, Cambridge University Press.

Moretti, Franco (1988) *Signs Taken for Wonders: Essays in the Sociology of Literary Forms*, revised edition, London, Verso.

Morris, Wesley (1972) *Towards a New Historicism*, Princeton, NJ, Princeton Univerity Press.

Mueller-Vollmer, Kurt (1985) *The Hermeneutics Reader: Texts of the German Tradition from the Enlightenment to the Present*, Oxford, Blackwell.

Nietzsche, Friedrich (1966) *Beyond Good and Evil: Prelude to a Philosophy of the Future*, translated with commentary by Walter Kaufmann, New York, Vintage Books.

——— (1983) *Untimely Meditations*, translated by R.J. Holingdale, introduction by J.P. Stern, Cambridge, Cambridge University Press.

Norbrook, David (1984) *Poetry and Politics in the English Renaissance*, London and New York, Routledge.

——— (1989) 'Life and Death of Renaissance Man', *Raritan*, vol. 8, no. 4: 89–110.

Norris, Christopher (1982) *Deconstruction: Theory and Practice*, London, Methuen.

Nuttall, A.D. (1989) *The Stoic in Love: Selected Essays on Literature and Ideas*, Hemel Hempstead, Harvester Press.

Oakeshott, Michael (1983) *On History and other Essays*, Oxford, Blackwell.

Ong, Walter J. (1982) *Orality and Literacy: The Technologizing of the Word*, London, Methuen.

Palmer, Richard E. (1969) *Hermeneutics – Interpretation Theory in Schleiermacher, Dilthey, Heidegger and Gadamer*, Evanston, Ill., Northwestern University Press.

Patterson, Annabel (1993) *Reading Between the Lines*, London, Routledge.

Plant, Raymond (1983) *Hegel: An Introduction*, 2nd edn, Oxford, Blackwell.

Plato (1963) *The Collected Dialogues, Including the Letters*, edited by E. Hamilton and H. Cairns, Princeton, NJ, Bollingen Series LXXI, Princeton University Press.

Popper, Karl (1986) *The Poverty of Historicism*, London, Routledge and Kegan Paul.

Prawer, S.S. (1978) *Karl Marx and World Literature*, Oxford and New York, Oxford University Press.

Pufendorf, Samuel (1991) *On the Duty of Man and Citizen According to Natural Law* (1673), edited by James Tully, Cambridge, Cambridge University Press.

Radcliffe Richards, Janet (1982) *The Skeptical Feminist: A Philosophical Enquiry*, Harmondsworth, Penguin.

Rhys, Jean (1968) *Wide Sargasso Sea*, Harmondsworth, Penguin.

Ricoeur, Paul (1981) *Hermeneutics and the Human Sciences*, edited and translated by J. Thompson, Cambridge, Cambridge University Press.

Roberts, Julian (1982) *Walter Benjamin*, London, Macmillan.

Rose, Gillian (1993) 'Walter Benjamin – Out of the Sources of Modern Judaism', *New Formations*, no. 20: 59–81.

Rosen, Stanley (1987) *Hermeneutics as Politics*, New York and Oxford, Oxford University Press.

Rousseau, Jean-Jacques (1994) *Discourse on the Origin of Inequality*, translated by F. Philip, edited by Patrick Coleman, Oxford, Oxford University Press.

Royle, Nicholas (1990) *Telepathy and Literature: Essays on the Reading Mind*, Oxford, Blackwell.

Said, Edward (1984) 'On Repetition' in *The World, The Text, The Critic*, London, Faber.

—— (1985) *Orientalism* (1978), Harmondsworth, Penguin.

Santayana, George (1905) *The Life of Reason or The Phases of Human Progress*, 4 vols, London, Constable and Co.

Schleiermacher, F.D.E (1959) *Hermeneutik*, edited by Hans Kimmerle, Heidelberg, Carl Winter, Universitätsverlag.

—— (1977) *Hermeneutics: The Handwritten Manuscripts*, edited by Heinz Kimmerle, translated by James Duke and Jack Forstman, Atlanta Ga., Scholars Press.

Scholes, Robert (1974) *Structuralism in Literature: An Introduction*, New Haven, Conn., Yale University Press.

Schopenhauer, Arthur (1966) *The World as Will and Idea 1818-1859*, 2 vols, translated by E.F.J. Payne, New York, Dover.

Schorske, Carl E. (1981) *Fin de Siècle Vienna: Politics and Culture*, London, Wiedenfeld and Nicolson.

Shepherd, Simon and Wallis, Mick, eds (1989) *Coming on Strong: Gay Politics and Culture*, London, Unwin Hyman.

Showalter, Elaine, ed. (1986) *The New Feminist Criticism*, London, Virago.

—— (1989) *Speaking of Gender*, London, Routledge.

Sloterdijk, Peter (1988) *Critique of Cynical Reason*, translated by Michael Eldred, foreword by Andreas Huyssen, London, Verso.

Sophocles (1984) *The Three Theban Plays*, translated by Robert Fagles, Harmondsworth, Penguin.

Spinoza, Benedict de (1951) *A Theologico–Political Treatise* (1670), translated by R.H.M. Elwes, New York, Dover.

Spivak, Gayatri Chakravorty (1987) *In Other Worlds: Essays in Cultural Politics*, London, Methuen.

Stendhal [Henri-Marie Beyle] (1958) *The Charterhouse of Parma* (1839), translated with an introduction by Margaret Shaw, Harmondsworth, Penguin.

Stern, Fritz, ed. (1970) *The Varieties of History, from Voltaire to the Present*, London, Macmillan.

Strauss, David Friedrich (1898) *The Life of Jesus* (1835–36), translated by Otto Pfleiderer, London, Macmillan.

Swift, Jonathan (1959) *Gullivers Travels* (1726), edited by Herbert Davis, introduction by Harold Williams, Oxford, Blackwell.

Taylor, Charles (1975) *Hegel*, Cambridge, Cambridge University Press.

—— (1991) 'The Importance of Herder' in *Isaiah Berlin, A Celebration*, edited by E. and A. Avishai Margalit, London, Hogarth Press.

Thomas, Brook (1991) *The New Historicism and Other Old-Fashioned Ideas*, Princeton, NJ, Princeton University Press.

Thucydides (1972) *History of the Peloponnesian War*, translated by Rex Warner, introduction by M.I. Finley, Harmondsworth, Penguin.

Timpanaro, Sebastiano (1976) *The Freudian Slip*, translated by Kate Soper, London, Verso.

Todd, Janet (1988) *Feminist Literary History*, Cambridge, Polity Press.

Troeltsch, Ernst (1934) 'The Idea of Natural Law and Humanity in World Politics' (1922) in *Natural Law and The Theory of Society 1500–1800* by Otto Gierke, translated with an introduction by Ernest Barker, Cambridge, Cambridge University Press.

Vandiver, Elizabeth (1991) *Heroes in Herodotus: The Interaction of Myth and History*, Frankfurt, Peter Lang.

Veeser, Aram, ed. (1989) *The New Historicism*, New York and London, Routledge.

Vermes, Geza (1976) *Jesus the Jew, a Historian's Reading of the Gospels*, London, Collins.

Vico, Giambattista (1970) *The New Science of Giambattista Vico* (1725), translated by T.G. Bergin and M.H. Fisch, Ithaca, NY, Cornell University Press.

Voltaire [François-Marie Arouet] (1759) *An Essay on Universal History, The Manners, and Spirits of Nations . . .* , 4 vols, 2nd edn, revised and considerably improved by the author, translated by Mr Nugent, London.

—— (1965) *The Philosophy of History* (1765), first English edition with a preface by Thomas Kiernan, London, Vision Press.

Waller, Gary, ed. (1991) *Shakespeare's Comedies*, London and New York, Longman.

Weber, Samuel (1982) *The Legend of Freud*, Minneapolis, Minn., University of Minnesota Press.

—— (1991) *Return to Freud: Jacques Lacan's Dislocation of Psychoanalysis*, Cambridge, Cambridge University Press.

Weinsheimer, Joel (1991) *Philosophical Hermeneutics: Hermeneutics and Literary Theory*, New Haven, Conn., and London: Yale University Press.

—— (1993) *Eighteenth-Century Hermeneutics: Philosophy of Interpretation in England from Locke to Burke*, New Haven, Conn., and London, Yale University Press.

White, Hayden (1973) *Metahistory: The Historical Imagination in Nineteenth-Century Europe*, Baltimore, Md., Johns Hopkins University Press.

—— (1978) *Theories of History*, Los Angeles, Cal., William Andrews Clark Memorial Library Publications.

—— (1978) *Tropics of Discourse*, Baltimore, Md., Johns Hopkins University Press.

—— (1987) *The Content of the Form: Narrative Discourse and Historical Representation*, Baltimore, Md., Johns Hopkins University Press.

Williams, Patrick and Chrisman, Laura, eds (1993) *Colonial Discourse and Post-Colonial Theory: A Reader*, Hemel Hempstead, Harvester Wheatsheaf.

Wilson, Richard (1993) *Will Power: Essays on Shakespearean Authority*, Hemel Hempstead, Harvester Wheatsheaf.

Wilson, Richard and Dutton, Richard, eds (1992) *New Historicism and Renaissance Drama*, London and New York, Longman.

Woolf, V. (1975) *To The Lighthouse* (1927), Harmondsworth, Penguin.

Young, Robert, ed. (1981) *Untying the Text*, London, Routledge.

—— (1990) *White Mythologies: Writing History and the West*, London, Routledge.

—— ed. (1991) 'Neocolonialism', *Oxford Literary Review*, no. 13.

—— (1995) *Colonial Desire: Hybridity in Theory, Culture and Race*, London, Routledge.